THE WOMAN MOVEMENT
FEMINISM IN THE UNITED STATES AND ENGLAND

Edited with an Introduction by

WILLIAM L. O'NEILL

QUADRANGLE PAPERBACK Q

THE WOMAN MOVEMENT

William L. O'Neill was born in Big Rapids, Michigan, and studied at the University of Michigan and the University of California, Berkeley, where he received a Ph.D. His most recent book is *Coming Apart: An Informal History of America in the 1960's.* His study of feminism in American history, *Everyone Was Brave,* has been widely acclaimed as the first important interpretation of the subject. Mr. O'Neill has also written *Divorce in the Progressive Era* and edited *Echoes of Revolt:* The Masses, *1911-1917,* and *American Society Since 1945.* He is now Professor of History at Rutgers University.

THE WOMAN
MOVEMENT

Feminism in the United States and England

Edited with an Introduction by

William L. O'Neill

QUADRANGLE PAPERBACKS
QUADRANGLE BOOKS/CHICAGO

CONTENTS

THE WOMAN MOVEMENT

INTRODUCTION

INTRODUCTORY

This essay endeavours to explain the course of feminist development in America and, to a much lesser extent, in England during the past century and a half. The American material derives from my own research, the value of which readers may judge for themselves from my interpretive history *Everyone Was Brave: The Rise and Fall of Feminism in America* (Quadrangle Books). The English material is derivative. There is abundant printed matter on the English women's movement available in the United States, and I have gone through much of it, but, as every scholar realizes, there is no substitute for a close familiarity with the primary sources. I do not pretend, therefore, to have anything new to reveal about English feminism. All the same, I have found it valuable to view the movement in both countries from a common vantage point. Since the beginning there has been a trans-Atlantic flow of people and ideas in both directions. While feminists in each country responded first of all to local conditions, neither movement grew up in isolation. Some knowledge of these reciprocal influences is necessary to understand fully what was happening in either country at any given time. Moreover, by comparing the two groups one gains a better understanding of what was distinctive about each, as well as some idea about the peculiarities of the societies to which they belonged.

Since this book is intended for an Anglo-American audience a further word of explanation is in order. In some instances I have felt obliged to explain what to many readers will seem common knowledge. But what is obvious in one country is often obscure in another. To take a simple example, few Americans realize that a Bill must pass three readings in each House of Parliament before it becomes law. On the other hand, how many Englishmen know that a Bill need only secure a majority once in each chamber of Congress? Apart from differences in spelling (labor-labour), usages sometimes cause trouble. In America all the people and activities which helped in any way to expand the role of women were known collectively as the Woman Movement. In England the preferred term for this was the Women's Movement. Similarly, Americans spoke of the Woman's Rights Movement and woman suffrage, English people of the Women's Rights Movement and women's suffrage. The advocates of votes for women were known in both countries as Suffragists. In England the term Suffragette was coined to describe the militant followers of Emmeline Pankhurst. First used as an epithet, it was later adopted by the English militants to distinguish themselves from orthodox feminists. In America, however, Suffragette was nearly always a derisive label. I have generally tried to use the terms favoured by the women themselves, with one important exception. Feminists did not distinguish between those women who put woman's rights before everything else, and those who favoured woman suffrage and the like in order to advance other interests. But after 1920 this distinction became crucial, and so I have coined the term social feminist to identify those women who placed particular social reforms ahead of woman's rights. In both countries they were far more numerous than the militant (or radical, or extreme, or hard-core) feminists.

In the Beginning

All histories of feminism properly begin with the appearance of Mary Wollstonecraft's *A Vindication of the Rights of Women* in 1792. Scattered attempts had been made earlier in both England and North America to secure a redress of feminine grievances, but with little effect. Miss Wollstonecraft's book was, however, both sensational and ineffective. Although widely read, or, at least, commented upon, it met with universal disapprobation. Coming as it did on the heels of Olympe de Gouges' tract *The Declaration of the Rights of Women* (1789) and Thomas Paine's *The Rights of Man* (1791–92) the book was unpleasantly, and correctly, associated in the English mind with revolutionary France. Even had it not been tainted in this fashion, her *Vindication* would still have fallen on deaf or hostile ears. The English-speaking peoples of her day were quite satisfied with their domestic arrangements, and Miss Wollstonecraft's demands seemed to them unsettling, if not actually immoral. In later years prominent feminists were to call the book their Bible. Inferior as it was to the Scriptures in literary power, it obviously possessed a pertinency and vigour insensible to both modern readers and her own contemporaries. This was her tragedy. Had she been born a generation or two later, when numbers of women were beginning to press against the laws and customs that confined them, her life would have been very different; not necessarily happier, but certainly more productive and more obviously relevant to the needs and interests of her sex. Of course the position of women in 1840 was no worse, and in some respects better, than in 1790, but by this time they were becoming conscious of their disabilities and interested in removing them.

No one can speak with certainty of the reasons why women emerged in the early nineteenth century as a distinct interest group. Few areas of human experience have been more neglected by historians than domestic life, and at this stage we can only speculate about it. In the past it was thought that the family had changed little throughout the Christian era until very recent times. The Victorian family was believed to be, therefore, not a modern institution but the most highly developed expression of an ancient way of ordering domestic life. By the same token such developments as woman suffrage, mass divorce, and the employment of women in large numbers could only be understood as radical departures from long-established traditions. The trouble with these assumptions is that they do not explain why a family system which had worked so well for so long suddenly came under attack in the nineteenth century. As a rule two explanations have been offered to account for this. In the first place, it is argued, the libertarian sentiments generated by the Englightenment and the French and American Revolutions gained such force that they came to influence women as well as men. The demand for personal freedom, natural to an egalitarian age, was further stimulated, in the case of women, by an industrial revolution which created jobs for women in great numbers and gave them the opportunities for independence in fact which the rise of liberalism inspired them to demand in principle.

This line of reasoning is plausible enough; it gains strength from the indubitable fact that the first important agitations for women's rights in the 1830s coincided with reform movements in both England and the United States, and came at a time when industrialization was far advanced in one country and well underway in the other. But the problem of timing is more complex than it seems. Why did it take so long for the libertarian sentiments of the Revolution to move American women to action? The first women's rights convention was not held until 1848, nearly three-quarters of a century after the Declaration of Independence was signed. If the prevalence of jobs for women made feminism possible, why were so few leading feminists in both England and America gainfully employed? Middle class women were least affected by the industrial revolution, but they were the backbone of feminism everywhere. I could go on in this vein indefinitely, but the point is obvious. Simply because certain developments take place at approximately the same time, it does not follow that they are causally related. The ideological argument is in some measure self-justifying, but the influence of the industrial revolution cannot similarly be taken for granted.

However, there is another way of explaining the origins of feminism that is suggested by Philippe Ariés' remarkable book *Centuries of Childhood*.[1] This historian and demographer argues, mainly on the basis of French materials, that the history of the family is quite different from what we have thought it to be. In his view the medieval family was large, loose and undemanding. Children were unimportant so long as they were numerous, and all but the poor apprenticed them out at an early age. The family existed chiefly to maintain the

[1] Philippe Ariés, *Centuries of Childhood: A Social History of Family Life* (New York, 1962).

continuity of name and property, and its members had relatively few obligations to one another. Men lived in society, not in the family. But, he continues, in the sixteenth century this began to change. Domesticity in the modern sense started to emerge. The family concentrated itself and turned inward, privacy became important, the education of children assumed major proportions, and women acquired a great many new duties and responsibilities. This process, which began with the middle class, was completed in the nineteenth century when all classes developed at least a formal commitment to bourgeois standards of familialism. If Ariés' speculations (and they are rather more than that since he adduces much unconventional evidence to support them) are well-founded, the history of women comes into better focus. Medieval woman enjoyed a considerable freedom. Standards of conduct were broader and more flexible, for noblewomen positions of great authority were not unusual, and even lower class women enjoyed substantial economic opportunities in certain crafts and trades. By the seventeenth century, however, the old ways were being modified. Although some authorities believe that at least a few women voted as late as the eighteenth century in England, and although they were not specifically excluded from the franchise until 1832, the erosion of their legal and political position seems to have begun with the great jurist Sir Edward Coke (1552–1634). In the seventeenth and eighteenth centuries as domestic life became, from the woman's point of view, more demanding and confining, the alternatives to it diminished. They were squeezed out of certain traditional occupations, and by the early nineteenth century women, and especially married women, possessed few legal or political rights of their own.

The merit of this hypothesis is that it enables us to see the organization of the family and the status of women on the eve of the Victorian era as the results of processes that were just culminating, rather than as fixed arrangements of great antiquity. So long as the role of women was assumed to have been stable over long periods of time it was hard to explain why in the early nineteenth century it suddenly became onerous. But when we view the position of women in 1800 or 1825 as one that had only recently been established, then the reaction that in fact took place seems perfectly natural, an appropriate if somewhat overdue response to repressive conditions still, in some instances, being formed. The gap between women's narrowed sphere and men's expanding one appears to have reached its greatest extent at a time when liberal and libertarian ideas were in ascendance. In both England and America the exclusion of women became more obvious as the suffrage was broadened, and more difficult to defend. This was particularly true in the United States, as Harriet Martineau pointed out. 'One of the fundamental principles announced in the Declaration of Independence is, that governments derive their just powers from the consent of the governed. How can the political condition of women be reconciled with this?'[2] Even in England, however, where eligibility was more strictly construed, the disenfranchisement of women was becoming less a matter of course. The very Parliament which in 1832 specifically denied votes to women was also the first to debate the issue. Thus, while thinking to put an end to it, Parliament in fact legitimized votes for women as a serious public question. Congress, by way of contrast, was not to recognize woman suffrage as a matter of legislative concern until almost forty years later.

Despite Parliament's initiative in this respect, the emergence of women proceeded more rapidly in the United States—until the twentieth century at any rate. This fact alone casts doubt on the usual thesis that the emancipation of women was a consequence of industrialization. America was much less developed than England in the 1830s, but even at this early date American women enjoyed certain advantages over their English counterparts. It has always been supposed that the frontier circumstances in which many women lived in the early nineteenth century, and which were part of the ancestral experience of most Americans, improved the status of women. Women were scarce on the frontier, and consequently more valuable. In truth, woman suffrage prevailed first in the raw Western states, and in Wyoming the territorial legislature specifically hoped thereby to encourage the migration of women. The pioneer woman's legendary courage and fortitude gave the lie to those innumerable assumptions about women's inferior physiology and nervous system that justified their civil disabilities. This did not, of course, prevent most men from continuing to cherish their prejudices and admire their own superior physical and mental constitutions.

Probably of greater importance to American women was the tendency toward association that made such a deep impression upon Tocqueville, and that continues to be so distinctive a feature of American life. In church auxiliaries and missionary societies, and then in philanthropic and charitable bodies, thousands of women found outlets for their altruism and wider fields of enterprise beyond the domestic circle. Barred from the society of men they discovered among themselves talents and resources enough to advance many good causes and perform many good works. By the 1830s there were literally thousands of separate women's groups holding meetings, collecting funds, discussing public issues, and variously improving themselves. In this manner a revolution of rising expectations was launched. The more women did, the more they wished to do, the more they pressed against the barriers that prevented them from exercising their full powers, and the more eager they became to equip themselves

[2]Harriet Martineau, *Society in America*, (London, 1837), i, 107.

for the tasks ahead. An early expression of this desire was a substantial expansion of educational opportunities. In 1821 the first real secondary school for women was founded in Troy, New York. Later Oberlin College became the first institution of higher learning to admit women and in 1841 produced its first woman graduate. By this time American women were not only better organized than their English sisters, but better educated as well, even though the United States was still comparatively poor and underdeveloped.

An important reason for this rising curve of feminine activism was the extraordinary ferment that characterized American society in the 1830s and '40s. Religion, politics, philanthropy, education and, indeed, almost every part of the national life experienced great changes, or attempted changes, for which there were few English counterparts. Orthodox religion was challenged by the great Western revivals, by the emergence of new sects like the Mormons, by a radical Perfectionism that led in some cases to the formation of Utopian communities with bizarre and threatening sexual practices. The most radical European social and political philosophies found institutional expression in hundreds of experiments from Robert Owen's New Harmony to the many Fourierite Phalanxes that spung up at the end of the period. Prison reform, educational reform, moral reforms of every kind agitated the American conscience and contributed to the happy confusion of those years. Eventually anti-slavery became the most important issue, swallowing up or obscuring many of the others, and finally securing the most durable triumph. Abolitionism was especially important because it became a great field for feminine enterprise. William Lloyd Garrison was a fervent supporter of women's rights, as were other Abolitionist leaders. The two causes were linked by a number of marriages. Elizabeth Cady, who was to become perhaps the greatest single figure in the history of feminism, married Henry B. Stanton, a noted Abolitionist. Angelina Grimké, who with her sister was the first respectable woman to speak in public (on slavery) married Theodore Weld, a towering figure in the Abolitionist crusade.[3] Lucy Stone married Henry Blackwell without taking his name, and their joint labours on behalf of women's rights and anti-slavery became legendary.

This generalized reform spirit had two important effects on the women's cause. In the first place it created new opportunities for women and a more enterprising spirit. Few reform movements can afford to turn away volunteers, and where the appeal is especially stirring, women as well as men will respond if allowed. Thus, in the

[3] Frances Wright was actually the first woman to speak regularly in public, but although wonderful she was not respectable. The Grimke sisters came from a wealthy Southern family and their public work was conducted under impeccable circumstances.

1830s there were perhaps a hundred female anti-slavery societies, and women played some part in most other reforms. By this time women had been organizing long enough so that some precedent existed for this further expansion of their extra-domestic operations. They played a crucial role in the Abolition movement. More than half of the signatures on the great petitions that forced Congress to take up the slavery question were women's. Most of these were obtained by female circulators. Precedent and necessity alike, therefore, compelled doubtful males to swallow their qualms and allow the women a part, however limited, in these activities.

A second and more direct benefit to feminists that stemmed from this yeasty situation was the tendency of one reform to lead to another. Many abolitionists (or temperance workers or whatever) were single-issue reformers. Others were capable of embracing a multitude of reforms, their sympathies were generous enough to include an infinite number of exploited or oppressed groups. In a more immediate way female reformers who were not feminists took up the cause as a way of advancing their initial interests. Innumerable women became suffragists because they believed women's votes were essential to their dearest wishes. Others became feminists because they were discriminated against by male reformers. Susan B. Anthony began her public life as a temperance worker, but was driven to feminism by arrogance and male chauvinism.

American feminism in the 1830s and '40s was a slight thing by comparison with later years, but that it existed at all was owing to these two large developments—the organization of women on a local level and the surge of reform that to some degree carried women's rights along with it. English feminism, on the other hand, languished during this period. English women had not yet begun to form associations to any large degree, and the English reform movement was less vigorous and diverse than the American. There were a number of women's groups formed to support the Charter or the Anti-Corn Law League, but neither of these causes was as compelling as the struggle against slavery—itself but one of many movements prodding the American conscience. It is important, however, to bear in mind that the differences were relative rather than absolute. The American feminist movement was in the van, but its actual accomplishments by the middle of the nineteenth century were slight. Feminists supported the expanded educational opportunities afforded to women, but the leaders in this movement were not themselves feminists. Emma Willard and Mary Lyon founded secondary schools mainly to educate future mothers and teachers, while Catherine E. Beecher who helped develop the Normal School (in later years the principal source of public school teachers) became a noted anti-suffragist. Beecher believed that motherhood was woman's chief profession, but since not all women could marry they needed something to fall back on, and teaching seemed to her, as to most people in her day, the most suitable alternative. It was, indeed, a kind of symbolic motherhood and in most respects consistent with the prevailing beliefs about women's role and nature. By the same token, the improvement in women's legal status which began in the 1820s originated in Southern states where feminists had no influence. It seems to have been inspired mainly by the liberal spirit of the times, the progress of equity law, and the desire of male debtors to save their property from seizure.

By mid-century, however, American feminists could point to several achievements that formed the basis for most of their subsequent work. They had begun to make their case known. Although earlier attempts were made, a consistent and effective propaganda did not develop until the 1830s when the Grimké sisters began speaking publicly for anti-slavery and women's rights. The most concrete result of their tours was the publication in 1838 of Sarah Grimké's *Letters on the Equality of the Sexes and the Condition of Women* (Doc. 1). First published separately, these letters sought to answer the charges made against the Grimké sisters' public activities by the General Association of Congregational Ministers of Massachusetts. In forceful, lucid terms Miss Grimké made it clear to the ministers that they had no right to fault women for their obvious shortcomings. Man, she observed, 'has done all he could to debase and enslave her mind; now he looks triumphantly on the ruin he has wrought and says, the being he has thus deeply injured is his inferior'. Miss Grimké further demonstrated her own keenness of mind by shrewdly manipulating and commenting upon Biblical texts to demonstrate that Scripture did not authorize women's present status as the ministers had insisted. Soon the sisters were persuaded not to compromise anti-slavery by associating it with women's rights, but the *Letters* remained in circulation, bringing to literate women everywhere fresh arguments and inspiration. Other feminist anti-slavery workers were not so easily convinced that women's rights should give way so completely to anti-slavery. Lucy Stone was willing to give separate addresses on behalf of these two causes, but she refused to give up her feminist propaganda altogether. In 1845 Margaret Fuller published *Woman in the Nineteenth Century*. Although her essay was more confused and pretentious than Grimke's, it reached a wider audience. Her readers doubtlessly found much of her argument nebulous, and she made more concessions to current opinions than radical feminists thought necessary, but in some manner her readers could not escape learning that she believed women could and should do more than law and custom allowed. Together with Mary Wollstonecraft's *Vindication* and Harriet Martineau's influential *Society in America* these works, and other lesser ones, constituted a reasonably substantial base of support for the feminist speakers and writers of the future.

The first organizational fruit of these literary and rhetorical exercises was the calling of a woman's rights convention in Seneca Falls, New York in 1848. It was a small and provincial affair by later standards. Held in an obscure village which happened to be the home of Elizabeth Cady Stanton, author of the call, and limited to those people in the vicinity who subscribed to the *Seneca County Courier* in which it was published, the meeting (there were no elected delegates) was yet the first of those convocations that eventually played a key role in the struggle for woman suffrage. The group was addressed by, among others, Lucretia Mott, better known at the time than Mrs Stanton, and Frederick Douglass, the leading Negro abolitionist who lived nearby in Rochester. It ended by adopting a Declaration of Principles written by Mrs Stanton and modeled on the Declaration of Independence, that declared the history of mankind to be 'a history of repeated injuries and usurpations on the part of man toward woman, having in direct object the establishment of an absolute tyranny over her' (Doc. 2). The meeting also narrowly passed a resolution calling for woman suffrage. It was thought so dangerous and excessive that Henry Stanton refused to attend the meeting at all on account of it. Even Mrs Mott considered it too far in advance of public opinion. Nonetheless, although the press treated it unkindly for the most part, the convention led to others during the next few years that carried the feminist message to remote parts of the country. There were four in Ohio alone.

At almost the same time the women of England, never too far behind in any case, began to move. In 1848 and 1849 Queen's College and Bedford College were founded to give women a good secondary education. The first suffragist group, the Sheffield Association for Female Franchise, held its inaugural meeting in 1851. In 1855 a Married Women's Property Bill was brought forward and a committee of women created to circulate petitions on its behalf. The Bill failed to pass, but in 1857 a Marriage and Divorce Bill which met the most urgent needs of married women did become law. In 1859 the Society for the Employment of Women was organized and the following year it was affiliated with the National Association for the Promotion of Social Science. Soon the Educated Woman's Emigration Society was born. Also in the 1850s Louisa Twining founded a Workhouse Visiting Society which brought middle class women into contact with the frequently appalling character of these institutions, and inspired the campaign for female Poor Law Guardians. At the end of the decade the *Englishwoman's Journal* came into being. Thus, by 1860 English-women in some numbers were engaged in roughly the same kinds of activities as their American sisters: on the one hand those broadly charitable, philanthropic, educational and reformist enterprises in which men and women had an equal interest but that women were only just becoming active in, and on the other hand the more strictly defined efforts designed to improve their status which were symbolized by woman suffrage.

At this point the United States suffered a war that affected American women in several ways. All American reformers, feminists among them, have traditionally been handicapped by the regional character of government in the United States. The great variety of governmental units, their differing powers and laws, and the inability or unwillingness of Congress (especially in the nineteenth century) to legislate in a host of areas, force American reformers to organize locally if they are to be effective. Until 1860 the woman movement had been largely provincial, a matter of scattered groups and individuals addressing themselves to local questions. But the Civil War gave them a common tragic experience. Moreover, Union women in particular had unknowingly prepared themselves for a part in the national drama. Having become accustomed in some measure to confront public questions and to organize for specific purposes they were able to respond quickly when war broke out, and to deal with one another on a national scale.[4] The Sanitary Commission and other relief agencies, although in the main controlled by men, gave large numbers of women public work to do. Thousands served as nurses. Daring individuals such as Clara Barton, Mary Livermore and Louisa May Alcott, not to mention the eccentric few who became spies, soldiers and the like, distinguished themselves. On the ideological front Elizabeth Cady Stanton and Susan B. Anthony formed the National Woman's Loyal League to inspire patriotism, support the Thirteenth Amendment, and secure for women an honourable role in the war effort. Most importantly, perhaps, the war gave Union women a heroic myth that echoed down the generations. No single woman achieved the reputation of a Florence Nightingale—the honours were spread among many notable women—but this helped to universalize the experience. It also had the effect, from a feminist point of view, of giving women a claim on the nation. One great woman might well be ignored, but a heroic generation was something else again.

The chief consequence of the war was not, therefore, an actual revolutionizing of the status of women—some new jobs came their way, although the best of these were lost after the war as often as not—

[4] These remarks do not apply to Southern women who participated in public affairs on a very small scale, even during the war. However, they did suffer in the end much more than Northern women. This had the peculiar effect of giving their daughters a legendary background equal to that of Northern women. Their shared misconceptions about the past made possible the reconciliation of Northern and Southern women at the century's end.

but a change in their self-image and expectations. In particular it persuaded the most ardent that their war services entitled them to vote. This conviction was further stimulated by the rush of events that led to Constitutional amendments guaranteeing the political and civil rights of ex-slaves. Feminists were buoyed up by the libertarian spirit of the moment. Having helped to crush the great evil of slavery, they found it easy to think that the lesser evil of sex discrimination would be similarly dealt with. Moreover, as their heated debates on the question amply demonstrated, most of the radical feminists, for all their genuinely liberal sentiments, could not believe that men would humiliate them by enfranchising black males while leaving white women beyond the pale. It soon became clear, however, that Northern politicians intended to do just that. Their best friends, men such as Wendell Phillips and William Lloyd Garrison, assured the feminists that not only would Congress refuse to give women the vote, but that any attempt to secure such a Bill would jeopardize black suffrage. 'This is the Negro's hour', they were told repeatedly; women would just have to wait their turn (Doc. 5).

This situation placed insupportable strains on what could now properly be called the woman suffrage movement. Since the call had gone out in 1848, woman suffrage had progressed from being an unthinkable idea to becoming merely unlikely. This was sufficient gain to hearten moderate suffragists, but it was not enough for the radicals. The gap between these two factions, one based in New York and led by Susan B. Anthony and Elizabeth Cady Stanton, and the other centred in Boston where women like Julia Ward Howe and Lucy Stone were supported by a cadre of male allies, grew steadily wider. Not only did they disagree over the wisdom of striking for immediate enfranchisement, but on the relationship between woman suffrage and other liberal causes. In 1868 the Stanton-Anthony wing began publishing a weekly journal called *The Revolution* (Doc. 6). Its primary function was to agitate for women's rights, but it also endorsed a host of other causes, some of which were extremely controversial. The Boston group preferred a conservative policy of working exclusively for women's legal and political rights. Moreover, they disapproved of *The Revolution*'s financial sponsor, a mentally unbalanced, morally unsound speculator named George Train whose Fenian sympathies soon landed him in an English jail. His defects, and his racial prejudices, were outweighed by his virtues, so far as the Stantonites were concerned. These consisted mainly of an enthusiasm for women suffrage and a willingness to give them complete editorial freedom. In return he asked only that the paper carry news of his dubious financial schemes. Soon *The Revolution* was cheerfully flailing away at marriage, the currency, the law, customs, morals, labour practices, and everything else that Mrs Stanton considered in need of reformation.

Two years later it was bankrupt, Susan B. Anthony as publisher was saddled with debts that were to burden her for a decade, and two entirely separate, largely hostile, woman suffrage organizations had come into being. In 1868 the New Yorkers formed their National Woman Suffrage Association. The next year Boston organized its American Woman Suffrage Association. Efforts to reunite the two wings of the suffrage movement were frustrated by the differences in principle and tactics responsible for the rift, personality clashes between the leaders of each bloc, and the Boston group's reluctance to become associated with New York's more radical and dangerous enterprises. Chief among these was the reform of marriage.

Before the war a sort of underground agitation had been conducted against marriage on a variety of fronts (Doc. 3). Perfectionists like John Humphrey Noyes regarded it as fundamentally immoral, a source of rivalry, jealousy and possessiveness, a mechanism for dividing mankind, a human perversion of the natural order. At Oneida and elsewhere marriage was, in fact, done away with. Other groups like the Shakers had discarded not only marriage but sexual intercourse as well. Some feminists were attracted by these approaches, both because marriage laws seemed to them so discriminatory that women could find true equality only outside of them, and for the very practical reason that marriage and motherhood made it all but impossible for most women to function in an extra-domestic capacity. Angelina Grimké's marriage to Theodore Weld ended her public career, even though Weld himself was sympathetic to it. Elizabeth Cady Stanton's five children prevented her playing a very active role in the movement until late middle age. She always said that her real life began at fifty when her children no longer needed her. Lucy Stone was spared these complications only because she had but one child.

In the largest sense feminists were quite right to think that marriage sharply limited their prospects. Experience has demonstrated that the formal barriers to women's full emancipation—votelessness, educational and occupational discriminations and the like—are less serious and more susceptible to change than the domestic, institutional and social customs that keep women in the home (Doc. 4). As long as women are mainly responsible for child-rearing, and for managing homes with continually rising standards of living entailing higher and higher levels of performance, they cannot be expected to play as active a part in the world as men do (Doc. 9). Broadly speaking there are only two ways that women's domestic and maternal obligations can be made compatible with their public aspirations. One way is to erect an effective welfare state on the Swedish model which guarantees that children of working mothers will be well cared for, offers paid maternity leaves, and in every manner possible gives women equal employment opportunities with men. The other way is to alter the institution of marriage itself. The welfare state was not a real possibility in nine-teenth century America. Therefore, far-sighted women were led inevitably to speculate on the means by which marriage could be altered to permit the widest use of their talents.

The handful of women who reached this point were, however, faced with two all but unanswerable questions. What was to replace ortho-dox marriage? How could the transition to a higher form of union be made socially acceptable? The first question was answerable in principle. John Humphrey Noyes had succeeded, admittedly under unique and probably unduplicatable conditions, in abolishing marriage and raising women to a state of absolute equality with men. However, Noyes had not only a kind of genius, but possessed charismatic powers enjoyed by few others. In addition his system rested on religious con-victions of limited appeal. The Mormons had moved beyond monogamy, and while polygamy was in one sense a reactionary marital system, in theory there was no reason why it could not lead to a new division of labour by which some wives could shoulder the entire domestic burden to free others for outside work. However, Mormons were everywhere hated and despised, largely because of polygamy. Thus, while serious feminists knew that alternatives existed, none of them were able to devise an acceptable variation on traditional monogamy. Their writings are full of elusive hints on the subject, but nothing more than that.

The problem of devising alternatives, however sticky, was nothing compared with the task of making such alternatives acceptable to public opinion. The Victorians were obsessed with family life. If Ariès is correct, the nineteenth century was the first in which every class, from top to bottom, was expected to observe bourgeois family norms. The universalization of these standards having just been effected, the Victorians had no intention of permitting any relapse into the bad old ways. In America this determination reached its peak in the post-Civil War era. Not that earlier generations had welcomed novel opinions on the subject of marriage. Still, it was possible even into the 1860s to propagate the varieties of free love through the United States mails, and there was plenty of room in an underpopulated country for Shakers, Mormons, Perfectionists and the like to experi-ment. In 1873 the Comstock Act was passed, denying the mails to 'obscene literature'. It ended the dissemination not only of radical literature on marriage and the family, but of birth control information and related matter as well. Thus the act was not only a symbol of the hardening public temper, but, together with the state and local statutes modelled on it, the chief instrument by which public opinion was put into effect.

The high Victorian era was, therefore, the worst possible time for feminists to cast doubt on the perfection of America's domestic arrangements and marital customs. The Stanton-Anthony group did so in two ways. They attempted to criticize the existing order in their own right, and they became involved with a group of notorious free lovers of whom Victoria Woodhull was most conspicuous. Mrs Stanton was a persistent advocate of liberalized divorce laws. In principle divorce and marriage were entirely compatible; indeed, I have argued elsewhere that divorce was an essential feature of the marital system which had become general in the nineteenth century.[5] However, at the time divorce was considered the chief threat to marriage as an institution, and by supporting it Mrs Stanton put her reputation in jeopardy. Although by no means a believer in free love, she was actually something of a skeptic on the marriage question. In private she condemned it as 'opposed to all God's laws'. *The Revolution* abounded with intimations to this effect, the plainest statement being made by one of her followers who cautioned women not to expect too much from the ballot.

'Woman's chief discontent is not with her political, but with her social, and particularly her marital bondage. The solemn and profound question of marriage ... is of more vital consequence to woman's welfare, reaches down to a deeper depth in woman's heart, and more thoroughly constitutes the core of the woman's movement, than any such superficial and fragmentary question as woman's suffrage.'

Even such delicately phrased remarks compromised the movement, but the Woodhull affair was nearly fatal to it. Victoria Woodhull had arrived in New York in 1868 with her sister Tennessee Claflin. The beautiful and raffish pair attracted the attention of Commodore Vanderbilt, whose taste in women was almost his only engaging quality, and with his support they became stock brokers and editors. Although their business was more sensational than profitable, their magazine, *Woodhull and Claflin's Weekly*, initially attracted some favourable comment. It was a lively and interesting journal that promoted all manner of causes from Marxism (which the sisters completely misunderstood) to spiritualism. Their intellectual mentor was a curious figure named Stephen Pearl Andrews. Best known for his advocacy of free love, he had also devised a synthetic universal language (Alwato) and discovered the key to all knowledge (Universology). Mrs Woodhull rapidly won a commanding position among the New York suffragists and scored a great coup when in 1871 she persuaded the House Judiciary Committee to hold hearings on a proposed constitutional amendment to give women the vote. This was the first time Congress formally recognized woman suffrage as an issue, and Mrs Woodhull further enhanced her stature by testifying to good

[5] William L. O'Neill, *Divorce in the Progressive Era*, (New Haven, 1967).

effect before the sub-committee. Mrs Stanton was charmed, and even the more reserved Susan B. Anthony recognized her gifts.

Unfortunately for the cause Victoria Woodhull was nothing less than a human time-bomb. Sensual, reckless, mentally unstable at the least, she was attracted to bizarre fads and cults into which she poured her immense, volatile energies. Always promiscuous, under the guidance of Stephen Pearl Andrews she moved closer and closer to declaring in principle what she had already put into practice. On November 20, 1871 she announced her belief in free love from the stage of Steinway Hall in New York City. Open season was immediately declared on her. Denounced by press and pulpit, turned out by landlords, excoriated by all the organs of respectable society, Mrs Woodhull became increasingly irrational. After threatening to carry 'the war into Africa' she finally struck back at her critics by telling all she knew of the Beecher-Tilton affair. Her choice of targets left something to be desired. Henry Ward Beecher was not only the most famous preacher of the day, but a good friend of woman suffrage. Elizabeth Tilton was the wife of Mrs Woodhull's principal champion, Theodore Tilton, a liberal editor who had written a biographical sketch of her and was the only man in New York with the courage to chair her Steinway Hall meeting. When Mrs Woodhull revealed that Beecher and Mrs Tilton had been lovers she embarrassed her friends, not her enemies. She was angry with Beecher for having criticized her spiritualist activities, but she professed only to disapprove of his hypocrisy. She insisted that he too was a believer in free love, and only his fears kept him from saying so in public. Apparently she had no grievances against Tilton who was not only a friend, but possibly also a lover.

The consequences of her exposé were entirely predictable. Tilton sued Beecher. Beecher denied everything and, although probably guilty, was essentially acquitted by both the courts and public opinion. Tilton fled the country a broken man, and before long the Claflin sisters were compelled by an indignant populace to follow him. They landed on their feet, however. Settling in England, they waged skilful campaigns against their own reputations. Both succeeded in marrying men of money and position and lived out the balance of their long lives in, for the most part, respectable obscurity.

Their former friends in America did not fare so well. The Stanton-Anthony group was smeared and ridiculed, both because of its association with the Claflins and because several of its members had played minor roles in the Beecher-Tilton affair. For years a taint of free love clung to woman suffrage, embarrassing its partisans and, most importantly, inspiring in them a profound revulsion against everything unorthodox. In the course of rehabilitating itself the National Woman Suffrage Association adopted the policies of compromise and expedience that already dominated the American Woman Suffrage Association. Increasingly the National focused on the comparatively safe legal and political problems that it had once scorned the American for failing to see beyond. Soon only personal animosities separated the two. By 1890 these had sufficiently abated, so that the woman suffrage movement could be reunited in the cumbersomely titled National American Woman Suffrage Association, hereafter to be known as the NAWSA.

The Woodhull affair, therefore, despite its grotesque and accidental features, marked a decisive turning point in the history of American feminism. Until it happened, a small but important group of suffragists were prepared to think deeply and radically about the position of women. It is true that they had had but small success, yet their minds were open to the possibility that the entire domestic system would have to be restructured as a pre-condition for sexual equality. This was the central insight of early American feminism, and the losing of it crippled the movement intellectually. Of course the period running roughly from 1860 to 1890 was so hostile to radical speculations on marriage and the family that feminists would have had to be more discreet in any event. But the Woodhull affair did not simply inspire caution, it literally destroyed the possibility that feminism would be able to generate a body of theory adequate to its later needs. This was to become evident after 1920 when, having won the vote, feminists were confronted with all those problems that had been suppressed in its favour so long before.

As the American feminist movement became more conservative and respectable it also became more like its English counterpart. Serious English feminists seem not to have been tempted by the dangerous speculations which nearly ruined the Stantonites in America. Although English suffragists began to coalesce at approximately the same time as the Americans, they operated in an entirely different atmosphere. Woman suffrage in America was stimulated by the reforming spirit of the 1830s and '40s. In England these years were less expansive and optimistic. England was faced with the consequences of industrialization earlier than America, and the English mood in the thirties and forties was nervous and defensive—in some respects like the American atmosphere a generation later. In the 1850s, with the Corn Law struggle resolved, Chartism disposed of, and a period of great prosperity beginning, the English temper mellowed. Thus, while the woman suffrage movement got under way in both countries during the same decade, their respective heritages were quite different. The first generation of American feminists matured in a buoyant era that was already passing away when they began to agitate. This was not without its advantages, but it did not equip them to withstand the challenges presented by the more conservative age to come. English feminists, having passed through a less sanguine time, were not disposed to take chances or flirt with radical notions in the American manner. Thus, woman suffrage in England from its inception enjoyed all the orthodoxy and respectability which a generation of American suffragists laboured to secure.

Oddly enough, however, woman suffrage in both countries peaked out at almost exactly the same time. In America the extension of male suffrage in the 1860s stimulated women suffragists, and in England the Reform Bill of 1867 had a similar effect. Talk of expanding the suffrage always encouraged English feminists to think that they might be included too, but in this instance they had additional reasons for hope. In 1865 John Stuart Mill was elected to Parliament, even though he was an open advocate of woman suffrage. The next year Disraeli announced his belief in votes for women. Thus encouraged, women suffragists collected 1,500 signatures for a petition that was presented to Mill in June 1866. In October Miss Lydia Becker founded the first durable suffragist organization, the Manchester Women's Suffrage Committee. In 1867 Mill introduced a women's suffrage amendment to the Representation of the People Bill which secured 74 aye votes as against 194 noes. This was a respectable showing and encouraged feminists to think that some kind of women's suffrage might be obtained in the very near future. Under the leadership of Miss Becker the tempo picked up. In 1868 the first public meeting on behalf of the cause was held in Manchester, and Miss Becker was among the speakers. She was the first Englishwoman to speak in public for woman suffrage, but other meetings were soon held and other women followed her example. In 1869 Lady Amberley, whose husband had voted in Parliament for Mill's amendment, caused a sensation by addressing a suffrage meeting in Stroud. In 1870 Jacob Bright introduced a Suffrage Bill in Parliament that passed its first reading and was only defeated on the second. This proved to be the early suffrage movement's high water mark.

The chief reason for the failure of women's suffrage after the 1870s would seem to have been simply that it was much in advance of its time. To get so far as a second reading in Parliament within five years of their first spokesman's election was a remarkable accomplishment for the suffragists. The American movement, although older, larger, and better organized was in the nineteenth century[6] never able to get its Bills out of committee. But these initial gains were misleading. Apparently they were easy to get because the public did not at first take woman suffrage seriously Some thought, no doubt, that after the

[6] The two situations were not exactly comparable. Since Congress votes on a Bill only once, many Bills that in Parliament would get a first or second reading never reach the floor. Congress was even more careful about amendments to the Constitution, which had then to be passed by two-thirds of the states.

Court of Common Pleas ruled in 1868 that women were ineligible to vote, ancient precedents not withstanding, the suffragists would give up. When, instead, they increased their efforts and began to speak publicly on their own behalf resistance increased. Lady Amberley's appearance in Stroud provoked Queen Victoria to say privately that the noble suffragist ought to be horsewhipped. Henceforth her influence was exercised to dissuade women from pursuing what the Queen called, in a letter not then made public, 'a mad, wicked folly'. Gladstone threw his great weight against Parliamentary suffrage and although a Bill was brought in and debated every year in the 1870s except 1874, none passed the first reading after 1870. In the 1880s the matter came to a division only once, when a small majority was secured in 1886. This did not happen again until 1897.

In both countries, therefore, the development of woman suffrage followed similar lines. From small beginnings in the 1850s unique events led to high hopes and intense efforts in the late '60s and early '70s. Failure in both countries led to a long period of organizing and agitation at a lower level of intensity and under discouraging circumstances. These naturally had the effect of keeping woman suffrage alive (sometimes only just) and gradually conditioning the public mind for its eventual acceptance. In England Parliament remained the chief theatre of war. Having been induced in 1869 to extend the municipal franchise to women ratepayers, and in 1870 to allow women to vote for and serve on the School Boards brought into existence by the Education Act, it had at least established a means by which women could acquire political experience and render some public service during the long years when they vainly sought the right to do for the nation what they were beginning to do for their communities.

Because in America the States could establish their own voting requirements, suffragists turned to them once it became clear that Congress was not to be moved. Until the turn of the century, their most important work was done on the state and local level. Some good resulted. In 1869, Wyoming became the first territory to give women the vote, and in 1890 the first state. This was a source of considerable satisfaction to its several thousand female residents. In the next ten years the women of Colorado, Utah and Idaho were similarly blessed. On the whole, the attempts to secure woman suffrage by amending state constitutions were more exhausting and hardly more productive than efforts to amend the Federal Constitution. In both countries, therefore, the political situation of women was about the same. Large numbers of English women acquired a very limited vote in the nineteenth century, while a small number of American women were fully enfranchised.

The most significant difference to emerge in this period was that while American suffragists remained obdurately non-partisan, female auxiliaries to the major parties were formed in England—the Primrose League in 1885 and the Women's Liberal Federation a bit later. The relationship of the parties to women's suffrage was, however, a complicated one. Liberals nominally favoured votes for women, but in an age when the suffrage was based on property it was believed that female voters, because they would be propertied, would naturally incline towards the Conservative Party. Conservatives, on the other hand, while they stood to benefit by an accession of female voters, were resolutely opposed to women's suffrage in principle. Thus, the suffragists' ideological allies were reluctant to assist them for very practical reasons, while those who had practical grounds for supporting them were ideologically unable to do so. In America, where universal male suffrage already obtained, enfranchised women were not expected to alter the political balance. American politicians were consequently free to indulge their prejudices (or principles, as the case may be), and so neither party gave suffragists any reason to abandon their neutrality.

In summary, then, while the history of woman suffrage in England and America followed roughly parallel lines during the nineteenth century, the two feminist movements were at one time quite different. Both came in the end to look much alike, yet at first the Americans were not only more colourful and electric, but capable of entertaining more radical speculations than their English sisters. The suppression of these qualities after 1870 was a crucial event in the history of Anglo-American feminism. Respectability was won at the expense of intellectual adventurousness. Possibility gave way to propriety. A mental calcification set in that prevented suffragists in both countries from taking advantage of the opportunities that matured in the next century.

2

The Rise of Social Feminism

In the nineteenth century women's rights enjoyed little direct support. For every active suffragist there were a hundred women engaged in club work, education, charity and various reforms. Suffragists were not bothered by this disparity in numbers. They knew that many who gave their public energies to other causes believed in woman suffrage and would support it when the time came. Moreover, reforms and philanthropies were often stepping stones to suffragism. Women who began by promoting temperance, or child welfare often became converts. Sometimes they discovered that votelessness handicapped them in the struggle to gain their special objective. Other times they were converted by co-workers who were also suffragists. Frequently a social conscience once awakened turned out to be unexpectedly elastic. Having taken up one cause women found themselves with an increased capacity for others. Even when women did not themselves become suffragists, almost every kind of public work that women did was thought to advance the cause. The achievement of a single woman reflected credit on all women. The achievements of masses of women generated, as a by-product, an irresistible momentum that would eventually sweep away the barriers to their full emancipation. When suffragists spoke of the 'woman movement', therefore, they meant not only themselves, but all women who were engaged in non-manual, extra-domestic pursuits. The most useful of these were involved in reforms or philanthropies that directly benefited women, or were of special interest to women. These social feminists demonstrated by their works that they believed in expanding women's sphere of interest and influence, but they were not necessarily in favour of woman suffrage (especially in the nineteenth century) and those who were failed to give it the highest priority. For them women's rights was not an end in itself, as it was to the most ardent feminists. However, since suffragists usually favoured other reforms, the differences between social feminism and hard core or extreme feminism were not clearly apparent until after they were enfranchised.

The very first women's organizations foreshadowed the emergence of social feminism. Well before women's rights found organized expression, women were coming together for benevolent and religious purposes. Sometimes inspired by the writings of pioneer English philanthropists like Sarah Trimmer and Hannah More, more often in response to local conditions, American women organized to assist their unfortunate sisters and to spread the Gospel. As early as 1800 the Boston Female Society for Missionary Purposes was raising funds for Congregational missions in the West. Soon a multitude of local women's groups were collecting money, distributing tracts, founding Sunday Schools, and so forth. A Female Humane Association was formed in Baltimore in 1798 to aid indigent women, and its example was contagious. By the 1830s maternal societies were commonplace. Starting with an interest in child welfare, many of these became concerned in the 1830s and '40s with suppressing vice and rehabilitating prostitutes. Sometimes separate organizations were formed to this end, such as the New York Female Reform Society of which Mrs Charles G. Finney, wife of the great revivalist, was a director. At the same time middle class women began to associate for more private reasons. What became known as women's clubs sprang up in scattered places to meet the need of women for social intercourse, education, and entertainment—self-culture was the phrase they most often used to describe their ambitions.

By mid-century the characteristic patterns of women's social development were largely established. Their historic religious associations made the church a natural point of departure for concerned, energetic women. Soon, however, they expanded into contiguous areas. The care of children and distressed women was an extension of their maternal and religious functions. Somewhat harder to justify were their own interests, and women did not organize on any scale for self-culture until after the claims of religion and philanthropy had been satisfied. The significance of these ventures was masked in the early nineteenth century by their local and evanescent character. Thousands of women were organized before the Civil War, but almost entirely in local societies. Many of their efforts were abortive or shortlived. Sometimes they functioned as auxiliaries to male associations. A number of distinguished women in both countries did useful work of an independent nature. Often this led to the formation of societies to carry on and expand their activities. In 1817 Mrs Elizabeth Fry began visiting Newgate prison. Later she organized the Ladies Association for the Female Prisoners in Newgate which helped the prisoners in a variety of ways. Women's 'sphere' was thus greatly enlarged and the foundations laid for the tremendous growth in women's organizations that took place later in the century.

This tendency was especially marked in the United States for reasons that are not entirely clear. No doubt it was related to the American proclivity for associations of every sort. Associationism itself may have been rooted in the frontier experience. Certainly the uneven character of government in America was a factor. Government was commonly remote, often inadequate, and frequently limited by custom, insufficient resources, divided authority, and constitutional prohibitions of one sort or another. In any event, Americans became accustomed in the nineteenth century to view governmental solutions to social problems as the last resort. There was no American equivalent of the English Poor Law, and the tradition of public responsibility that it reflected was weak or localized. In some places, like Philadelphia where the Quaker influence persisted for many years, welfare and relief were considered public trusts. Elsewhere, notably in the South, private philanthropies bore the entire burden. Most attempts to induce the Federal Government to accept responsibility in these areas failed. During the Civil War Congress passed an act making grants of land to the states for the support of agricultural colleges, but this was an isolated event. More common was the response of President Pierce. In 1854, Congress, at the behest of Miss Dorothea Dix, apportioned public land among the states for the support of insane asylums and institutions for the deaf. Pierce vetoed the Bill saying that the Constitution did not authorize the government to be 'the great almoner of public charity throughout the United States'.

From the start, then, distressed citizens had almost unlimited needs that women could organize to meet. As the century wore on, the population expanded while industrialization and urbanization made want ever more appalling and insistent. This inspired larger efforts to deal with indigence, efforts from which women could not be excluded. Having demonstrated philanthropic interests and abilities long before the Civil War, and having made up a large part of the Sanitary Commission's rank and file during it, women were becoming essential to such undertakings. The new philanthropy of the late nineteenth century made good use of them. 'Lady Visitors' who investigated relief cases were the backbone of the Charity Organization movement. The London Charity Organization Society which began in 1869 to rationalize and put on a scientific basis the scattered efforts of private charities, was widely imitated in America. Its emphasis on rehabilitation rather than relief, and its discrimination between the deserving and undeserving poor were greatly admired. This austere approach was not entirely alien to philanthropists in the United States. The Sanitary Commission which supervised welfare work in the Union Army had declared its end to be 'neither humanity nor charity. It is to economize for the National Service the life and strength of the National soldier'. The Sanitary Commission, like the COS after it, worried about 'irresponsible' benevolence. The men and women

drawn to charity organization in the 1870s and '80s were informed by
a similarly stern, uncompromising spirit. The unregenerate poor were
to be cast aside, and the rest instructed in self-help. This unfeminine
philosophy appealed to certain women all the same. Josephine Shaw
Lowell, whose husband and brother were killed in the war, helped
found the New York Charity Organization Society in 1882. Louisa
Lee Schuyler moved on from the Sanitary Commission to launch the
New York State Charities Aid Association in 1872. It opposed public
relief as 'undermining the self-respect of recipients, fostering a spirit
of independence opposed to self-support, and interfering with the
laws governing wages and labor'.

Although scientific philanthropy flourished in the post-war era, it
failed for obvious reasons to capture the tender heart of middle class
American womanhood. Few women were interested in becoming
professional social workers, fewer still were aroused by the abstract,
intellectualized formulas of the charity organizers. Having been
assured for generations that morality and sentiment were their forte,
it was hardly surprising that women were most responsive to moral
and emotional appeals. Temperance and anti-slavery exemplified this
trait. They were among the first causes to enlist the energies of
women on a large scale, and temperance continued to do so well
into the twentieth century. Of the two major temperance organizations
the Women's Christian Temperance Union was composed entirely of
women, while the Anti-Saloon League relied heavily on them. Simplified, moralistic enterprises of this type produced astonishing effects.
The WCTU, for example, had its origin in what was called 'the crusade',
an extraordinary outburst in the 1870s marked by 'praying bands' of
women who invaded saloons and fell upon their knees petitioning for
divine aid all the while. Faced with these unnerving spectacles,
distraught publicans were said to have poured their whisky into the
streets.

England had its own crusade at about the same time. This was the
great struggle against regulated vice led by Josephine Butler. The
'revolt of women', as it was also called, was in many ways the English
equivalent of the American temperance movement. There was, of
course, an English temperance movement but it did not have anything like the impact of its American counterpart. This may have
been because the English working classes preferred beer, a mild drink
compared with the whisky favoured by the American workers. Moreover, that part of the American working class that drank beer or wine
was mainly foreign-born and aroused other emotions. Temperance in
America was middle class and rural, and directed against the urban
working class. The native-born worker was to be saved from his drinking habits, the immigrant punished through his. The saloon was also
a political agency as the English pub was not. By attacking it American

reformers struck at the centre of Boss rule in the great cities, for the saloon was the principal institution linking the machine with its constituents. Temperance was, therefore, a more complicated affair in America than in England.

The crusade against prostitution tapped deep moral and emotional wellsprings. It was a much more profound and, in some ways, dangerous cause than temperance which had few avowed enemies. No other reform came so near to the heart of wounded femininity, nor touched so directly the sources of masculine guilt. The double standard of morals embodied in the vice regulations mocked the ideal of purity it was supposed to protect. The Contagious Diseases Acts passed by Parliament in 1864 and thereafter were designed to protect the health of soldiers and sailors by curtailing the civil liberties of prostitutes. Women living within specified areas were liable, on police accusation, to be designated common prostitutes and as such subject to compulsory medical examinations. Refusal to comply meant imprisonment, compliance meant accepting the designation. The C. D. Acts violated, therefore, Christian moral standards, feminine integrity, and the most fundamental principles of English justice—all in the name of public health. Josephine Butler called them in her memoirs an 'outrage on free citizenship, and an outrage on the sacred rights of womanhood'.

Mrs Butler, the wife of a college principal, had done rescue work among prostitutes before deciding in 1869 that regulation must be abolished. Her abolitionist crusade met an immediate response. Thousands of women who felt as she did were encouraged by her brave example to defy the canons prohibiting women from public agitations. Soon a petition was presented to Parliament. Even more dramatically, Mrs Butler in 1870 led the fight against a candidate for Parliament who was closely identified with the Acts. Sir Henry Storks was the Government candidate in a by-election for Colchester. He had enforced the Acts as governor of Malta, and Colchester was a garrison town where they applied. Sir Henry was defeated after a tumultuous campaign during which he unfortunately admitted that he favoured extending the Acts to include servicemen's wives. The people having spoken, Parliament responded by appointing a Royal Commission to investigate the Acts. Mrs Butler testified to their moral defect, John Stuart Mill exposed their threat to personal liberty, and the Commission duly reported against them. Thirteen years were to pass before its recommendations were acted upon. This was a blow to Mrs Butler and her friends, but without the delay there would have been no great crusade. Instead of staging a short blitz, the women were forced to organize and propagandize on a large scale, thereby making a deep impression upon the public consciousness and stimulating the growth of related movements.

Mrs Butler's initiative had reverberated through both countries. In England efforts to gain women's suffrage, to secure a Married Women's Property Act, to raise the age of consent and obtain other benefits were launched or furthered by the crusade. She herself thought that the Association for the Defence of Personal Rights, which embodied the highest principles of English Radicalism, was the most important outgrowth of her campaign. In America attempts were made during the 1870s in most important cities to regulate vice, and the resistance to them was crystallized by two emissaries from Mrs Butler who arrived in New York at the end of the decade to rally public sentiment. They were warmly received, especially by ministers, suffragists, and veterans of the anti-slavery movement. In Boston they were sponsored by William Lloyd Garrison, and their public meeting was chaired by Wendell Phillips. Women from both suffragist organizations cooperated in the work. Mary Livermore and Lucy Stone addressed their Boston meeting. In New York, Elizabeth Cady Stanton and Susan B. Anthony had already spoken on behalf of social purity (the favoured American term for vice suppression). Vigilance committees were organized in many communities and the country grew accustomed to hearing ladies speak against prostitution. In 1883 the WCTU, at that time the most broadly based and effective social feminist body in America, established its own anti-vice department.

By this time the English movement was reaching its climax. In 1883 Parliament voted to suspend the C.D. Acts, stimulated by the knowledge that while it debated Mrs Butler and her fellow crusaders were wailing and praying in the Westminister Palace Hotel. Three years later the Acts were formally repealed and regulation laid permanently to rest. The crusade was over, but much remained to be done. Twelve was still the age of consent. The white slave traffic was comparatively unrestrained. A Bill to remedy this state of affairs languished in Parliament for five years until in 1885 Mrs Butler persuaded W. T. Stead, editor of the *Pall Mall Gazette*, to publicize these facts. Stead, a brilliant and imaginative journalist, resolved to expose the criminal law's shortcomings in the most dramatic way possible. Assisted by the Salvation Army he bought a thirteen year old girl for five pounds, kept her (suitably protected) overnight in a brothel, and then sent her to Paris. The details of this entirely lawful transaction he then published in his paper as 'The Maiden Tribute of Modern Babylon'. It was the sensation of the age, and his articles were reprinted throughout the English-speaking world, while the *Gazette* exhausted its stock of newsprint. On the fifth day the Criminal Law Amendment Bill was rushed through its second reading. A month later it became law. The age of consent was raised to sixteen, procuring became a criminal offence, and other reforms were secured. Stead's reward for this astonishing feat was a three-month prison term, ostensibly for making an illegal contract with the girl's mother, actually for having outraged and embarrassed respectable opinion.

In America the sensation was almost as great. The lagging social purity movement was stung to action. Mothers' meetings were organized by the WCTU's Social Purity Department. Later it added another devoted solely to eradicating obscene literature. Before long Social Purity Congresses were organized that brought a measure of coherence and solidity to the movement. In 1895 these led to the formation of a national organization, the American Purity Alliance. Purity reformers in America were, of course, faced with a rather different problem from their associates in England. Regulation was a purely local question. There were no Bills in Congress to serve as symbols and rallying points for the women's fervour. Social purity won out nonetheless, not chiefly through legal means, but by altering the climate of opinion so that while in the 1870s attempts to regulate vice were commonplace, they had become virtually nonexistent by the century's end. Most physicians and public health officers were converted to abolition. As in England prostitution continued to flourish, but public opinion was firmly set against any official toleration of commercial vice.

The exact meaning of these events is hard to determine. On the face of it there were good reasons for women to oppose legalized prostitution. Prostitution was clearly an evil, and its legal recognition did not make it any less wrong. In this sense it resembled drink and slavery. But unlike them, slavery in particular, there was a good case to be made for regulated vice. If vice was always going to exist, and would always be a source of disease, there was some reason for putting it on a rational, scientific basis. Moreover, it was argued, brothels drained off sexual tensions that might otherwise lead to sex crimes. Certainly regulation was the only way to control venereal diseases and save innocent women from being infected by their own husbands. In both these ways regulation protected the great majority of women at the expense of a rather small minority. The prostitute herself benefited in some respects from the system. Compulsory medical inspections safeguarded her health as well as her customers'. Legalization reduced, where it did not eliminate, the graft and police corruption inevitably associated with the vice trade. Victoria Woodhull, almost the only American suffragist to favour legalized prostitution, was especially impressed with this last argument, thanks no doubt to her unique personal experience.

Vice reformers responded to these contentions in several ways. Since they believed that most prostitutes were compelled by economic necessity, it followed that a more just and equitable economic order would dry up the supply and eliminate commercial vice. A cure for sex crimes was not to be had by degrading women, but through better laws and more efficient police. The C.D. Acts in particular had a pernicious aspect offensive to the English love of liberty that alarmed people who might not have opposed regulation in principle. Mrs Butler was herself steeped in the Radical tradition which despised that 'Socialistic State-Worship' embodied in the Acts. Yet, anyone who reads much of the social purity literature cannot fail to be impressed by its emotional flavour. Crusaders did not hate the prostitute as such. More often they seemed to view her as a kindred victim of masculine depravity. Middle class women were violated by husbands legally entitled to possess them by force. Extreme feminists called this state of affairs 'prostitution within the marriage bond'. It was not until 1884 that Parliament abolished imprisonment as the penalty for denying a spouse's conjugal rights. Many feminists in both countries believed that only easy divorce would entirely secure the wife's sexual integrity. Women who felt this way must have found it easy to see in the prostitute only a more deeply wounded version of themselves.

The opposite of sympathy for the prostitute was hostility to the masculine world that created and abused her. In saving the prostitute one also struck a blow at the men she pleasured. If visiting a prostitute profaned the sanctities of womahood, the denial of her services had an opposite meaning. Symbolic rape was met with symbolic castration. Extreme feminists expressed this by forgetting the help social purity everywhere got from sympathetic men. Reflecting on Stead's disclosures an American suffragist said 'one thing is evident, without the votes of women no vice that appeals peculiarly to the appetites of man can ever be suppressed or the laws enacted for the suppression of such be properly enforced'. Parliament's hasty response to the 'Maiden Tribute' showed the falsity of this charge, but it did contain an emotional truth. Similarly, feminists derived much satisfaction when public men were damaged by sexual transgressions. Many were disappointed when Grover Cleveland, a confessed fornicator, was elected President of the United States, but a few years later they were heartened by the Parnell affair. When the great Irish leader's career was ruined by the exposure of his relations with a married woman, Mrs Stanton was one of the few feminists to speak in his behalf[1] (Doc. 8). More typical was the response of Frances Willard who thanked God 'that we live in an age when men as a class have risen to such an appreciation of women as a class, that the mighty tide of their public sentiment will drown out any man's reputation who is false to woman and the home'.

A certain underground interest in free love notwithstanding, (Mrs Woodhull was neither the first nor the last woman attracted by it) the great majority of feminists wanted to restrict the sexual franchise. That is to say, they believed not simply in chastity for all, but to a considerable degree in celibacy as well. Many leading feminists were

[1] See Doc. 8.

spinsters by choice. Those who did marry often maintained their reservations about it even after they became wives and mothers. Charlotte Perkins Gilman, the most radical American feminist theoretician, was married twice but rarely addressed herself to sexual questions except when condemning the 'sexuo-economic' theories of Freud and his emulators. Many feminists believed in family limitation, but in the nineteenth century they usually opposed contraception as yet another effort of the bestial male to exploit women for his own benefit. Indeed, as J. A. Banks has pointed out, while the middle class birthrate fell in the 1870s, contraceptives were not then generally available and continence seems to have been the customary method of limiting family size.[2] Those feminists critical of marriage usually wanted fewer rather than more sexual opportunities. Mrs Stanton's distaste for marriage has already been noted, and this attitude persisted for generations. Mona Caird, an English journalist whose critique of marriage caused a sensation in the late 1880s and early '90s, advocated separate rooms for husbands and wives as the best way of refining domestic life. The unfortunate Edith Ellis carried this position to its logical conclusion by calling for separate residences (Semi-Detached Marriage).

The foregoing is not intended as support for those who dismiss the woman movement by libelling its members as 'castrating feminists'. This tiresome cliche originated in the 1920s, for reasons I will explore later, and retains a certain vitality even yet.[3] Obviously there is some truth to the charge that feminism involved an attack on masculinity. Feminists did try, and with considerable success by the end of the century, to limit man's sexual field of operation. Easier divorce, the suppression of vice, family limitation without contraception, restricting man's conjugal rights through changes in law and custom were all, in this sense, counter-phallic devices. Even so, feminism stood for much more than the curbing of masculine appetites. To dismiss it as a mere castration reflex is to ignore the countless other ways in which feminists strove to better their own position and to elevate the quality of social life. Justice is still desirable when pursued in curious ways by confused and misunderstood people. Nor is there any point in saying that feminists ought to have been something other than what society had made them. The cult of pure womanhood justified both the double standard of morals and the social isolation of women by insisting on the unbridgeable moral gap between men and women. In giving

[2] James A. Banks, *Prosperity and Parenthood: A Study of Family Planning Among The Victorian Middle Classes* (London, 1954). See also J. A. and Olive Banks, *Feminism and Family Planning in Victorian England* (Liverpool, 1964).
[3] See, for example, Warren and Marianne Hinckle, 'A History of the Rise of the Unusual Movement for Woman Power in the United States, 1961-68,' *Ramparts*, vi (February 1968), 22-31.

women a monopoly on virtue, it made them the only fit associates for one another. The sororital feelings thus inspired led naturally to that flowering of associationism which became the woman movement. Moreover, the morality gap thus created inevitably led women to question why beings as pure as themselves should be subject to the lusts of men, even when such relations were sanctioned by law and religion. The movement to give women power over their own bodies, to make them, as it was said, 'the monarch of the marriage bed', was an outgrowth not only of an expanding liberalism but of an understandable revulsion against compulsory intercourse with their moral inferiors. The Victorian moral code, therefore, in this crucial respect was self-defeating.

Is it fair, then, to criticize women for denying their sexuality when to admit it made them vulnerable to such risks and humiliations? If intellect was defined as a purely masculine quality, if achievement was restricted to men only, if motherhood meant numberless pregnancies, if marriage demanded complete subjection to one's spouse, who would wish to be a woman? Feminists may have overstated it a bit, but the subjection of women was very much a reality in the nineteenth century. A slave could escape to freedom, a very light-skinned Negro could 'pass' into the White world. A woman could not change her sex, but she could deny it—or, at the very least, deny that it made any difference. Who can blame her for doing so? Certainly the men who thus abused woman's sexuality were hardly in a position to criticize them for reacting against it. On the other hand, feminists could attempt to take advantage of the cult of pure womanhood, either, as I have suggested, by using their purity as a defence against masculine sensuality, or by regarding themselves as a separate and superior race. This was the root of their repeated claim that public life would be transformed when women gained the vote. In her essay on 'the Matriarchate or Mother-Age' Mrs Stanton carried this argument about as far as it would go.[4] She posited a remote Golden Age dominated by women. Under their beneficent sway peace and plenitude had been the rule. Masculine depravity undermined this idyllic state reducing humanity to the sad condition later generations accepted as normal. This interpretation was of course, hardly more comforting to most men than the customary feminist rejection of sexuality.

Another assumption commonly made by those who malign feminism as a castration reflex is that the entirely domesticated female had a wholesome influence on family life. There is no way of either proving or disproving this contention, but Victorian literature, the principal source of our knowledge about such things, hardly lends substance to it. As Ronald Sampson has recently pointed out, in

[4] In Rachel Foster Avery, ed., *Transactions of the National Council of Women of the United States* (Philadelphia, 1891).

such novels as Butler's *The Way of All Flesh* patriarchal authority was offset by the informal yet potent maternal influence. The memoirs of contemporary figures demonstrate that mothers commonly gained power within the family over their children, and through them over posterity. John Stuart Mill in his great essay *The Subjection of Women* put it very plainly:

'An active and energetic mind, if denied liberty, will seek for power: refused the command of itself, it will assert its personality by attempting to control others. To allow to any human beings no existence of their own but what depends on others is giving far too high a premium on bending others to their purposes. Where liberty cannot be hoped for, and power can, power becomes the grand object of human desire.'[5]

Just so! Like many another good thing domesticity, when compelled, doubtlessly became a corrupting force. Tyranny is not less odious, or dangerous, for being employed in so small an arena. If only one family had suffered from a perverted maternalism that would have been a tragedy; multiplied a thousandfold, a millionfold, it was a disaster.

The development of social feminism in the late nineteenth century was probably most important, therefore, for the good it did women themselves rather than for the good women succeeded in doing. In opening up new fields of action, organizations like the WCTU, the National Council of Women, the YWCA and so forth became safety valves by which frustrated women could find an outlet for talents and ambitions that home life could neither satisfy nor healthily contain. Some organizations were more successful than others from the standpoint of social utility, but virtually all of them had a useful effect on their members. By the century's end middle class women had a wide range of organizations to choose from. These ran the gamut from conservative, patriotic groups like the absurdly misnamed Daughters of the American Revolution to the venturesome bands of women who were founding social settlements in the great cities. Two organizations especially demonstrated that intelligent self-interest (Jane Addams called it the 'subjective value') which informed these enterprises—the Association of Collegiate Alumnae and the General Federation of Women's Clubs.

By 1882 the higher education of American women was an established fact. The best state universities admitted them on essentially the same basis as men. In the Sage College of Cornell and the Harvard Annex (later to become Radcliffe College) they had separate but more or less equal facilities. A handful of women's colleges had developed to the point where they were as good as, if not the best, at least the next

[5] John Stuart Mill, *The Subjection of Women* (New York, 1869), 181-82. Ronald V. Sampson, *The Psychology of Power* (New York, 1966).

best men's colleges. Prejudices and discriminations were not wholly abolished. Post-graduate and professional training was still hard to obtain. Now and again protests were voiced and alarms raised. In 1873 Professor Edward H. Clarke published his *Sex in Education* which argued that higher education damaged women's reproductive capabilities. No one wanted to see the race enfeebled but so few women earned the bachelor's degree in these years that the controversy never amounted to much (Doc. 16). Clarke's book was angrily refuted, of course, but the increased emphasis on physical training in women's colleges was probably a more effective response. Yet, these irritations notwithstanding, the progress of educated women was steady and encouraging. As early as 1880 the 40,000 women enrolled in American institutions of higher learning constituted more than a third of the entire student body. This was in striking contrast to England where at the same time only London University granted degrees to women scholars. The handful of the students in the women's colleges of Cambridge and Oxford (less than 200 in 1882) took the same examinations given to men, but were not allowed to receive degrees until after World War I. There were a number of independent women's colleges in England at the century's end, but they were in reality institutions of secondary education. The gap between the two countries was, however, not quite so great as the above suggests. Many of the colleges for women in America were not true institutions of higher learning. Some of them remained female seminaries in all but name, others were so weak that their graduates were unable to pass even the entrance examinations of the better colleges and universities. Still, American women enjoyed significantly better educational opportunities than their English counterparts.

By the 1880s the chief difficulty facing ambitious American women was not in getting an education, but in using it. Teaching was virtually the only profession open to women, and to teach in the lower schools, where most were employed, a college degree was not required. Women teachers had usually a high school diploma or, at most, two years of preparation in a teacher training institute, usually a Normal School. The handful of women graduates from reputable institutions of higher learning thus found themselves in an uncomfortable position. They could either perform work for which they were over-qualified, or, more commonly it appears, do nothing at all. Their situation was all the more vexing because as students they had undergone a unique experience—especially in the independent women's colleges where the majority of them earned their degrees before 1900. Having become undergraduates, often against heavy odds and with much trouble and expense, they enjoyed for four years an intense communal experience. Sororial ties of an intimate and rewarding character were established. A sense of high purpose informed their studies. They regarded them-

selves, quite rightly, as an elite with special privileges and responsibilities. But upon graduating they discovered that society did not
place the same value upon their education, and that they were in
effect a functionless élite. Their education was of little worth in the
job market. Moreover, graduation meant the end of those communal
intimacies that had loomed so large in their college years. They were
expected to marry and settle down as housewives, but their education
had isolated them from their male peers while imbuing them with
ambitions that housewifery could not satisfy. It was hard enough for
single woman to make a career for herself in the Victorian era; for a
married woman it was all but impossible.

The formation of the ACA was a direct response to these peculiar
difficulties. Its founder, Marion Talbot, was one of the first women
to earn a degree from Boston College. Frustrated by her meagre prospects, she issued a call to her similarly dissatisfied friends. In 1882
some sixty-five graduates of eight institutions organized themselves
into the Association of Collegiate Alumnae. Their nominal objectives
were to provide a kind of university extension that would refresh them
intellectually, and to raise the standards of female education. Subjectively the ACA was to be a means of recreating the satisfactions of their
college days—friendship and a shared interest in some higher purpose.
The first members were mostly single, all recent graduates suffering
from a kind of culture shock. Few of them, apparently, were teachers.
As time went on, however, the proportion who taught increased, and
the ACA came more to resemble what M. Carey Thomas was to call a
trade union for educated women. More married women came in also,
but the proportion of single women remained high throughout the
organization's early years. This reflected the aversion to matrimony
characteristic of the graduates of women's colleges. In the nineteenth
century about half of them never married at all, and those who did
were much older than the average—about twenty-seven as against the
usual twenty or twenty-one.

The ACA did not become an important national organization until
after World War I when, as the American Association of University
Women, it acquired a large membership. But the ACA merits attention
for several reasons. It was the only significant women's organization
in its day made up entirely of college graduates. Thus, it suggested
how middle class women would function when college training became
commonplace. Moreover, it was one of the most clearly interest-
oriented women's organizations and therefore gave the lie to certain
assumptions made about the woman movement. The ACA was not only
élitist, but self-consciously so. Its members knew themselves to be the
best educated women in the country and were determined to associate
only with their peers. When a comparable group founded the Western
Association of Collegiate Alumnae in 1884 they were compelled to

wait for five years until the ACA was satisfied that a merger would not compromise its standards. From the first, admission was restricted to graduates of institutions specifically approved by the Association. In 1889 only fourteen colleges and universities were deemed suitable, and for generations the number of institutions it recognized was very small. In 1903 the Southern Association of College Women was organized because the ACA did not accept graduates from even one of the more than 140 women's colleges in the South. Thus, while the ACA claimed to speak for all college women, it in fact represented comparatively few.

The ACA justified its highly restrictive membership policy by arguing that it would lead institutions to reform themselves. The ACA was never able to demonstrate that its policies actually had this effect. The best institutions were indifferent, while the worst, even if capable of improvement, were hardly likely to do so merely to win a token of unproven value. The few instances where recognition was decisive did little to validate policies that were stubbornly adhered to until 1963. For example, the University of Cincinnati's first application for membership was denied because it did not provide suitable facilities for its women students. A women's building was then constructed after which its graduates became eligible to join the ACA. But, helpful as the building may have been to the female students of Cincinnati, it did not affect the value of their degrees in the slightest, nor markedly improve the quality of their education. These incidents suggest that restricting membership served mainly to reinforce the ACA's stature as an élite organization. Just as a college sorority gains status from those it rejects, so did the ACA guard its eminence by jealously confining its attentions to the graduates of prestigious institutions.

This is not to say that the ACA was motivated by mere snobbishness. Its standards were rational and based to a considerable degree on achievement rather than prescription. But the whole character of the organization was self-centred. Apart from its own members those who benefited from its admission policy were graduates of institutions strong enough so that a little push was all it took to bring them up to standard. That is to say, the women of the ACA were chiefly interested in others like themselves. Its remaining activities were of the same order. One of the Association's first acts was to make a study of the students at a leading preparatory school in Boston to show that studying did not injure their health. It investigated in numerous ways the position of female teachers, teaching being the principal occupation of its employed members. It inaugurated a scholarship programme. In an age of cooperation among women's organizations it was noticeably uncooperative. For a few years it jointly sponsored a post-graduate fellowship with the College Settlement Association. In 1915 it finally got around to joining the innocuous National Council of Women. This was about the extent of its ties with other organizations until after the Great War.

There was, let it be said again, nothing shameful about the Association's policies. Even the best women's colleges were not so good that they could do without outside help. A small organization like the ACA (only 6,000 members in 1914) could not spread itself for fear of becoming entirely ineffectual. Educated women continued to be at a disadvantage in the job market, and female teachers were consistently discriminated against (as they are even today). The ACA behaved in a manner consistent with its members' interests. But in doing so it showed how little middle class women understood themselves. Social feminists assumed that women were above the mean partisanship and class-consciousness of the male world, and that their emancipation and fuller participation in public life would reorient public affairs in a broad, humane direction. They differed among themselves as to what were the unique feminine virtues that would effect this transformation, but few doubted that they existed and would lead to the redemption of mankind. The higher education of women was understood to be an important step towards the liberation of these energies. Yet the ACA showed all this to be nonsense. As college students women, although more self-conscious and emotional about their roles than men, functioned exactly like them. As professionals women, when allowed to be, did not differ noticeably from their male peers. The ACA in this period existed mainly because women were denied the treatment men received as a matter of course. Still, by the turn of the century its members had freed themselves from most of the limitations imposed on women by law and custom, and, as most of them were single, from the burdens of motherhood as well. The effect of their new freedom was to inspire policies and programmes very much like those of purely professional organizations except that they were aimed at a group still felt to be disadvantaged. In this the ACA anticipated what would happen to middle class women generally once the main barriers to their individual advancement were breached. Thus, while the ACA was regarded as a part of the woman movement, it really had little in common with most women's organizations. This becomes apparent when it is compared with the largest, most representative, and probably most influential of all the social feminist organizations, the General Federation of Women's Clubs.

As we saw before, what were in fact women's clubs developed at the start of the nineteenth century. Doubtlessly there were informal associations of women even earlier. However the history of the club movement proper begins in 1868 when the first of the great clubs was founded. Mrs Jennie Cunningham Croly, wife of a noted journalist, herself well known to newspaper reading women around the country under her pen name 'Jennie June', and the mother of Herbert Croly whose career in journalism was to be even more brilliant than his parents', was not allowed to attend the New York Press Club's dinner for Charles Dickens in March 1868, nor was any other woman. This insult to her sex inspired her to organize a feminine equivalent of the Press Club which she called Sorosis. At first it was made up entirely of professional women, mainly writers and teachers. Soon it attracted a broader membership and while numerous other clubs were later established in New York, Sorosis remained pre-eminent for years. Almost immediately a group of distinguished Boston women organized the New England Woman's Club. Unlike Sorosis it was open to men and in fact attracted representative figures from the city's moral, intellectual and social élite. By 1890 it had grown to the point where some kind of association seemed in order. Sorosis took the initiative and in that year the General Federation of Women's Clubs with fifty-two member organizations was formed. In 1892 when its first biennial convention was held the Federation had already expanded to 190 clubs with 20,000 members. Another eight years brought it up to 150,000 members. By 1910 perhaps a million women were enlisted in its ranks.[6]

This astonishing growth, unmatched by any other middle class movement during the Progressive era, marked the real emergence of women as an influence in American life. There were several basic types of clubs represented in the General Federation. Most common, perhaps, was the relatively small, largely social, club that flourished in the towns. Ostensibly devoted to self-culture, often with a literary title such as The Shakespeare Club, they frequently gave the impression, as one critic put it, of being 'a body of women banded together for the purpose of meeting together' (Doc. 12). The backbone of the GFWC, and of the State Federations that soon sprang up, were, however, the great department clubs of which the Chicago Woman's Club was best known. Large, well-financed, and organized into departments concentrating on specific interests from the promotion of art to the suppression of child labour, these clubs often exerted a considerable influence in their communities. They produced most of the Federation's high officers. Also important were the civic clubs organized to improve the level of municipal services. Although women usually could not vote on these matters, the civics clubs proved that women could influence enough votes, or enough office holders, to initiate juvenile court systems, pass bond issues and the like.

Subjectively, clubs met the need of middle class, middle aged women of leisure activities outside of, but related to, their traditional

[6] The exact number is impossible to determine because the General Federation had several classes of membership, some of which overlapped. Not all clubs were affiliated with the GFWC, but a majority, including virtually all the important ones, probably were.

sphere. There were, it soon became clear, literally millions of women whose lives were not filled up by domestic and religious pursuits. Poorly educated for the most part, unwilling or unable to secure paid employment, they found in club life a solution to their personal dilemma. Those with more ability and ambition, or with a greater need to serve, could move up the ladder from positions of responsibility in their clubs to offices in the state federations, or even the General Federation itself. The club movement, requiring no special education or expertise, non-partisan, non-denominational, relatively uncontroversial by comparison with the suffrage and reform momvements, was perfectly suited to the developing need for self-expression of this very large class of women.

Objectively, the club movement for a time came near to being the woman movement. Clubs were the chief organs of support for the compact organizations upholding organized women's highest ideals and most ambitious reforms. The Women's Trade Union League, the Consumers Leagues, the settlement houses, and, until almost the end, the National American Women's Suffrage Association were tiny by comparison with the GFWC. The clubs gave them money and support, and club women made up the rank and file in the woman's army of reform. They drew into public affairs women who could not otherwise have been reached. Feminists, and social feminists in particular, appreciated the club movement's value. Charlotte Perkins Gilman reviewing the progress of organized women put it this way.

'The most wide-spread and in a way the most important of these various associations was the Woman's Club, which reached almost every one and brought her out of the sacred selfishness of the home into the broader contact and relationship so essential to social progress.'[7]

The Clubs mobilized in support of the Pure Food and Drug Act, threw their weight behind every conservationist effort, and struggled to raise the status of women and children, especially working women and children.

Club women embodied the social feminists' most characteristic traits. They were flexible, open-minded to the point of naivety, and sympathetic. They were not analytical, politically sophisticated, or especially self-aware. Guided by their instincts, semi-isolated from the intellectual and political mainstreams of the day, they were capable of the most innocently radical statements. The 1890s was a tumultuous decade in America, a time of large and often bloody strikes. The greatest industrial depression the country had yet seen spanned its

[7] Charlotte Perkins Gilman, *The Living of Charlotte Perkins Gilman* (New York, 1935), 257

middle years. At the end of the decade America suddenly found itself in possession of a colonial empire and had become, overnight as it were, a world power. The response of club women to these events was erratic, uncertain, but always spontaneous and warm-hearted. They deplored war but patriotically supported the country's foreign policy. Clubwomen were heartily against strikes, yet even in the 1890s, with the gunfire of the Homestead and Pullman strikes echoing in their ears, important club women rose above the prejudices of their class. In 1895 the General Federation's principal organ carried an article declaring 'since capital is too often but the incarnation of the spirit of modern greed, is the laborer to be blamed if he looks upon the strike as his only weapon of defence against existing conditions that rob him of all power over his own subsistence and that of those dearer than self?' (Doc. 11). Strong stuff, this, too strong no doubt for most club women. But throughout the Progressive era similar remarks appeared in the Federation's magazine and similar sentiments were expressed at its biennial conventions. If no great pieces of legislation were passed at the Federation's behest, it did make sterling resolutions at every biennial. It persuaded Congress to authorize a major study of working women and children, and it contributed in many ways to the more wholesome public opinion of those years.

However, the General Federation could not escape the defects of its virtues. Numbers were its chief asset. Because it was so large it automatically elicited the respect of politicians and journalists who had to assume, in the absence of contradictory evidence, that the Federation's officers spoke for their rank and file. As women did not vote there was no way of measuring their impact. It behove cautious public men, therefore, to play it safe by conceding the Federation's right to be heard on certain issues. On the other hand, the Federation grew so great because it did not ask much of its members. Attempts to secure a tighter organization prompted fears of secession. Most officers cautiously relied on persuasion and exhortation to implement their policies. They played a numbers game in which large membership figures masked the Federation's lack of real authority. This also meant that by definition the GFWC could not embark on controversial programmes. Its endorsement of a specific proposal signified that a consensus had been reached. Obviously this was worth knowing, even though agreement did not necessarily lead to action (Doc. 13).

The fear of conflict inspired by this loose structure exposed the Federation to a kind of moral blackmail. Since a determined group could prevent action by threatening to withdraw the GFWC was sometimes put in very equivocal positions. Its stands on racial segregation and the suffrage strikingly illustrate this. In 1900 Mrs Josephine St Pierre Ruffin, a cultivated Negro woman active in the Massachusetts State Federation, demanded recognition as an accredited delegate to the biennial convention. This precipitated the gravest crisis in Federation history. Club women were proud of their liberal, democratic sentiments (Doc. 15). The Federation had risen above denominational and sectarian rivalries. Many club women were not only heirs of the Abolitionist tradition, but like Julia Ward Howe had been themselves Abolitionists. Scarcely a biennial passed without the delegates rising to sing or recite her 'Battle Hymn of the Republic'. However, the Federation was equally proud of its national character. It believed itself to be playing a key role in the sectional reconciliation then taking place. Except, perhaps, for the WCTU it was the only national women's organization with a strong following in the South. Southern club women were a minority of the whole, but an important one because they represented the mass of conservative womanhood that the Federation's leaders were most eager to reach. Thus, the race issue touched not only the members' own prejudices, but jeopardized what most club-women felt to be the essential harmonizing and conciliatory function of the GFWC.

Put in these terms, and this is exactly how the matter was put in the very full discussions carried on at two biennials and in the pages of the Federation's journal, there could be but one response. The GFWC decided to sacrifice the handful of Negro clubwomen to its larger mission. The Federation was determined to be an instrument of sectional, not racial, reconciliation. Mrs Ruffin was not seated in 1900. Southern clubwomen were not forced to carry out their secessionist threats. Southern women failed to secure their ultimate ambition, a whites-only clause in the GFWC's constitution, but the next biennial voted overwhelmingly for a membership policy that permitted the South to veto any club whose racial composition gave offence. This is not to single out the GFWC. Almost every national organization upheld similar policies. Even the NAWSA, virtually all of whose founders had been Abolitionists, took an equivocal line on race during its salad days. The General Federation truly reflected the views of most social feminists, and in doing so demonstrated the limits of their liberalism.

Even more suggestive was the Federation's policy on woman suffrage. Most of its leaders, and perhaps a majority of its members, favoured equal suffrage well before it was enacted into law. The election of Sarah Platt Decker, an especially outspoken suffragist, as President of the GFWC in 1904 implied a substantial commitment on the issue. Yet it was not until 1910 that a convention session was devoted to woman suffrage. When in 1912 a resolution endorsing woman suffrage reached the floor it was ruled out of order. President Moore reminded her listeners that when the race question had been raised they had given way to a minority of Southerners to preserve the Federation. 'Your majority vote at any time in support of suffrage,'

she continued, 'would be your weakest argument, because it would
take out of the organization the minority that we want with us, the
timid and conservative women from all over the United States who
are working toward citizenship.' Finally, in 1914 a resolution endorsing woman suffrage was passed. The delegates sang the 'Battle Hymn
of the Republic' and 'Praise God from Whom All Blessings Flow'. No
one defected. Thus, the Federation was shown to be a victim of its
own fears. Of course suffrage was not so emotional an issue as race.
Certainly many, if not most, Southern women would have withdrawn
had Negroes been admitted to the GFWC. But the Federation would
not have been gravely diminished even so. By consistently passing up
its chances to seize the initiative in controversial areas the GFWC
narrowed the area of feminist manoeuvre. No doubt it did embrace
women who otherwise could not have been mobilized for the public
good. To this end it compromised and curtailed its activities so that
when women were liberated a tradition of limited action had been so
firmly established that it could not be overcome. Nor, having become
habituated to a policy of safety first, did these women wish to transcend
it. The innocuous effects of woman suffrage were, therefore, prefigured
in the workings of this most representative of all social feminist organizations.

The relative conservatism of the Federation was not, as the above
might suggest, entirely situational. There was another sense in which
club women were genuinely conservative. The notion that an evil
social condition, once clearly identified as such, ought to be abolished
is not unique to liberals and radicals. The vigorous strain of Tory
democracy that has periodically infused the English Conservative
Party is a case in point. But in America the reluctance to admit class
lines, the odium attached to paternalism, the frequent similarities
between major parties, and the generally low level of ideological
sophistication and self-awareness make it difficult for groups and
individuals to know what it is in fact that they stand for. Where
women at the turn of the century were concerned this confusion,
normal to Americans, was complicated by their artificial exclusion from
formal politics. Few women conceded the need for something like a
philosophy peculiar to themselves, but this did not mean that they
did not have one—or, rather, the elements of one. Women tended
to react impulsively and sympathetically to specific problems. Reporting on a local Bill favoured by clubwomen an inland newspaper noted
that it 'passed in a rush of gallantry in which gush, good sense, and
sentimentalism were combined'. Their confusion was compounded by
an oratorical style that relied on phrases like 'universal brotherhood',
'the Mother instinct', or 'true wisdom and divine love' to justify
specific policies.

What gave a certain coherence to the work of clubwomen, despite their hopelessly trite, sentimental and obscurantist rhetoric, were the beliefs, habits of response and assumptions common to them. Astute women recognized that the great emphasis the cult of womanhood placed on women's service and maternal functions was capable of exploitation. Having been taught from their earliest days that it was their duty to serve, leisure class women suffered from underemployment in middle age. Still vigorous, but with lessened maternal and domestic responsibilities, they were capable of redirection. The best clubs filled a vacuum in their personal lives by teaching them to see their duty in a larger context. Such women brought to civic work, child labour reform, and the like homely attitudes of considerable value. Domesticity gave them an awareness of the practical and concrete that resulted on the local level in better streets, sewers, and public services. Informally educated, isolated from the abstract principles of the day, they were impatient with formalistic objections to particular improvements. The Federation magazine complained that 'to some men all law is tyrannical and contrary to the American system'. They failed to understand why desirable legislation should be frustrated simply because it 'tended toward socialism'. On the contrary, it seemed to them, viewing the damage created by generations of men in the name of sound business and safe politics, that it was the women who were truly conservative, or, as they more often put it, conservationist.

'Conservation, then, in its best and highest sense is the raison d'être of the General Federation of Women's Clubs—conservation of life, of liberty and of happiness; conservation of child life, of womanhood, of civic and national integrity in matters of public and private import.'[8]

These were deeply conservative ambitions, and should have been recognized as such. They were misunderstood for several reasons. At the turn of the century conservatism was identified with preserving a *status quo* based on *laissez-faire* and social Darwinism. Opposition to the existing order was invariably regarded as radical or progressive, even though it often was not. The business men in the Progressive Party of Theodore Roosevelt sought to rationalize the economic structure and regulate competition. These were in a real sense conservative goals, but the Progressives were denounced as radicals nonetheless. It was not to be expected that in this climate the ambitions of club-women, requiring as they did more vigorous governmental action on every level, would be appreciated for what they were. Clubwomen further confused the issue, and themselves, by their ignorance of, and contempt for, the conventional wisdom on economic and social questions. They repeatedly condemned economic competition. They

[8] Mary I. Wood, *The History of the General Federation* (New York, 1914).

admired co-operation, sometimes to the point of calling for a
'co-operative commonwealth', the very phrase used by Eugene V. Debs
to describe the Socialist Party's vision of the good society. There was
something splendid about this freewheeling, spontaneous eclecticism.
Women did not yet possess the ideological early-warning system that
was to frustrate so many reforms in the post-war era. At the same time,
however, this openness to experience and hostility to theory prevented
women from understanding the realities of their position. It kept them
from developing an ideology appropriate to their long term needs. It
confused their friends as well as their enemies (Doc. 14). When the
vote was won it became clear, as we shall see later, that for clubwomen
as well as suffragists the symbols of feminine unity had functioned as
a screen for their disunity and uncertainty. The decline of the General
Federation's prestige and authority after 1920 was an inevitable consequence of these analytical failures.

3

Social Feminism Reaches Maturity

While mass organizations like the GFWC, the WCTU, and, at its end, the NAWSA played a key role in women's emergence, they were not necessarily more important than the smaller, although more vivid and dramatic movements allied with them. Of these, none had greater impact than the social settlements. Unlike women's clubs, which originated in America and never really caught on elsewhere, the social settlement had its genesis in England. It began with the example of Arnold Toynbee. A university graduate of compelling personality, much influenced by John Ruskin, Toynbee settled in the slums of East London, where until his death in 1883 at the age of thirty-two, he attempted to share the lives of working men to their mutual advantage. His idea was institutionalized by Samuel A. Barnett, the vicar of an East London parish, who in 1884 founded Toynbee Hall. Barnett conceived of the Hall as a place where university men like Toynbee could live among the poor, sharing in their struggles while bringing to them the benefits of a higher culture. In practice Toynbee Hall had an exemplary and educational effect. Barnett was not so much interested in social reform as in the spiritual and aesthetic poverty of the urban masses. His initiative was immediately successful, however, because it touched the romantic conscience of his age and seemed to offer a practical outlet for the imaginative sympathies of educated youth. By 1911 there were forty-six settlements in Great Britain.

It was in America, however, that the movement reached its fullest development. There were numerous reasons for this. Urban conditions deteriorated rapidly in the late nineteenth century under the pressure of an immense population growth. Chicago, for example, doubled in size between 1880 and 1890, when its population reached the million mark. In that same year the slum population of New York alone exceeded one million persons. The Federal government accepted no responsibility for conditions in the city, while the cities themselves lacked the resources, and usually the statutory authority, to address their problems directly. Most were governed by corrupt political machines whose power rested on the votes of immigrants inaccessible to middle class reformers. The transformation from a largely rural society without great disparities in wealth and characterized by, for the most part, a common tongue and a common political and religious heritage, to an urban society marked by severe class, religious, and ethnic differences proceeded rapidly in those years. The urban crisis was more severe in the United States than in England, while at the same time the political instruments for attacking it were less effective. This situation impelled Americans to place their hopes on voluntary, non-political approaches to the problem. Politics was, of course, not entirely ignored. There were municipal reform efforts, inspired to some degree by the example of Birmingham and the London County Council. The Progressive era saw repeated attempts to prod every level of government into action. Few of them accomplished much. Voluntary associations, the normal American response to social ills in any event, became, therefore, all the more important.

Apart from these objective considerations, the social settlement met the personal needs of a certain kind of young American woman. In England the movement was largely masculine, in America it was chiefly feminine. Of the best known American settlement leaders at least half were women like Jane Addams, Lillian Wald, Mary McDowell and Mary Simkhovitch. The great majority of residents were women. Jane Addams, the movement's most notable spokesman, offered the best explanation of this fact in her remarkable essay, 'The Subjective Necessity of Social Settlements'. While she spoke in general terms of the problems of 'young people' from comfortable backgrounds who lived 'unnourished, over-sensitive lives' and felt themselves shut off from the real world of struggle and service, she meant especially the frustrating dilemma of young women such as herself who had been caught in what she elsewhere called 'the snare of preparation'.

'Parents are often inconsistent. They deliberately expose their daughters to knowledge of the distress in the world. They send them to hear missionary addresses on famines in India and China; they accompany them to lectures on the suffering in Siberia; they agitate together over the forgotten region of East London. In addition to this, from babyhood the altruistic tendencies of these daughters are persistently cultivated. They are taught to be self-forgetting and self-sacrificing, to consider the good of the Whole before the good of the Ego. But when all this information and culture show results, when the daughter comes back from college and begins to recognize her social claim to the "submerged tenth", and to evince a disposition to fulfill

it, the family claim is strenuously asserted; she is told that she is
unjustified, ill-considered in her efforts.'[1]

Miss Addams rejected the family claim only after long struggle
and a nervous indisposition lasting seven years. By moving into a slum
she found not only opportunities for service, but relief from the
anxieties and contradictions that had marked her whole adult life. Other
women in similar circumstances were to find less drastic solutions to
their dilemma. For some the civic altruism of club life was a respectable and satisfying outlet. College women who did not, like Jane
Addams, repudiate their education found in alumnae groups and the
ACA outlets for the emotional energies generated by their school years.
Miss Addams' resentment of her education was in this respect unusual.
She felt that college had pushed her farther away from the world by
teaching her to see life in terms of literature and cutting her off from
the direct perception of reality. But few of the women graduates who
moved into settlements would have agreed. Most believed that life in
a settlement was a kind of post-graduate education, a continuation
on a higher level of what they had done in college. Jane Addams did not
have to fight her way into college as most of them had, and so she
understandably did not share their heavy emotional investment in
higher education (Doc. 16). Moreover, they found in the *camaraderie*
and sociability of the settlement a facsimile of the associations they
had learned to cherish in school. Few of them, however, devoted their
lives to settlement work. Most stayed for a few years and then either
married or moved on into careers in social work or allied fields.

For a time the female settlement worker had a considerable impact
on feminism in America. This seems not to have been the case in
England, apparently because of the disparity in size. Smith College
alone had more women students than Oxford and Cambridge. In 1890
the Women's University Settlement in Southwark, supported by the
four women's colleges of Oxford and Cambridge, had only five residents. The College Settlement in New York, supported by the leading
Eastern women's colleges, started out with seven, and quickly
expanded even as the parent association founded other college settlements in Boston and Philadelphia. By 1911 when the English settlements were numbered in the dozens there were literally hundreds of
settlements in America. Nor did the English settlement movement
attract women like Jane Addams or Lillian Wald. Thus, the settlement movement had a unique effect on social feminism in America.
It produced individual women of much influence who built their
settlements into great engines of reform. Jane Addams' Hull House
embraced fourteen separate buildings. Lillian Wald's Henry Street

[1] First published in 1892, the essay is conveniently available in Christopher
Lasch, ed., *The Social Thought of Jane Addams* (Indianapolis, 1965), 37-38.

Settlement in New York owned property worth half a million dollars. If their physical plants commanded respect, their character and accomplishments were still more impressive. Their energy, dedication, courage, and, in the case of Miss Addams, fluency, made them known the country over and gave middle class women heroic examples to follow and admire.

Equally important were the thousands of women who did not give their lives to the settlement, but contributed to the spread of its influence. The settlement was a transitional institution in several respects. Most women did not stay long in it, and the settlement lost influence after the war for reasons too numerous to deal with here. But from about 1895 to 1915 it met the needs of thousands of young women, inspired by their education to play a larger role in society than custom permitted. In the twentieth century as women's opportunities expanded the settlement's subjective importance diminished. It had emerged when educated young women most needed it, however, and thus played its part in the great drama of their emancipation. Most importantly of all, perhaps, it undermined the Victorian stereotype. When the first College Settlement's founders set to work a Boston newspaper remarked dolefully that 'the falling of their young unsullied lives in this wretched vicious dismal quarter seems like the falling of a lily in the mud'. When instead of falling they flourished, as did the thousands who came after them, the image of middle class woman as a flower of rare delicacy and useless refinement was shattered forever. Even if most settlement residents had not been feminists, they would still have rendered the movement a signal service. That most of them were suffragists was simply one more reason for gratitude on the part of the women's rights movement.

Although settlement workers were generally the most celebrated social feminists, they were by no means alone in their attempts to aid the disadvantaged. Among the other feminine reformers two organizations in particular exemplified alternative modes of action—the National Consumers' League and the National Women's Trade Union League. In the beginning, before settling down as neighbourhood service agencies, the settlements possessed a mystical element. The first women in the College Settlements had a Franciscan ambition to share in their neighbours' lives. Often settlement residents were strongly religious, although by inclination and necessity non-sectarian. Even Robert A. Woods, the most pedestrian of settlement apologists, expressed in his early writings a vision of the city redeemed through neighbourly intercourse. Organizations like the NCL and NWTUL, by way of contrast, were both more ambitious and less messianic. They did not imagine themselves to be the agents of universal regeneration. On the other hand, while settlements lavished attention on local problems, the national organizations, as their titles demonstrated, aimed for continental and sometimes international influence. They wanted to accomplish a limited number of reforms on the very largest scale possible.

The first Consumers' League was founded by a committee led by the remarkable Josephine Shaw Lowell. Although steeped in the severe doctrines of Charity Organization, and a member of that generation of philanthropists most influenced by Social Darwinism, Mrs Lowell was a woman of uncommon sympathies. Her work with the State Board of Charities in New York convinced her that what the labouring poor most needed was not institutional assistance but higher wages and better working conditions. This insight led her to resign finally from the State Board in order to assist directly the struggling masses. She was one of the first of her class to appreciate the value of trade unions, and so informed her colleagues in the National Conference of Charities and Corrections. Labour unions were, however, uninterested and, in some ways, ill-suited to the fight for working women and children who were at once the most distressed, and the least able to help themselves, of all workers. They needed immediate aid in the form of protective legislation, and to secure this a sympathetic public opinion was required. Influential, upper class women qualified for this work, and once she realized it Mrs Lowell moved quickly to implement her discovery.

In 1890 a mass meeting was held in New York at the behest of a society of working women to publicize their needs. It resulted in a committee which in January of the following year decided to call itself the Consumers' League, as an organization with that name had been formed in England a few months earlier. Mrs Lowell was its first president. She was assisted by many friends acquired during her long career in philanthropy, the most important of which was Maud Nathan. Mrs Nathan was in every respect the Jewish counterpart of Mrs Lowell. Both were of old upper class stock. Mrs Lowell came from the Boston Brahmins, Mrs Nathan from the Sephardic aristocracy of New York that dated back to the middle of the seventeenth century. Their wealth, social connections, and charitable experiences enabled them to mobilize a small but strategically placed group of elite women. The Consumers' League focused initially on the retail clerks of New York. It publicized their low pay and deplorable working conditions. It published annually a 'White List' of approved stores with good labour policies, which people of conscience were asked to patronize exclusively. It agitated with considerable success for shorter store hours during the Christmas season, and waged 'shop early' campaigns to diminish the Christmas rush that made such demands on store personnel. The Consumers' League was not, therefore, as the name suggested a band of consumers organized to advance their own interests, but rather to assist the people who served them. In the next few years other Consumers' Leagues were formed in major American cities. In 1899 these scattered branches met to organize formally as the National Consumers' League.

Far more significant than its decision to go national was the League's hiring of Florence Kelley as general secretary. Although not well known at the time, she was destined to become one of the greatest women in American history. Florence Kelley was born in Philadelphia in 1859. Her mother's family were mostly Quakers. Her father was a lawyer who sat in Congress for thirty years, earning the title 'Father of the House'. His enthusiasm for protective tariffs, and his passionate devotion to the needs of heavy industry, made him known throughout the country as 'Pig-Iron Kelley'. (His friends called him Judge Kelley.) He was, however, neither a profiteer, nor a callous servant of the new rich, nor a stern, unbending Tory. Rather he combined in his person both of the dominant strains in the Republican Party of his day. He was, on the one hand, a Unionist, an Abolitionist, and an early supporter of woman suffrage. On the other hand, he was also completely dedicated to making America an industrial power at whatever cost. These two strains, the altruistic and the materialistic, were not warring impulses within him. He saw industrialization as a patriotic duty, even an ideal. He promoted it for the same reasons as he opposed slavery, disunion and sex discrimination. He looked to the future when America would be a just, powerful and affluent society. In the short run this meant paying a certain human price in terms of labour exploitation and the accumulation of capital by men who did not share his own high standards. He saw it, as he told Florence when she was still a girl, to be the duty of his generation to create the wealth which it would be her generation's duty to equitably administer.

A remarkable father produced a remarkable daughter. Miss Kelley shared her father's energy, enthusiasm and ambition, while surpassing him in social consciousness and altruism. She was a pioneer woman university graduate earning a bachelor's degree from Cornell in 1882. Denied the opportunity for further study by the restrictive policies of most American graduate schools, she then went to Zürich where the university accepted women on an equal basis with men. Zürich was then a centre for political exiles. Most of them were socialists of one sort or another, and before long she herself was converted. She began translating one of Engels' early works into English. In 1884 she married Lazare Wischnewetzky, a Russian revolutionary and physician. They settled in America where she gave birth to three children. The marriage was not, however, a success. Wischnewetzky was addicted to fads and impulses, and although a socialist was inspired by the heady American business atmosphere to dabble in speculative enterprises of a consistently unfortunate nature. Her political life was equally unpromising. The only Marxist group in the United States was the Socialist Labor Party which the Wischnewstzkys joined as a matter of course. Dominated by German immigrants, fiercely sectarian, the SLP was not excited at having recruited a native born American woman of ability and good family. During the next few years a series of bizarre incidents and misunderstandings led to the Wischnewetzkys' expulsion from the SLP. Dr Wischnewetzky's professional fortunes languished and the marriage seems gradually to have decayed. In 1891 Florence Kelley, having resumed her maiden name, moved to Chicago to secure a divorce under the more lenient laws of Illinois, and took up residence in Hull House.

During these years she also abandoned her commitment to revolutionary socialism. This was not simply the result of her expulsion from the SLP for, as she ruefully explained later, speaking English, but because she came to feel the need for an immediate attack on the pressing social problems she saw all around her. Socialism was for the future, but the needs of working women and children could not, in her mind, be left to that distant day when the revolution would put everything to rights. This was hardly a surprising conclusion for one of her class and background. Except for Vida Scudder, a Boston settlement worker and academician, no other prominent social feminist went so far as to join the socialist movement, and Miss Scudder was essentially a Christian Socialist, not a revolutionary (Doc. 17). The odd thing is that Florence Kelley became a socialist in the first place. Doubtlessly the bracing political air of Zürich was responsible, although other young American women—notably M. Carey Thomas, the president of Bryn Mawr College and a leading figure in the ACA—studied in Zürich without being affected by its politics. Mrs Kelley never stopped being a socialist. When the Debsian Socialist Party was formed she joined it, and she held numerous offices in socialist organizations throughout her career. But she was an intensely practical, impatient woman. Revolutionary movements gave her no way to employ those overflowing energies that led her to be called 'Niagara Falls'. She wanted to be effective at once and the only way to take instant action was to become a reformer. Hull House offered her a start as a reformer, and she took the chance gratefully. Even before her divorce she had begun investigating the child labour problem. She continued investigating, reporting, and agitating as a resident. Soon the election of John Peter Altgeld, the great reform governor of Illinois in the mid-1890s, gave her a wider field of action. He appointed her Chief Factory Inspector of the state to enforce a new Anti-Sweat Shop Bill. The celebrations of reformers were, however, premature. The Bill was soon declared unconstitutional by the state Supreme Court and when Altgeld failed of re-election Mrs Kelley lost her job.

In 1899, when the Consumers' League began shopping for a General Secretary, Mrs Kelley had been comparatively unemployed for two

years. Her term as Chief Factory Inspector, however abortive in
the end, had given her a reputation, invaluable experience, and a
permanent commitment to social reform through governmental action.
It had also showed her the importance of changing public opinion.
The National Consumers' League offered her a platform from which
to speak, and a vehicle for implementing reforms. Its socially prominent members commanded both the public eye and the official ear.
They were equally ready to publicize and to lobby. Under Florence
Kelley's inspired leadership they did both. Mrs Kelley's genius was
hortatory rather than organizational (Doc. 19), yet within a few years
the NCL had grown to include 90 local leagues, 20 state leagues, 35
student branches, and 35 auxiliary leagues. She travelled and spoke
constantly, and her words frequently fell on responsibe ears. However,
the NCL's size was in a sense misleading. The branches were, for the
most part, small, scattered, and subject to fits of enthusiasm punctu-
ated by long periods of lassitude; only the key branches in New York,
Boston, and Chicago were continuously effective. Mrs Kelley was, of
course, always busy. She recruited a body of women who became
professional reformers like herself. One of them, Frances Perkins,
became Secretary of Labor under President Franklin D. Roosevelt—
the first woman to be a cabinet officer. Others, like Pauline and
Josephine Goldmark shuttled between the Consumers' League and a
variety of governmental posts. Together with the wealthy philanthropists who supported the National and local leagues, and often gave of
their time as well as their money, they constituted a highly trained
striking force backstopping Mrs Kelley's formidable efforts.

The NCL's specific accomplishments were numerous. It helped
secure protective legislation for working women in many states during
the Progressive era. It played a key role in the successful campaign to
have a Children's Bureau added to the Department of Labor. Together
with the National Child Labor Committee, of which Mrs Kelley was
also an officer, it helped persuade Congress to pass a Bill restricting
child labour in 1916. Among the most durable of its victories was its
struggle for minimum wage and maximum hour legislation. In 1907 Mrs
Kelley and Josephine Goldmark persuaded Miss Goldmark's brother-
in-law Louis Brandeis, the great liberal attorney and later Supreme
Court Justice, to defend the Oregon Ten Hour Law before the Supreme
Court. Brandeis took the case, and with logistical and research support
from the League, argued it successfully. *Muller v. Oregon* marked a
turning point in the struggle for protective legislation for women and
children. The court had previously taken a dim view of legislative
attempts to control the hours of labour. In this, and subsequent cases
required to nail down the many points of law, the court took another
tack. Later the NCL similarly supported minimum wage legislation.
When Brandeis moved up to the bench he was replaced by Felix

Frankfurter, who in turn became a Justice of the Supreme Court. Thanks to them the League was able to win judicial approval for state laws protecting working women and children. This proved to be even more important than it seemed at the time for the Supreme Court later invalidated two congressional child labour bills. The state laws that the League helped validate proved, therefore, to be indispensable.

Florence Kelley and her League illustrated both the strengths and weaknesses of social feminism. We have seen how they showed what a handful of upper and middle class women could do. But they also demonstrated the limits of that type of reform. Many of the local laws they secured were never properly enforced. More seriously, the campaign to abolish child labour nationally, the cause closest to Mrs Kelly's own heart, ended in complete failure. Although a Constitutional Amendment permitting Congress to legislate in this area was presented to the states, only a handful ratified it. This was no small defeat. The campaign against child labour was not only Mrs Kelley's favourite cause, but the single most important reform espoused by social feminism as a whole. Mrs Kelley was pre-eminent among those women who wanted the vote chiefly to effect such reforms as the abolition of child labour and the full protection of working women. Both efforts bogged down after the First World War. Child labour became a dead issue while feminists divided among themselves as to whether minimum wage and hour Bills did not unduly restrict female workers in their competition with men. Although the vote was supposed to unleash the maternal instincts of women prevented by their unenfranchised status from reforming the condition of working women and children, it had no such effect. Social feminists were, in fact, comparatively more successful without the vote than with it. This was demoralizing to feminists and reformers alike, but especially to the social feminists who were both. It also made doubtful the other propositions on which women like Mrs Kelley built their lives: that social reforms were a more practical alternative to the sweeping and presumably Utopian aims of socialists; that the altruism and social sympathies of women, upper and middle class women in particular, were a realistic substitute for the unawakened self-interest of the masses.

The National Women's Trade Union League casts further light on the problems facing social feminists. Unlike the NCL, which owed only its name to England, the NWTUL was copied from an English original. The English WTUL, in turn, was inspired by several American examples. In 1873 Mrs Emma Paterson came to the United States on her honeymoon and was struck by the limited success of several female unions in New York City. On her return to England she called a conference, attended by such notables as Canon Kingsley, Arnold Toynbee, Harriet Martineau and George Shipton of the London

Trades Council which organized the Women's Protective and Provident League. In 1890 it changed its name to the Women's Trade Union League. At first the League reflected its leader's sternly Liberal principles. It opposed protective legislation for working women and concentrated on organizing female trade unions. These usually proved to be short-lived. In 1886 when Mrs Paterson died only about 2,500 women belonged to League-sponsored associations. Thereafter the League worked for protective laws and the opening up of existing unions to women workers. The Trades Union Congress did not accept delegates from the WTUL, because of its middle class character, but did hold a 'women's conference' in connection with its annual meetings. In 1889 the League changed its membership policies and invited all trade unions with female members to affiliate with it by paying dues of a half-penny a year for each woman member. At this time some 118,000 working women were unionized, mainly in the cotton unions. The WTUL, now led by Lady Dilke whose husband, Sir Charles Dilke, spoke for them in Parliament, won a fair share of these union women, although its greatest growth came after 1903 when Mary MacArthur became secretary.

In that year William English Walling, an American intellectual and socialist, visited England and was much impressed by the WTUL's progress. On his return he contacted Mary Kenney O'Sullivan, a labour veteran closely associated with the settlement movement, and together they induced some of the prominent reformers and labour leaders gathered in Boston for the annual convention of the AFL to organize an American counterpart to the WTUL. This was done, but the infant National Women's Trade Union League developed little momentum. Union labour had no interest in working women. President Gompers of the AFL gave the women little encouragement and less money. As in England, many unions barred women from membership. Most union leaders thought women's place was in the home, and not in industry filling jobs that otherwise would go to men. Although there were some five million working women in 1900 they made, on the average, about half the wages of working men. Thus, they could not pay the same dues as union men and the money it cost to organize them brought a lesser return than the same money invested in organizing men. Working women in both countries tended to think of their jobs as temporary and most left the work force upon marriage. They lacked, therefore, the long-term commitment required of union members. Moreover, in both countries they were mainly unskilled workers, notoriously the hardest sector of the work force to organize.

At the outset, the NWTUL relied upon settlement houses for its support. Branches were established in Boston, New York, and Chicago with the help of settlement workers. However, settlement workers were already over-committed. They gave the League what help they could, but it was pathetically little in relation to the job ahead. In 1906 the League's fortunes improved when it was joined by Margaret Dreier, the handsome daughter of a prosperous German immigrant. Although she soon married and left New York for Chicago, she retained her interest in the League and in 1907 was elected president of the NWTUL. With the encouragement of her husband Raymond Robins, a young man who had struck it rich in the Klondike and now was working full-time as a reformer, she held the position for twenty-two years. Mrs Robins brought to her work a number of important advantages. Her relatively high social position gave her self-assurance. More importantly, perhaps, it intimidated some labour leaders—notably Gompers himself—into giving the League more attention than they liked. The social standing of Mrs Robins, her sister Mary, and other prominent women was helpful also in assuring working girls that they would not lose status by joining the trade union movement. This was of considerable importance in the fluid American social order where status anxieties were particularly acute. Working girls, especially native Americans threatened by the competition of immigrant women, were understandably reluctant to jeopardize what little standing they enjoyed. The most ambitious and upwardly mobile girls of greatest value to the trade unions were precisely the ones most repelled by their proletarian character. The League's middle class leadership was, therefore, often a point in its favour among working women, and, although resented by union men, an asset in negotiating with them.

Mrs Robins understood, however, that a trade union league had finally to be made up of trade union women. She believed that middle class dominance was only a temporary condition. From the outset she began recruiting a cadre of working women, a job she did so well that at her retirement most league offices were filled by her working class protegées. During her presidency the League operated on a variety of fronts. New branches were added and a training school for organizers established in Chicago. When in 1909 the New York shirt-waist makers spontaneously went out on strike the League rendered important services to them. This great strike, the largest ever to be made up entirely of working women (mainly single, Jewish girls), lasted for months and involved twenty to thirty thousand people. The League provided bail money for arrested pickets, conducted an effective publicity campaign, and supplied large sums for the strike fund. The strike was lost, but it proved to be a springboard for the International Ladies' Garment Workers Union that later effectively organized a large part of the industry. It also established the WTUL as a legitimate friend of labour. In 1910 the Chicago branch rendered even greater services to the more than 40,000 garment workers who went out on strike in that great city. In the next few years the strikes came thick and fast. The League's tiny force of organizers shuttled back and forth across the country organizing a branch here, a union there, rallying in support of embattled strikers everywhere that its resources permitted.

Yet the tangible results of all this activity were few. Membership grew, income rose, but most of the new branches waxed and waned in response to local conditions and, like the NCL, the League could only count on the key branches in New York, Chicago, and, sometimes, Boston. In large measure this was a consequence of the AFL's surly attitude. Although the League made great efforts to conciliate Gompers and his like, they could never compromise enough or defer sufficiently to merit the Federation's steady approval. Most of the time it got no money at all from organized labour, even though the women it organized and the unions it formed generally affiliated with the AFL. When one of the League's organizers, Rose Schneiderman, resigned after four years of work it was estimated that she had recruited 7,000 women for garment unions that did not contribute a penny to the WTUL. When the Federation did provide funds they were earmarked for specific purposes, and often withdrawn for arbitrary or capricious reasons. Throughout its life the WTUL depended almost entirely on private donors. The League's unreciprocated devotion to the AFL was, therefore, destructive of its larger purposes. It might have been impossible to organize women workers without the AFL's help, but it was clearly impossible to do so under the conditions imposed by the Federation.

The small measure of success that the League did enjoy was chiefly the result of its affiliation with the woman movement. Women philanthropists supported it financially. The League, in turn, supported equal suffrage and co-operated with other social feminists in the areas of mutual concern. Its organizational failures made it psychologically more dependent on woman suffrage than its English counterpart. The League existed because some middle class women understood that the vote was not enough, that the condition of working women depended on their organizing as men had done. But their grave difficulties undermined this perception to a degree. Without ever giving up their central insight, they could not but feel at times that woman suffrage offered another way of achieving the same ends; that in co-operation with feminists they could achieve what they had failed to do by working with labour leaders. This was a natural response to an essentially impossible situation. As time was to show, however, it was a forlorn one.

The English parallel is instructive in other ways. In 1903 Mary Macarthur, the daughter of a prosperous draper who moved from working in his store to becoming an officer of the Shop Assistants (retail clerks) Union, became secretary of the WTUL. At that time its strength depended largely on one or two affiliated unions in the cotton industry. These unions were, in fact, composed mainly of women and the unionization of working women was pretty much confined to them. Miss Macarthur launched a membership drive that brought in 16,000 male members in two years, raising the League's total membership to 70,000. In 1906 she took a step of great importance by organizing the National Federation of Women Workers, which she served as president and later as secretary. Membership in it was open to all unorganized working women, and to women in trades where male unions would not admit them. The NFWW had several advantages over the WTUL. As an entirely working class organization it was able to join the Trades Union Congress. It was also eligible for membership in the General Federation of Trade Unions, a strike insurance organization formed by the TUC in 1899.

The WTUL transferred some of its functions to the NFWW. It concentrated on lobbying and propaganda, while the NFWW worked directly at organizing working women. In 1910 it won a great token victory by organizing the women chain makers of Cradley Heath. The women chain makers were few in number, but they had come to symbolize the sweated labour of women. Working at small forges they made coarse iron chains on a contract basis, often in their own homes. Their tiny income, arduous work, and distressing home life aroused widespread sympathy, but, as was usually the case with sweat shops, the subcontracting system made them extremely hard to organize. Miss Macarthur overcame these obstacles by securing a Parliamentary Bill setting up Trade Boards in four sweated industries, including the chain industry, consisting of employer representatives.[2] The idea was to make the policies of the best employers universal. Not all contractors complied with the Trade Boards' recommendations. It took a combination of pressure from the co-operating employers together with a strike against non-compliers, organized by Miss Macarthur, to make wages uniform throughout the industry. Thanks to these flexible tactics organization proceeded apace in both the sweated and conventional industries. By 1914 there were 400,000 women in trade unions. The death of Sir Charles Dilke three years earlier had not retarded their progress, for his parliamentary role was assumed by Miss Macarthur's husband Will Anderson, chairman of the Labour Party.

When the war broke out Miss Macarthur had succeeded in making the WTUL and its offspring the acknowledged representatives of working women, although few were then organized, and fewer still affiliated with the WTUL and the NFWW. The flood of women workers who poured into industry as the result of acute labour shortages greatly

[2] The Bill passed with the help of the Home Secretary, Winston Churchill, whose lack of enthusiasm for woman suffrage did not blind him to the evils it was supposed to eradicate.

strengthened her hand. By 1918 over a million women belonged to trade unions. The Standing Joint Committee of Industrial Women's Organizations, made up of all the organizations interested in working women and chaired by Miss Macarthur, was recognized by both the Government and the Labour Party as the chief authority on working women. It was extremely successful in having its recommendations made official policy, and the fair wages and good working conditions enjoyed by English industrial women during the war were a tribute to its efficacy.[3] When the war ended the women's trade union movement had developed to such an extent that its incorporation by the regular union organizations was possible. In 1919 the NFWW became a section of the National Union of General Workers. In 1921, following her premature death, Miss Macarthur's plan to have the WTUL become a part of the General Council of the Trades Union Congress was executed.

The NWTUL in America fared quite differently during these years. It experienced no surge of growth comparable to the British WTUL. During the war, that is, during the approximately eighteen months when America was a combatant, the NWTUL was depleted as government agencies drew off many of its key members. The war created few new openings for women workers and in consequence the number of trade union women did not increase markedly. There was no American equivalent of the Standing Committee of Industrial Organizations. The government endorsed but did not enforce equitable policies for the protection of women workers. After the Armistice the NWTUL recovered slightly, and then fell into a decline that continued until the generation of working women recruited by Mrs Robins was too old to carry on. The NWTUL then dissolved. Its fate, therefore, was almost exactly the reverse of its English counterpart. This does not mean that the millennium was brought to pass in England. Even today working women earn less than men, and their representatives have less influence than the number of working women might suggest. But a larger percentage of the female work force is organized in England, and they play a larger role in the labour movement. The first woman cabinet member in England was Margaret Bondfield, Mary Macarthur's old colleague in the Shop Assistants Union. Had she lived, Miss Macarthur herself would probably have gone to Parliament, as trade union women still do. No comparable development has taken place in America. Women have only a small voice in the AFL-CIO. Union women are not elected to Congress. The first woman to secure a cabinet office was appointed by President Roosevelt as Secretary of Labor, but although an ally of labour Frances Perkins was not a trade union woman, having been associated

[3] Which is not to say that there were no abuses. For a harrowing if scrappy account of them see E. Sylvia Pankhurst, *The Home Front* (London, 1932).

with the Consumers' League and the New York State Department of Labor. She had, in any event, no successor.

Several factors would seem to account for these disparities. The union movement as a whole has been more successful in England than in the United States. A much larger percentage of the work force is organized, and through their political organ, the Labour Party, trade unions exercise a much greater influence on public policy. Women have been carried along by the victorious march of their male colleagues. This was not, however, a foregone conclusion. Female trade unionists and their allies shrewdly capitalized on their advantages. They aligned themselves with the Labour Party and the socialist movement at an early date. They did not waste their energies on woman suffrage which they rightly saw to be, in some respects, marginal to their real needs. When it became clear that the bourgeois character of the WTUL was an impediment to close co-operation with the union movement they formed organizations that were acceptable to labour leaders, notably the NFWW. At the earliest possible time they sunk their separate organizations into the mainstream of organized labour.

Trade union women in America, it must be admitted, faced insuperable obstacles. The labour movement itself was weak through this whole period. The socialist movement was suppressed during the war and largely collapsed in the 1920s. The large immigrant population in the cities made organizing extraordinarily difficult, as did the vast size and decentralized structure of the United States. But the women further compounded their difficulties. The NWTUL overlapped with the NCL to some degree. At the same time its bourgeois leadership was a barrier to close association with the trade unions. Obviously these women would have been better advised to divide as their English sisters did into a pure union organization and a supporting but separate group of allies. Their peculiar difficulties also led them to exaggerate the vote's usefulness. Some union women, the mine workers' legendary Mother Jones for example, were critical of the emphasis on equal suffrage, but union women and their allies persisted in spending time, money, and energy on suffrage campaigns of doubtful value to themselves. The insistence of the NWTUL on maintaining its own identity was also self-defeating. A policy of working from within the union movement might very well have failed, but it was worth trying and women had nothing of importance to lose in the attempt.

It should be remembered, however, that the problems I have been discussing were not apparent in 1917 when America entered the war, or even in 1920 when the vote was won. Hindsight alone enables us to see that the woman movement at its peak was burdened with contradictions and difficulties that would prove fatal to it. However, the movement never seemed more united and vigorous than on the eve of its dissolution. To appreciate why this was so we must understand that in its final stages the suffrage campaign generated such momentum as to inspire even the most sober feminist with expectations grounded in little more than momentary enthusiasms. Since feminists as a whole were not much given to introspection and self-criticism, it was hardly to be expected that they would pause on the edge of victory to consider its consequences. A closer look at the mechanics of the suffrage campaign will indicate how this came about.

4

Winning the Suffrage

The history of woman suffrage in both England and America during the late nineteenth century makes drab reading. In America, after a vigorous beginning in the 1850s and 60s, the demand for equal suffrage (American feminists insisted that they be enfranchised on the same basis as men) encountered a deadly mixture of feminine apathy and masculine resistance. Suffragists were by no means inactive during this period. Between 1870 and 1910 they staged 480 campaigns in thirty-three states to have the issue voted upon. Yet only seventeen resulted in actual referenda, and just two of these were successful. Even the growing conservatism of the Stanton-Anthony group failed to make the cause generally acceptable. The 1890s did see women suffrage prevail in four states. Wyoming and Utah, which had enfranchised women while still territories, were admitted to the Union. In 1893 Colorado granted votes to women, and in 1896 Idaho followed suit. Colorado was especially important for, unlike most Western states, it had some industry and one urban centre. Thust, it approximated the conditions under which Americans commonly lived. Surprisingly enough, however, the example of Colorado, even though it disproved the arguments usually employed against woman suffrage, had a negligible effect. At the beginning of the twentieth century equal suffrage seemed hardly more popular than it had been forty years earlier.

In England woman suffrage, having begun more modestly, progressed more slowly. A flicker of interest was aroused in 1884 when the Parliamentary franchise was broadened. Women were encouraged for a moment to think they would be included also. They were not, and the suffrage movement fell back into a sullen torpor enlivened only by quarrels that divided suffragists for a time into separate factions. During these years the movement often consisted of little more than Miss Lydia Becker who edited the *Women's Suffrage Journal*, and continued to lobby Parliament until her death in 1890. A few gains were registered. In 1869 women ratepayers were given the municipal franchise. In 1875 women became eligible to serve as Poor Law Guardians, and later as Borough and County Councillors. In 1897 a women's suffrage Bill got a second reading in Parliament and interest quickened. A monster petition was organized, and the movement reunited as the National Union of Women's Suffrage Societies under the leadership of Mrs Henry (later Dame Millicent) Fawcett. As usual, however, the Bill failed. English suffragists continued to be thwarted by the baffling parliamentary situation. Liberals, while nominally in favour of women's suffrage, feared that it would strengthen the Tories; the Conservative Party, on the other hand, was against women's suffrage in principle. Further complicating matters was the tendency of such Liberal prime ministers as Gladstone and Asquith to resist women's suffrage, while Conservative prime ministers like Disraeli and Salisbury personally favoured it. Liberal duplicity and Tory obstinacy alternately baffled and enraged suffragists. For decades they could find no way out of the impasse thus created.

To a degree, of course, the relative quiescence of the Anglo-American suffrage movement was misleading. Women were organizing in clubs, reform societies and the like, and this development generated streams of feminine energy that eventually flowed back into the rights movement. Moreover, in both countries the old leadership was passing away and new women were coming to the fore. In America the generation whose ideas were based on the reformism of the pre-Civil War era and, especially, the great anti-slavery movement, faded in the 1890s. Mrs Stanton resigned her presidency of the National American Woman Suffrage Association in 1892.[1] Lucy Stone died in 1893. Susan B. Anthony, who had succeeded to the presidency, resigned it in 1900. They were replaced by women of a different stamp. Victorian prudishness and repeated defeats engendered a more narrow-minded, hard-nosed approach to the suffrage question. The first generation had a broadly liberal view of social progress that was attenuated by time and disappointment. Susan B. Anthony abandoned her other interests for a single-minded pursuit of the vote; Mrs Stanton turned against universal suffrage and argued instead for an educational qualification. Their successors took up where they left off, making a narrow position narrower still.

This was a policy born of more than simple frustration. From the outset suffragists had considered the vote both just and expedient. Women, they argued, deserved it as a matter of right. In addition, if given the ballot, women would use it to advance certain desirable causes. By the century's end the balance shifted. While women continued to insist on their right to vote, they placed more emphasis

[1] In 1890 the two major suffrage groups, The National Woman Suffrage Association and the American Woman Suffrage Association, were combined. Mrs Stanton became the first president of the NAWSA.

on the consequences of woman suffrage. These included not only various reforms, notably in the condition of working women and children, but the preservation of Anglo-Saxon (or Nordic, or Teutonic, depending on the speaker) supremacy. The movement's growing nativism was produced by a variety of causes, as Aileen Kraditor has demonstrated in her careful analysis of this phenomenon.[2] For one thing, almost all middle class people feared and mistrusted the new immigrants from Southern and Eastern Europe who were pouring in at such a great rate. Many felt the foundations of American life were being undermined, democracy corrupted, and the social order itself imperilled. Middle class women naturally shared these fears. Suffragists were also willing to exploit them. Since native-born women outnumbered foreign-born women, who were themselves a minority among immigrants, the enfranchisement of women, it was pointed out, would secure a permanent electoral majority for native Americans. Moreover, suffragists had a private reason for their chauvinism. Most immigrants, coming as they did from patriarchal societies, had conservative ideas about the role of women. Many suffragists favoured an educational requirement for the vote because it would disenfranchise that part of the electorate most hostile to their cause. To some extent they were right. However, in time it became clear that not all immigrants opposed woman suffrage. The suffragists' great victory in New York State during the war was made possible because a small but crucial bloc of votes was cast by immigrants in their favour. Although the friends of woman suffrage in the foreign-born community were not numerous, they provided the margin of victory. Thereafter suffragists were more sympathetic to immigrants in general. This development, of course, came very late in the game.

The generation of suffragists who led the cause to victory differed from their predecessors in other ways. They were not women of the broadest vision or highest ability. Pioneer suffragists like Elizabeth Cady Stanton, Lucy Stone, and Julia Ward Howe were second to none in strength of mind and character. Anna Howard Shaw, Rachel Foster Avery and most of their associates in the mature NAWSA were less impressive. This was not because the quality of women as a whole had declined. The period 1890 to 1920 was actually a kind of feminist golden age. In no other time were there so many women of heroic stature. Lillian Wald, Florence Kelley, Jane Addams, and Margaret Dreier Robins, to name but a few, gave women a well-deserved reputation for intelligent generosity and high accomplishment. However, most of these great women, although suffragists, spent their energies on the struggle for social justice. Woman suffrage, while desirable, was not to them of overriding importance. Other women,

[2] Aileen S. Kraditor, *The Ideas of the Woman Suffrage Movement*, 1890-1920 (New York, 1965).

like Charlotte Perkins Gilman who did concentrate on feminist issues, believed that the ballot's value was exaggerated. Mrs Gilman had, perhaps, the best mind of any feminist, but she devoted it mainly to the larger questions concerning women's social and economic role (Doc. 9). She was also, except for Florence Kelley, the only major figure in the woman movement committed to socialism—a further indication of her unusual vision.

Anna Howard Shaw and Carrie Chapman Catt represented the worst and the best elements in the mature woman suffrage movement. Miss Shaw was a woman of immense tenacity who overcame the handicap of having been brought up in rural Michigan when it was still almost a frontier society. She became a physician and a minister of the gospel, formidable accomplishments both, then a protege of Susan B. Anthony, and finally president of the NAWSA. Dr Shaw was an orator of great force and effectiveness. Her rough, unpolished addresses do not read well today, but in their time won her many fervent admirers (Doc. 18). However, she was a poor organizer, insensitive of others' feelings, and a pronounced manhater. Her single-minded devotion to the suffrage issue displeased social feminists, some of whom believed her to be less interested in the problems of working women than she actually was. She was president of the NAWSA from 1904 through 1915, during which time almost no progress was made on the national level. There were energetic state suffrage campaigns, and Dr Shaw often participated in them, but little effort was made to secure a federal amendment. As early as 1910 dissatisfaction with Dr Shaw's leadership, or lack of it, was manifest in the NAWSA. Her most obvious rival was Carrie Chapman Catt, who had been president from 1900 to 1904, but resigned because of personal problems and the complications arising from her role as president of the International Woman Suffrage Alliance.

Mrs Catt was almost the reverse of Dr Shaw. Affable, witty, at least in private, and a woman of broad social sympathies, she also possessed a singular gift for administrative leadership. Her ideas on public questions resembled those of the most social feminists. Unlike them, however, she believed that woman suffrage was a pre-condition of effective reform. She first became interested in the suffrage from a desire to help working women and children, and she frequently wished aloud that she could work for peace (a cause which she did, in fact, take up seriously after the vote was won), but once persuaded that woman suffrage was the key to all other reforms she never entertained serious doubts about it. Mrs Catt attracted Susan B. Anthony's attention in the early 1890s after working in several gruelling state campaigns. She was made chairman of a newly created Organization Committee of the NAWSA in 1895. In 1900 Miss Anthony personally chose her to become the NAWSA's third president. The unpropitious times, her own comparative inexperience, family difficulties and her international obligations rendered Mrs Catt's first term as president unfruitful. Her resignation did not take her out of circulation, however. She continued with the IWSA, her powers as a leader matured, and in 1912 she once more began taking an active part in the American movement. At this point her most salient characteristic came into focus. Mrs Catt was what Americans call a 'major leaguer', which is to say that not only did she think in the largest terms, but that she was equipped by nature and temperament to execute successfully great enterprises. Other suffragists may have been more intelligent, or better speakers, yet none before her possessed this special quality. Of course, one cannot play in the big leagues if they do not exist. Woman suffrage was a minor league affair until around 1912. Mrs Catt lacked, therefore, a proper setting for her talents. But when the call to greatness came, she was ready.

In 1910 the state of Washington voted for woman suffrage. In 1911 California, after a dazzling referendum campaign marked by the use of electric signs, automobiles, essay contests, and a small army of energetic women, became a suffrage state by the narrowest of margins. In 1912 Arizona, Kansas, and Oregon followed suit. In that same year the short-lived Progressive Party headed by ex-President Theodore Roosevelt adopted a woman suffrage plank. In 1913 the Illinois legislature, where Progressives held the balance of power, gave women the right to vote in Presidential elections. These encouraging events signified that woman suffrage was on the move again. However, it was becoming evident that to win the ballot on a state by state basis would take forever and cost the earth. The Illinois situation was unique. While California was won for equal suffrage, Ohio, Michigan, and Wisconsin were lost. Moreover, California alerted the anti-suffragists who were not be caught off-guard again. The liquor interests, quite rightly fearing that votes for women meant votes for Prohibition, were spending large sums to counteract suffragist propaganda.

Under these circumstances suffragists turned their thoughts to the neglected federal amendment campaign. In 1912 the chairman of the NAWSA's Congressional Committee received ten dollars for her expenses, none of which was actually spent. Neither house of Congress had held hearings of the Suffrage Bill since 1896. All this was soon to change. In January, 1913 Alice Paul, fresh from years of service with the English militants, arrived in Washington. Miss Paul, a young, well-educated Quakeress, proved to be one of the most single-minded and tenacious controversialists ever to take up the women's cause. She had been fired with the evangelical spirit characteristic of radical English suffragettes and was determined to infuse the lacklustre American movement with some of their passion and drama. She had herself made chairman of the Congressional Committee, and on the day before Woodrow Wilson was inaugurated as President she and a small band of ardent spirits organized a march of 5,000 women through the centre of Washington. Suffrage marches were not unheard of, but this was the first to become a riot. Washington was jammed with people who had come for the inaugural festivities. The parade turned a crowd into a mob that literally overwhelmed the women. In the end it took the combined efforts of the police, army, and militia to protect the marchers and restore order. There were comparatively few casualties, by English standards at least, but the women had been sufficiently victimized to appear martyrs. A touch of martyrdom was just what was needed to dramatize the Federal amendment. Money and recruits poured in, petitions were collected, and a momentum generated that was to carry the women through to victory.

Welcome as this development was, it embarrassed more orthodox suffragists. Alice Paul meant to keep the pressure on. The NAWSA welcomed the rebirth she had stimulated, but feared it would lead to deliberate outrages as in England. Even worse, Miss Paul was determined to hold the party in power responsible for the failure of woman suffrage. This tactic made some sense in England where the majority party actually controlled Parliament and could almost always get the legislation it wanted. It was not appropriate in America where the administration's control of Congress was never very secure, and where votes from both parties would be needed to push the Bill through. Miss Paul persisted, and in 1913 formed her own organization, the Congressional Union. At first the Union was affiliated with NAWSA, but their differences were too great and in 1914 it became an independent organization. The distance between them widened year by year, but until 1917 the Congressional Union (which in 1916 became the Woman's Party) complemented rather than contradicted the NAWSA's efforts. Through 1915 the NAWSA continued to wobble along under Dr Shaw's uncertain leadership. It received little money, and on a national scale was outpaced in every respect by the Congressional Union. In 1914 the Union sent organizers into the nine states where women voted to campaign against Democratic candidates. It successfully induced both houses of Congress to act on the Suffrage Bill. They rejected it, but the Bill was alive and moving again. Both houses were persuaded to create Woman Suffrage Committees, an important step forward. By 1915 the Union was operating in all of the forty-eight states.

1915 proved to be the turning point, although this was not immediately apparent. While militancy was building the Congressional Union into a formidable organization, the orthodox suffragists were still plugging away on the local level. In 1915 major campaigns were waged in the populous industrial states of New York, Pennsylvania, Massachusetts, and New Jersey—all were lost. However, he failure in New York was anything but demoralizing. Mrs Catt, s president of the New York State Suffrage Association, had construc-ed a magnificent political apparatus. From the precincts upwards uffragists were thoroughly organized and co-ordinated. Every campaign device known to man was imaginatively employed. The women had plenty of money. More than that, they had so much confi-lence in Mrs Catt that defeat only spurred them on to greater effort. Mrs Catt had, in fact, expected to lose in 1915 and was really aiming t 1917. Two days after the referendum was turned down a mass meeting at Cooper Union raised $115,000 for the next campaign. This xtraordinary response convinced the majority of orthodox suffragists hat only Mrs Catt could pull the NAWSA together. In December at its nnual convention Mrs Catt, now known affectionately as the Big Boss, was swept into office. Dr Shaw accepted her fall from grace nobly, esigning her office in advance of the convention. As it happened her lay was not yet over. She still had one last great service to render women, as we shall see.

Mrs Catt, now fifty-five and at the peak of her powers, did just what was expected of her. The old board was dismissed and a new one, made up chiefly of wealthy women who could give all their time o the fight, was selected. They became working heads of a full-time professional staff. The state organizations were bombarded with uggestions and instructions, and brought into a close relation with eadquarters. In 1916 Mrs Catt worked out a six-year plan based on he following assumptions: that President Wilson, who had moved com hostility to neutrality on the suffrage issue, could be persuaded o endorse it; that a victorious referendum campaign in New York would break the back of Congress's resistance by showing that a najority of representative Americans favoured equal suffrage; and hat by concentrating on thirty-six state legislatures it would be pos-ible to secure a ratification of the constitutional amendment in another our years. She had not allowed for America's entry into the war which ook two years off her timetable. In all other respects her calculations roved accurate.

As described above the final suffrage drive sounds absurdly simple, ut, of course, it was not. It cost huge sums of money and required egions of women to execute. Mrs Catt was bequeathed several million lollars, but much more was actually spent by the various suffrage rganizations. No one knows the exact number of women involved; owever, the NAWSA alone soon counted its members in the hundreds f thousands. Perhaps two million women contributed to the effort in ome way making it the greatest independent political movement of nodern times. The true magnitude of this accomplishment cannot be rasped simply by looking at the formal structure that effected it. The women's victory was not inevitable. Serious mistakes in strategy could have compromised the entire effort—Mrs Catt made none.

The two major challenges faced by the renewed NAWSA were America's entry into World War I and the growing militancy of Alice Paul's Woman's Party. Organized American women, although more sympathetic to the Allies than to the Central Powers, generally opposed American entry. Like the majority of Americans they were horrified by the carnage in Europe, and did not believe that the United States had anything to gain by becoming party to it. Once war was imminent however, a combination of prudence and patriotism led to rapid changes of heart (Doc. 20). Even before the President's war message to Congress, voluntary offers of support were sent him by many leading women's organizations. The NAWSA pledged its aid more than a month in advance of need. Knowing that anything less than a complete endorsement of the American war effort would damage the cause, Mrs Catt suppressed her own pacifist tendencies and broke with the Woman's Peace Party of which she had been a founder. Mrs Catt was, however, no jingoist; few American suffragists were. In England Emmeline and Christabel Pankhurst had suspended suffrage activities for the duration, and went on to exceed even their government in sanguinary enthusiasm. But while the NAWSA did some war work, it continued to put votes for women first. The militant Woman's Party did no war work at all.

The NAWSA's tepid attitude towards the war did not escape notice especially by the anti-suffragists who, thanks to the passions of war and their own declining prospects, were growing more bloody-minded by the day (Doc. 21). However, Dr Shaw neutralized much of this hostile fire by accepting the chairmanship of the Woman's Committee of the Council of National Defense, the highest ranking body concerned with the women's mobilization. She did enough patriotic cheerleading to persuade doubters of the NAWSA's sincere desire for victory. She also did all that the feeble powers of her office permitted to see that women were not exploited during the emergency. The government successfully prevented her from gaining any real authority, but it could not keep her from drawing attention to its numberless shortcomings where women were concerned. By bluff and bluster, by threats of resignation, by all the means her rough and wintery character allowed she fought the government on every level she could reach. As an office-holder she was forced to wage her private war in secret so that few women ever learned of it. Nonetheless, it was her finest hour. Those critics who had complained of her feeble leadership and narrow sympathies would have felt differently had they known the truth about her role in government. Not that their opinions mattered to her. Dr Shaw had human feelings, but she was a dreadnought of a woman and ploughed ahead regardless of wind and weather. This was a disadvantage in the NAWSA where a sensitivity to others was called for. In the government, however, where she did not confront people of exquisite sensibilities, her temperament was invaluable. All that could be done for women by bulldozing her superiors was done. In the event, this was not much. Government agencies consistently ignored and evaded the needs of women, but Dr Shaw did not make it easy for them. If she had done nothing else in her life, this alone would entitle her to the respect and admiration of posterity.

While Dr Shaw was struggling with the Federal bureaucracy, events were telescoping the suffragist timetable. By now it was clear that women were going to get the vote. What was needed was some kind of device that would enable anti-suffragist politicians to change their position without loss of face. Time and experience had shown most of the arguments against equal suffrage to be false. Women now voted in many states and the political process remained unaffected. The old saw that women did not want the vote was laid to rest in New York where a million women signed suffrage petitions. The war was demonstrating that women were ready and able to do virtually all the jobs monopolized by men. The experience of most European countries showed that womanpower was essential to victory under modern conditions. Traditional ideas about woman's fragility, incompetence, and unique disabilities went by the board. Their performance on the home front won Englishwomen the vote. American women made a lesser contribution to the war effort, but a similar movement into government and industry took place enabling politicians to reverse themselves and confess that all doubts had been removed. In America, then, the convenient fiction that woman suffrage was a war measure got many prominent individuals, including President Wilson himself, off the hook. This was no small thing. It was for want of such a mechanism that the progress of equal suffrage had been so long delayed.

The greatest danger now was from the militants. The Woman's Party had campaigned against President Wilson in all the twelve states where women voted, only to see him carry ten of them. In January of 1917 the militants, embittered by their failure in the fall elections, began to picket the White House. Picketing was hardly a new technique, but it had never been used against a President before. At first nothing happened. Then war was declared and the picketing took on a new aspect. The Woman's Party included many Quakers who were against all war. It also had a number of radical socialists like Crystal Eastman who were opposed to this particular one. Continued picketing struck many Americans as unpatriotic. Worse still were the women's banners and placards with their references to 'Kaiser Wilson' and suggestions that 'Democracy Should Begin at Home'. Soon mob violence erupted. The pickets were repeatedly abused and their signs destroyed, often with official encouragement. In June the police began arresting pickets, and when this failed to deter them jail sentences of up to six months were imposed. Poor jail conditions prompted them to go on hunger strikes in imitation of the British militants. Since many of the women were prominent in society and the professions their ordeal was widely publicized. Eventually the government was forced to back down. At the end of 1917 they were released from jail. Subsequently the District of Columbia Court of Appeals invalidated every one of the original arrests. The militants' moral and legal position was thoroughly vindicated; their wisdom remained in doubt.

Mrs Catt and other leaders of the NAWSA were furious. Privately they denounced the militants. Publicly they took every occasion to repudiate the WP's tactics. By refusing to protest the pickets' treatment they silently acquiesced in what was not only illegal but contemptible as well. Although this point has often been debated, it seems to me that the NAWSA was absolutely right and the WP entirely wrong in their assessment of conditions. What the WP failed to realize, but Mrs Catt was entirely aware of, was that the war had provided suffragists with a unique opportunity. By injecting a fresh element into the stale controversy over equal suffrage it enabled the President and some congressmen gracefully to change their minds. The pressure had to be kept on, but it had to be done tactfully. The WP threatened to upset this delicate situation by putting Mr Wilson and the wavering congressional element in the position of being forced to act against their will. The NAWSA could not allow this to happen. It had to isolate and neutralize the WP. Did it also have to condone the pickets' brutal mistreatment? No one can be certain of this, but my impression is that the NAWSA went too far. This was, of course, the opposite side of its pragmatic coin. The NAWSA was forced to be practical, strike bargains, and accept positions that were not entirely in keeping with its lofty goals. These are the hard facts which every group that wants political power must face. Yet there are limits beyond which a movement cannot go without compromising its essential character. The NAWSA had given way on the peace issue. Now it shut its eyes to an obvious injustice. The subsequent demoralization of the feminist movement was probably not unrelated to the means by which victory was attained. Orthodox political groups seem able to survive quantities of cynicism and manipulation that are fatal to movements with a moral basis. This, too, is a fact of life. In the short run, however, the NAWSA's strategy was highly successful. Mr Wilson did call for woman suffrage as a war measure on January 10, 1918, and by the narrowest of margins the House of Representatives passed an amendment to the Constitution enfranchising women. Intense lobbying finally carried it through the Senate in June of the following year. Fourteen strenuous months later it was ratified by the thirty-sixth state legislature and became law. No such obviously desired and modest a reform ever required so much effort.

Englishwomen gained the vote in a somewhat different manner. The story is well-known, but worth summarizing for the light it throws on conditions in the two countries. The most striking difference was the emergence of militancy on a vast scale. This in turn reflected the rise of a new generation of English feminists. Whereas in America second generation suffragists were more sober and orthodox than their predecessors, in England the opposite was true. The tradition of cautious respectability did not die out—Miss Becker was followed by the equally proper Mrs Fawcett—but a different type of feminist personified by the fighting Pankhursts came into being. These women were called suffragettes, a term first used scornfully and then defiantly adopted by the militants to distinguish themselves from the orthodox suffragists, who were also known as constitutionalists. Apart from matters of personality and temperament, it is difficult to explain the suffragette phenomenon. In modern times no great nation has equalled England's record of social peace and order; few have enjoyed a more democratic political structure. Yet woman suffrage was the cause of greater violence and disorder in England than in any other major country. How is this paradox to be accounted for? In particular, why was it that the United States, a society characterized by savage outbreaks of violence, race riots, assassinations, bloody strikes, a terrible civil war—experienced little suffragist militancy, while England, an incomparably more stable and harmonious society, was shaken by it?

Several possibilities come to mind. It may have been precisely because the level of violence was so great in American life that suffragists avoided provocative confrontations. Knowing riot and rapine to be American institutions, they refrained from inflammatory acts. Then again, American women had a somewhat greater sense of power. Militancy was born of desperation. American feminists were often bitter and frustrated, but rarely desperate. Even in the nineteenth century they exercised some influence through their various national organizations. Moreover, the shortage of women, a defect not overcome until fairly late, made them as individuals correspondingly more valuable, esteemed, and deferred to than their English sisters. A handful of great English ladies enjoyed a power unknown in America where there was no aristocracy, no salon, and where the political structure favoured electoral popularity over the partisan intrigue at which some women excel. Englishwomen, however, were generally inhibited by patriarchal traditions of greater rigidity than the American variety, and had failed, perhaps for that reason to build an infra-structure of their own equal to the American social feminists' network of associations. American women were not so powerful and autonomous as foreign visitors liked to pretend, or as men like

Henry Adams and Henry James imagined in their gloomier moments, but they were better off than the majority of Englishwomen. Still, it would be a mistake to undervalue the Pankhurstian influence. Certain things made militancy possible in England; they did not make it inevitable. It seems unlikely that the suffragettes would have gone so far had the Pankhursts not been spurring them on to death or glory.

Little in Emmeline Pankhurst's early life suggested the leader she was to become. Even as a girl she was very beautiful, a quality that normally precludes greatness since its possessor has little incentive to develop her other faculties. Feminists invariably described their colleagues as beautiful, a fact not usually supported by the photographic record. They may have had beautiful character traits, which is actually most often what was meant, but had they all been physically beautiful few would have become ardent suffragists. Mrs Pankhurst's striking good looks, which lasted all her life, were, therefore, a distinct asset to the cause. In 1879 when she was twenty years old she married Dr Richard Marsden Pankhurst, a distinguished lawyer twice her age. Their union was blessed with five children, only the first of which, Christabel, was apparently desired by Mrs Pankhurst. She gave no more time to the others than she had to, but it was still considerable. While Dr Pankhurst was a nationally known lawyer, a supporter of many liberal causes from woman suffrage to trade unions, he was not prosperous. At his death in 1898 she was burdened with the support of five children, the eldest of them only seventeen. Nonetheless, for reasons that remain obscure, within a few years Mrs Pankhurst threw over her job as registrar of births and deaths in Manchester and poured her fabulous energies into the fight for woman suffrage, leaving her older children to look after themselves and trusting that Providence would care for her youngest. Providence, as sometimes happens, obliged.[3]

Since the existing suffrage societies had made little progress, she resolved to form her own and in October of 1903 the Women's Social and Political Union was established. Doubtless the first reason for its creation was Mrs Pankhurst's inability to work in harness. Another was her conviction that suffragists must hold whatever party was in power responsible for their plight. Dr Pankhurst had been defeated in a parliamentary election in 1885 by Home Rulers acting on this theory, even though he himself was a supporter of Home Rule. Mrs Pankhurst had been outraged by the tactic, but her husband assured her it was the only course open to the embattled partisans of Irish freedom.

[3] All but one of the children survived this experience. Mrs Pankhurst literally farmed out her only son, but rural life did not agree with him. Sylvia attributed his early death to her mother's negligence. Later Mrs Pankhurst adopted four war babies, then gradually passed all of them on to others. Her maternal instincts were never very reliable.

The failure of their effort ought to have planted seeds of doubt in her mind, but naturally it did not. A further point in favour of a new organization was the need for firm direction and unity of action. Mrs Pankhurst conceived of the WSPU as a suffrage army with herself as commander-in-chief. Anyone who disagreed with her was encouraged, indeed forced, to leave it. Among those who did was Mrs Charlotte French Despard, an elderly woman of splendid appearance who in 1907 formed the Women's Freedom League. Its aims paralleled the Union's, but were pursued with greater moderation.

The tactics of militancy which made the Union famous developed gradually. The first step was taken on May 12, 1905 when, after an unsatisfactory debate in the House over woman suffrage, a band of WSPU women held an impromptu meeting on the grounds of Parliament. In October the first arrests were made after Christabel Pankhurst and a young mill worker named Annie Kenney disrupted a political meeting. On refusing to pay their fines they were given short jail sentences. Instead of deterring them, such treatment only stiffened the militants' resolve. On February 12, 1907 a WSPU march on Parliament was broken up by the police who clearly, as photographs taken at the scene showed, used excessive force against the women. Private citizens sometimes reacted even more violently. In January, 1908, after the WSPU helped defeat a Liberal candidate for Parliament his outraged supporters threw Mrs Pankhurst to the ground, and but for the police would have rolled her down the streets of Newton Abbott in a barrel. Later in the year Mrs Pankhurst was given a six-week jail sentence, and then, when she persisted in speaking at illegal rallies, was sentenced to three months. Other militants were similarly treated.

In this short time the WSPU had already moved into high gear. The violence they encountered incited sympathy and won them publicity which, even when hostile, attracted supporters. Money and volunteers flowed in, notably the Pethick-Lawrences. Frederick Pethick-Lawrence, who was later to be ennobled for his services to the Labour Party, was already well-known as a reformer and anti-imperialist. His wife was a social feminist of considerable experience and ability. Pethick-Lawrence's money was useful to the Union, his executive talents even more so. He put its finances in order, for it was being showered with gold. From £3,000 in 1906–1907 the Union's income grew to a peak of £37,000 in 1913–14. No comparable organization, not even the Labour Party, commanded such resources. Pethick-Lawrence saw to it that they were expended carefully and efficiently. He also offered the best possible defence for the increasingly extreme methods, including damage to property, resorted to by the militants. In his little book, *Women's Fight for the Vote* (1911), he argued that while militant tactics would be wrong or inappropriate in most instances, an unenfranchised body had no other way to make itself felt. Previous extensions of the suffrage in 1832 and 1867 had been accomplished in the same manner. Heckling ministers was accepted practice in England, and the few cases in which excited individuals had gone beyond mere words were deplored by all serious members of the WSPU. His case was not altogether persuasive, but it does indicate that until 1912 Pethick-Lawrence could view militancy as a comparatively moderate programme largely consistent with English traditions. Some suffragists believed that he remained with the WSPU, even while dissatisfied with parts of its programme, in order to keep it from declaring a sex war. If so, he failed. Christabel saw every bad thing from venereal disease to original sin as a consequence of masculine depravity. Her influence over both her mother and the WSPU as a whole was very great, and at its end the Union was more anti-masculine than any major suffrage organization.

The tactics Pethick-Lawrence tried to justify became steadily more indefensible. The WSPU held rallies, distributed propaganda, campaigned against government candidates, and the like, but its peculiar mystique stemmed from its escalating violence. At first the militants were more sinned against than sinners. Heckling ministers and breaking windows were not acts confined to women, yet women were punished for committing them with unusual severity. They appeared to prick the heart of mankind in some secret, vulnerable place. Seemingly men felt diminished when women struck the attitudes and employed the robust vocabulary that were traditionally masculine perogatives. Perhaps their sense of self as well as their sense of decency was outraged, their concept of what it was to be a man obscurely violated. Certainly the government responded to provocation with unwonted savagery. Each new feminist outrage was met with longer jail sentences, hunger strikes led to forcible feedings by means of tubes through the mouth or nostrils that were always painful, and sometimes dangerous as when lungs were punctured and became infected. The government entirely abandoned those standards of civility and that tradition of amiable controversy which were England's pride and the world's envy.

Events proved the government to be guilty of bad judgment as well as bad form. Reprisals stimulated more violence. Ministers were attacked and mail boxes mutilated. On March 1, 1912, 200 militants were arrested after an orgy of window smashing in the heart of London. The Pankhursts now decided upon a campaign of secret arson and violence. The Pethick-Lawrences, who had supported open confrontations, refused to endorse a programme of anonymous sabotage and were expelled from the Union. In her memoirs Mrs Pankhurst serenely remarked that the policy was essential because 'every advance of men's political freedom has been marked with violence and the destruction of property'.[4] In fact, she continued, at the very moment when she herself was speaking of the need for greater violence, a cabinet Minister, C. E. H. Hobhouse, addressed an anti-suffrage rally in Bristol and cited the absence of large-scale violence as a reason for denying women the vote. Accordingly, during the years 1912–14 the WSPU committed outrages on a large, even lunatic, scale. A house under construction for Lloyd George was bombed, railway stations burned down, paintings slashed, a hatchet was thrown at Prime Minister Asquith, and other grotesque acts too numerous to mention perpetrated. In the first two and a half months of 1913 alone sixty-six suffragists went to prison. The government retaliated with the so-called Cat and Mouse Act which permitted it to release non-co-operating prisoners, but to re-commit them at any time. It helped only a little. Christabel fled to Paris where she continued to direct strategy. Mrs Pankhurst was equally dangerous in prison or out, and the government was unable to make up its mind about her. When she was in prison her sufferings dishonoured the government; when she was at large the situation was reversed.

After war broke out all this suddenly came to an end. The Pankhursts suspended hostilities for the duration. Christabel returned from Paris and fell to promoting the war with such vigour that the government was almost as embarrassed by her support as it had previously been by her opposition. The mobilization of women that freed millions of men for military service destroyed the opposition to women's suffrage. By 1916 it was evident that women would have to be included in the next Representation of the People Bill. After patient negotiations a compromise was worked out between the government and the constitutional suffragists. Women did not get equal suffrage until 1928, but in 1918 those who were thirty years of age and householders or the wives of householders were enfranchised.

What had the WSPU contributed to this victory? In the first place it is fair to say that votes for women seemed inevitable in 1916 not only because of the war, but also because of what had gone before. Frenchwomen made great sacrifices and contributed much to the war effort, but they were not enfranchised until considerably later. Englishwomen profited from the war because when it came they were ready to meet its challenges and opportunities. They owed something to the Pankhursts for this. The growth of the suffrage movement after 1903 was stimulated by militancy, and until 1911 or 1912 the WSPU did the cause more good than harm. At the same time, however, the movement's real strength lay not in the WSPU, but in the constitutional organizations, especially the National Union of Women's Suffrage

[4] Emmeline Pankhurst, *My Own Story* (New York, 1914), 213-14. According to Sylvia the book was actually written by an American journalist, Rheta Childe Dorr.

Societies. To it in later years were added groups like the Catholic Women's Suffrage Society, the Free Church League, The Jewish League, and the Scottish Churches League. The woman's movement in England was not so large and well-organized as in America, but it proved to be adequate. Again, as in America, the two wings, although hostile, complemented each other. The WSPU kept the heat on, while the NUWSA demonstrated that its aims were shared by masses of average women. The NUWSA's avoidance of sex antagonism, its publication was called *The Common Cause,* was a valuable counterweight to Christabel Pankhurst's programme of 'votes for women and purity for men'.

Between them, the suffragists and the suffragettes gained such momentum that by 1910 the government was seriously looking for some way out of its dilemma. In that year a Conciliation Bill was brought forward, only to be destroyed by Winston Churchill who condemned it as undemocratic. He disliked the property qualification. He also thought a national referendum should be held on the question. Finally, like other Liberals, he could not support a measure, however admirable in principle, that would strengthen the opposition party. In America the chief difficulty was in finding a graceful way for the opponents of equal suffrage to change sides without losing face. In England not only was face-saving called for, but some kind of technical resolution that would not change the balance of electoral power seemed necessary. The Prime Minister first tried to get off the hook by trickery. In 1911 Asquith declared that the government would broaden the suffrage without including women, but in such a way as to make it possible to include them at a later date. This play failed. It was neither devious enough to escape detection, nor sufficiently conciliatory to win approval. In 1912 the Labour Party resolved that no suffrage bill would be acceptable to it that did not include women. Later a Second Conciliation Bill came up, but although the uncertain Mr Churchill voted for it, it too failed.

By the middle of 1914, however, the government seemed to be in retreat. Lloyd George and other leading politicians began holding private talks with prominent suffragists including Sylvia Pankhurst. In June Asquith received a delegation of working-class women from her East London Federation. They explained to the Prime Minister that woman suffrage would ease their hard lot. He declared the experience to have been instructive. Sylvia believed Asquith was preparing to back down, but that he could not afford to imply that the WSPU was responsible. Dealing with the East London Federation was a clever way of getting around the problem. It was an autonomous body, having been founded by Sylvia to enlist working-class women in the cause. Initially it was affiliated with the WSPU, but as the Union was becoming Tory in sympathy, while the Federation inclined towards socialism, the alliance was not a stable one. Family ties counted for nothing. Mrs Pankhurst had already driven her youngest daughter, Adela, out of the country by making her promise never to speak in England. (Adela emigrated to Australia where she became an active socialist and feminist.) In 1914 Christabel, the WSPU's real head, expelled the East London Federation for left deviationism. The Federation was, therefore, an especially suitable vehicle for reconciliation between the government and the main body of suffragists. Sylvia was the most sensible and broadly sympathetic Pankhurst. The Federation's working-class base enabled Asquith to assert humanitarian motives for his prospective change of heart, while attempting to cut into the Labour Party's constituency. In this respect it gave Liberals a legitimate political reason for risking woman suffrage. The chances of winning labour votes may not have been good, but they were doubtlessly worth taking. It seems likely, therefore, that the government was in the process of working out a formula along these lines when the war began.

If this analysis is correct, then the last years of the WSPU's life were counter-productive. Its extravagant policies only delayed the working out of what was becoming an inevitable compromise. In this respect it anticipated what the militants in America would do under similar circumstances. Wrong as these tactics seem to have been, they were entirely understandable. Militants in both countries encountered extraordinary and unwarranted resistance. Lord Russell, who ran for Parliament on a women's suffrage platform, recalled that 'when, in later years, I campaigned against the First World War, the popular opposition that I encountered was not comparable to that which the suffragists met in 1907'.[5] As time went on conditions worsened. The cycle of action and reaction speeded up, and, accordingly, the militants' hold on reality slackened. The martyred women drew in upon themselves. Persecution made them more neurotic, and less able to communicate with outsiders. The expulsion of the Pethick-Lawrences, as it was meant to do, cut them off entirely from the real world. By then the role they played had become an end in itself, for many the most satisfying of their lives.

Years later Christabel declared grandly that 'mother and I had pledged and promised that we would get women their vote and we did'.[6] In fact, their actions after 1912 suggest the opposite. As the day of emancipation came nearer, the Pankhursts did everything in their power to delay it. Consciously they were still working for the vote, unconsciously they seemed determined not to have it. Perhaps they

[5] Bertrand Russell, *The Autobiography of Bertrand Russell* (London and Boston, 1967), 231.
[6] Christabel Pankhurst, *Unshackled: The Story of How We Won the Vote* (London, 1959), 210.

sensed that enfranchisement meant the end of their days of glory. Their response to the war suggests this. If the vote were all that mattered they would have, like the constitutionalists, continued to work for it, as conditions permitted. Instead, they abandoned the cause entirely. By 1914 the methods of the senior Pankhursts had displaced the ends they were nominally designed to attain. The hysterical passions, obsessive camaraderies, dramatic plots and revelations, and the whole messianic pattern of which they were a part, had become self-sustaining. The Pankhursts hurled themselves into war work because it was the only way of maintaining this emotional pitch now that the day of reckoning for suffragists was so near at hand. The war gave them a new lease on life, if a short one. In 1918 they discovered that the train of history had passed them by when Christabel ran for Parliamment and lost. Thereafter she deserted politics for enthusiastic religion. Mrs Pankhurst's last years were even more pathetic. Only Sylvia continued to fight the good fight. She became a partisan of Ethiopian independence and spent her last years as an honoured resident of that country.

In both England and America, then, the war enabled politicians to give painlessly what they could not have long withheld. Everyone now braced themselves for the great changes to come. Few grasped the truth, which was that they had already happened. Enfranchisement did not mark the beginning of women's real emancipation, but its end. While hardly anyone could see this in 1920, by 1930 it was patently obvious. Less comprehensible were the reasons for this surprising anti-climax to women's century of struggle.

5

The End of Feminism

Nineteen-hundred-and-twenty was the moral pinnacle of American feminism. The hopes and dreams of three-quarters of a century had matured at virtually the same moment. Prohibition and woman suffrage, the two objects most passionately desired by middle class women, had been secured. Child labour, to social feminists the greatest scandal of the day, was on the verge of extinction thanks to a congressional Bill passed in 1918. The problems of working women had been eased by the establishment of maximum hour laws and the progress of minimum wage legislation. Even the cause of peace, so dear to the hearts of women and only recently in such disarray, had gained a new lease on life through the League of Nations. With women ensconced in a variety of new occupations because of the war, with female students pouring into the colleges at an even greater rate than before, the feminist thrust seemed more powerful than ever. In England, too, morale was high. Many of the same conditions obtained as in America. The promise of a brilliant postwar reconstruction had not yet faded. The Labour Party's quick rise to at least a semblance of power made it appear that the wartime slogan of 'homes fit for heroes' was to become a genuine programme.

It soon became evident, however, that in neither country were there to be sweeping social reforms, and that in America even the gains already made were vulnerable. As always, woman suffrage once enacted became a dead issue, but it was not so with Prohibition. Within a few years the prevalence of bootlegging demonstrated that Prohibition was unenforceable and, indeed, almost unbearable. The 'drys' retained sufficient political strength to block Repeal until 1933, but they could not keep Americans from drinking, nor prevent the whole notion of reform through constitutional amendment from being discredited. Hence, when in 1922 the Supreme Court pronounced the national child labour law to be unconstitutional, social feminists were unable to secure a constitutional amendment permitting congressional action on child labour. Such a Bill passed easily through the Congress, only to be voted down in state after state, partly for fear that it was a Communist trick to nationalize children, chiefly because of a wholesale reaction against the regulation of morals symbolized by the Volstead Act and the Eighteenth Amendment. Similarly, when the Court struck down a minimum wage Bill social feminists were powerless to stem the adverse tide. Not until the Second New Deal did the court reverse its position on minimum wage laws for working women. The child labour amendment was never passed.

These defeats were but symptoms of a general malaise. Reforms of every type experienced heavy weather in the 1920s, and those women's organizations geared for reform foundered when they did not trim sail. The social settlements gave up their grander aspirations and were content to play small if useful roles as service stations in the city wilderness. The General Federation of Women's Clubs wobbled badly for several years and then recovered, but it never regained its old prestige and momentum. Hardest hit were the élite units in the women's army of reform. The National Consumers' League was devastated by Progressivism's collapse, red-baited savagely by the super-patriotic organizations then becoming a permanent part of American life, and demoralized by its failure to secure the child labour amendment. Rebellious member leagues and a wounding struggle over who was to be its president—the incumbent, former Secretary of War Newton D. Baker who had protected the NCL in wartime but was now in disrepute for criticizing organized labour, or John R. Commons, a distinguished liberal economist at the University of Wisconsin—almost finished off the League. It made something of a comeback in the 1930s and survives today, but with little of its original drive and elan.

The National Women's Trade Union League suffered also, especially from an abortive venture in international co-operation. Social feminists were always interested in kindred foreign organizations. The rise of a powerful, world-wide labour movement gave the NWTUL a further reason for developing its international contacts. In 1919 when the International Labor Conference met in Washington the League arranged for a congress of working women to meet in connection with it. Out of this congress developed the International Federation of Working Women established in 1921 with Mrs Robins as president. Trouble developed almost immediately. The European delegates (including England's National Federation of Working Women) were both too radical and too sectarian for the American delegates. Economic difficulties in their home countries made the European women unusually militant. They were also tied more closely to union movements of a social democratic complexion. On the other hand, they were far more suspicious of Catholics and Communists than the ideologically unsophisticated Americans. By 1923 when the

IFWW met for a second time most delegates wanted to merge with the International Federation of Trade Unions. The Americans resisted this, ostensibly because the AFL with which they were affiliated did not belong to the IFTU, really because they felt that as a section of the IFTU women would be merely appendages of a masculine structure. The American delegates put their roles as feminists ahead of their interests as trade unionists. Undeterred, the majority went ahead and became a department of the IFTU, while the NWTUL resigned from the movement it had brought into being. The Americans, thoroughly disconcerted by their European adventures, congratulated themselves on a lucky escape. Yet the NWTUL dwindled away until after World War II it was disbanded. Women never achieved an important position in the American trade union movement, while in England they became union heads and cabinet officers.

The relationship between feminism and the masses of employed women was, however, more complicated than this. In addition to the Anglo-American division on feminist priorities, there developed in both countries a dispute over the wisdom of protective legislation as such. In England, and especially in America, the multitude of laws regulating female employment were virtually the only benefits working women had derived from feminism, which was otherwise of, by, and for the middle classes. The value of these benefits was questioned even before the war ended. In America extreme feminists began turning up at legislative hearings to testify that protective laws handicapped women in the competition for jobs. In 1919 Mrs Sidney Webb, a late convert to woman suffrage but a steady friend of working women, filed a minority report of the War Cabinet Committee on Women in Industry which protested that special treatment for women workers only perpetuated their inferior status. Labour Party women, including Margaret Bondfield, the leading female trade unionist, did not generally agree with her. However, the three major feminist organizations—the Women's Freedom League, the National Union of Societies for Equal Citizenship (which succeeded the NUWSS) and the new Six Point Group—endorsed Mrs Webb's position. Broadly speaking, the division in England was between extreme feminists and the social feminists in the NUSEC, on the one hand, and the female Labourites who were not really feminists at all, on the other.

The American alignment was rather different. Only the militant Woman's Party opposed special protective legislation. Against it during most of the 1920s were ranged every important social feminist body, except for the American Association of University Women (formerly the ACA) which was neutral. Trade Union women and their allies in the NWTUL and the NCL, who did not constitute a separate force as in England, were included in the social feminist consensus. Because the American Federation of Labor supported them, social feminists found it easy to accuse the Woman's Party of being anti-labour. There was a grain of truth to this charge. It was also true that the Woman's Party's employed members were mainly business and professional women not covered by protective laws. But the WP was quick to point out that while the AFL favoured special legislation for working women, it considered independent trade union action to be the best protection for working men. It was liable to the charge, therefore, that it favoured the regulation of women precisely because such laws made them less competitive. Militant feminists believed the AFL was working both sides of the street. It evaded its obligation to organize working women by asserting their need for protective laws, knowing that these laws did not so much protect women as keep them from desirable employments.

For its part, the WP was accused of being more concerned with its proposed constitutional amendment than with the plight of working women. Even after 1920 women continued to be discriminated against by law in hundreds of different ways. The WP had attempted to redress each grievance by sponsoring specific pieces of legislation in state legislatures. But while it framed hundreds of Bills, few of them were enacted. The Party resolved, therefore, to solve the problem at one stroke by securing an amendment to the Constitution declaring that 'men and women shall have equal rights throughout the United States'. This equal rights, or blanket amendment would surely have nullified most industrial legislation that applied only to women. The WP had to defend itself against the charge that it cared nothing for the problems of working women, and did so by taking an offensive position against the whole concept of special protective legislation. The ensuing struggle sharply divided organized women who were forced to choose between their interests as women and their interests as reformers. Most of them chose the latter. In the process, however, the woman movement was destroyed. It had rested on the false assumption that women possessed a special unity independent of class and occupation, and untainted by self-interest. As much as anything else, the fight over the equal rights amendment made this position impossible to sustain.

The 1920s were subversive of the woman movement in other ways. Women were thought to be especially pacific thanks to their mother instinct, the lack of which made men destructive by nature. Yet, as Jane Addams sorrowfully observed, when women finally became members of Congress they were united only by their common enthusiasm for a larger army and navy. When women gained the ballot it was to be used for constructive social purposes, but the Nineteenth Amendment proved only that there was no women's vote. Women voted much as men did, except on a handful of issues concerning personal morality. Henceforth politicians had to be more careful of their drinking and wenching, but otherwise the enfranchisement of women meant little to them. In fact, once the women's vote was shown to be a paper tiger, female organizations often carried less weight with professional politicians than before.

Nor were women's concrete gains so durable as had been supposed. Women moved into the colleges in greater numbers, but their share of the total enrolment declined. In 1920 they constituted 47.3 per cent. of all college students; by 1950 their percentage had fallen to 30.2. In 1956 only a third of all master's degrees were awarded to women, as against 40 per cent. in 1930. In 1920 women earned one out of every six doctorates compared with one out of ten in 1956. Their role in the work force has been equally unimpressive. More and more women obtained jobs, but they continued to be at the bottom levels of business and industry. New occupations were opened up, but old ones were lost so that in recent years the degree of occupational sex segregation has been about the same as it was in 1900.[1] The income of employed women increased, the earnings of men rose even faster.

Conditions in England were somewhat less depressing. Women did not gain equal suffrage until 1928, and so the unifying effects of suffragism persisted longer than in America. There was no great surge of reform after the war, but this was offset to a degree by the Labour Party's growth. For reasons that are far from clear, Englishwomen did better in politics and the professions than their American sisters. A larger percentage of working women were organized in trade unions. Broadly speaking, however, women continued to play a subordinate role in England as in America. In neither country did the expectations of feminists come anywhere near realization.

Satisfactory explanations for the collapse of feminism are not easily come by. For nearly a hundred years the advancement of women had been a salient feature of Anglo-American life. Votes for women was the most dramatic accomplishment of this movement, but while it was thought a harbinger of things to come, it really constituted the last significant demand that organized women were able to make. Partly this was, as I have suggested, because the struggle for suffrage imposed a spurious unity. Once gained, there was nothing to take the vote's place as a rallying point. Even more, by the time women secured the vote they had sufficient experience as students, workers and professionals to appreciate the disadvantages of these public roles. To succeed in the world they had to abandon their sexual functions altogether. Or, they could attempt to combine their public and private lives to the disadvantage of both. Much had changed in the last several generations, but the old conflict between home and work had not.

[1] This fact has been established by Edward Gross, 'Plus ca Change . . . The Sexual Structure of Occupations Over Time', an unpublished paper delivered at the 1967 meeting of the American Sociological Society.

Women could be mothers, and they could be workers. They could not, however, perform with equal facility in both categories at once. Things might have been different if society had lightened their burden with extensive nursery facilities, paid maternity leaves, and the like. In the event, it did not. Again, if marriage had been redefined so as to give husbands and wives equal responsibilities women might not have found it more difficult to balance the demands of home and work than men did. This also failed to happen. Under the circumstances women could hardly be blamed for declining public roles that brought them few rewards and many hardships. By the 1920s it was becoming evident that their emancipation had been largely negative. The formal barriers to equal opportunity were down, yet the social changes which would enable them to take advantage of this fact had not been made. Thus, like racial minorities, they were free in theory but not in practice.

Added to this were social and ideological changes that made domesticity seem more attractive. Ambitious women had traditionally escaped the domestic trap by declining to marry, a decision made all the easier by the low esteem in which sexual relations were held. Victorians did not view celibacy as a particularly deprived state. One was denied children, of course; still, one was also spared the coarse and painful means by which they came into being—processes especially repugnant to women of taste and sensibility. By the 1920s this was no longer true. Sexual fulfillment was not yet regarded as an inalienable human right, but neither was it seen as a hopeless, if not actually unspeakable, dream. What is usually called the revolution in morals was, if not quite a revolution, real enough. For a variety of reasons women's sexual practices do seem to have changed after the war. Everyone felt this at the time, and the few sexual studies made then were confirmed later by the Kinsey report on women. The incidence of pre-marital intercourse among middle class women rose sharply in the twenties. Prostitution declined. The Victorians had resolved to destroy the double standard of morals by compelling men to be as chaste as women. This proved to be unfeasible. Women got what they wanted all the same. If men and women could not be equally chaste, they could, at least, be equally promiscuous. Of course, this is to overstate the change. Women continue to be somewhat less active sexually than men, and the double standard of morals was modified rather than abolished. But the convergence of masculine and feminine sexual practices that became manifest in the 1920s is still going on, which suggests that in time a rough parity will finally be reached. The flappers and jazz babies we associate with the Roaring Twenties may not have been typical, but they did reflect, however garishly, a fundamental and enduring alteration in the sexual lives of women.

These changes in sexual behaviour were accompanied by new, or apparently new, ideas. Radical feminists in the nineteenth century had gingerly explored the possibilities of free love in hopes of breaking out of the domestic trap. Orthodox feminists rejected this view, not only for its obvious dangers, but especially because they felt women's subjugation was based on those very sexual characteristics that radical women hoped to exploit. To theorists like Charlotte Perkins Gilman the exaggerated emphasis on women's sexual role was precisely the means by which they were chained to home and family. Women needed to be freed from sex, and not encouraged actively to pursue what could only lead to earlier marriages and larger families. Time was to prove her right. The increased awareness of feminine sexuality that developed in the 1920s resulted in the teenage marriages and the baby boom of the 1940s and 50s.

This was not only because early intercourse produces unexpected babies and promotes early marriage, but also because shifts in the climate of opinion encouraged women to develop both their erotic and maternal capacities. For functional reasons orthodox feminists had stressed the ways in which women resembled men. Women were urged to compete with men, to acquire the same training and fill the same jobs. In the 1920s, however, the tide turned. Now women were again asked to discover what was unique about themselves, to cease their vain and sterile competitions with men, to develop their special capabilities. Closer examination revealed, to no one's great surprise, that what was unique about women was their wombs. Betty Friedan, in her spirited polemic, calls this new orientation *The Feminine Mystique*. Andrew Sinclair, perhaps more accurately, terms it the New Victorianism.[2] To the old saw that 'woman's place is in the home' was added a codicil—'and in the bed'. Thus, the traditional domestic system was reconciled with the newer ideas about sex. Women were to enjoy more sexual opportunities before marriage, and, presumably, deeper gratifications within it, while discharging the same responsibilities as before.

The pioneer sexual ideologists, whom I elsewhere have described as New Moralists, seem not to have anticipated this development.[3] In the 1890s people like Edward Carpenter and Havelock Ellis began advocating sexual freedom and expertise for moral and aesthetic reasons. They wanted to clear away the layers of Victorian hypocrisy and obfuscation so that everyone could live full and beautiful sex lives. Because they were feminists they felt women would profit especially from the erotic revolution they hoped to launch. Most of them thought that sexual freedom would inevitably force other desir-

[2] Betty Friedan, *The Feminine Mystique* (New York 1963); Andrew Sinclair, *The Better Half* (New York 1965).

[3] See the chapters 'Origins of the New Morality', in my *Divorce in the Progressive Era* (New Haven 1967).

able changes in the relations between men and women. Few of them realized that their new wine would pour so easily from the old bottles. Nor did they anticipate the effects of psychoanalysis. When Freud first became popular in the 1920s he was thought to favour promiscuous sexuality. His teachings did help to sexualize the climate of opinion, but as Freud himself entertained conventional Victorian views on women his work in the long run lent strength to the anti-feminist reaction. Women who competed with men were now seen as victims of penis envy. They suffered from a castration complex. They were immature, fixated at an early state of development. Well-balanced adult women understood that fulfillment came from bearing and raising children. Their talent was for nurture, its proper setting was the home.[4] If this summary seems to caricature psychoanalysis, that is because the popular dissemination of complex intellectual systems depends on their being reduced to convenient formulae. Darwinism becomes Social Darwinism; Marxism becomes Maoism. Psychoanalysis became variously, a dogmatic religion, a parlour game of searching for 'Freudian slips', and a bag of labels marked 'penis envy' and the like.

Other factors were responsible too. Women grasped at psychoanalytic straws, after all, because the body of feminist thought was simply inadequate to their needs. Emancipation had not made women happier or more satisfied, and feminists were unable to explain why. American feminists conducted a rather elaborate post-mortem during the 1920s without coming to any reliable conclusions (Doc. 22). Clearly the woman question had not been successfully answered, perhaps it had not even been asked—at least in the proper way. Feminists had been unable to erect a suitable ideology during their glory years; who then could expect them to when the dimensions of their failure were just becoming evident? It would be rash indeed of me to offer here a solution to the feminist dilemma. What Elizabeth Cady Stanton and Charlotte Perkins Gilman could not do is surely beyond my powers. Yet, I think it possible now, because we have evidence that they lacked, to point out the direction that feminists ought to have taken. The success of Sweden, and the failure of Anglo-American society, have to be the key items in this respect. Women may not be entirely equal with men in Sweden, but Sweden is closer to that goal than any other country. Its combination of an advanced welfare state, and a willingness to re-examine traditional ideas about sex, maternity, and male-female relationships would seem to be responsible. The decline of feminism in England, and especially in America, was then, rooted in a failure of intellectual nerve.

[4] A valuable counterweight to the classical Freudian view is Karen Horney, *Feminine Psychology* (New York 1967). Ronald V. Sampson's *The Psychology of Power* contains an illuminating critique of Freud's attitude toward women.

Still, who can blame these splendid women for failing to accomplish what the whole of Anglo-American civilization, with its vast physical and intellectual resources, could not do? They dreamed of freedom, they dreamed of justice, most of all, they dreamed of equality, of a society in which every individual could reach the limit of his own possibilities. In America especially, where poverty and prejudice put such strains on the fabric of society, we can ill-afford to patronize any group, however mistaken, that laboured to make good the promise of our national life. Generations of valiant women struggled, not just for their own sakes, but for us all. If they had been wiser and more daring they would have come closer to building the good society of their dreams. Yet, of what reformers can this not be said? The Reverend Samuel J. May, who was both a feminist and an abolitionist, put it very well when, writing to a friend, he summed up his colleagues in the anti-slavery movement in terms descriptive of feminists too:

'You must not expect those who have left to take up this great cause that they will plead it in all that seemliness of phrase which the scholars . . . might use. But the scholars, and the clergy and the statesmen had done nothing. We abolitionists are what we are—babes, sucklings, obscure men, silly women, . . . sinners, and we shall manage the matter we have taken in hand just as might be expected of such persons as we are. It is unbecoming in abler men who stood by, and would do nothing, to complain of us because we manage the matter no better.'

A NOTE ON SECONDARY SOURCES

The best introduction to American feminism is Eleanor Flexner, *Century of Struggle: The Woman's Rights Movement in The United States* (Cambridge, Mass. 1959). No work of comparable depth and range has been done on feminism in England. Still the most useful is Ray Strachey, *The Cause: A Short History of the Women's Movement in Great Britain* (London 1928). Also helpful, although limited to woman suffrage, is Roger Fulford, *Votes for Women* (London 1957). The best primary source on American feminism, for which, again, there is no English equivalent, is the six-volume *History of Woman Suffrage*. This treasury of original materials on many aspects of the woman movement was edited variously by Elizabeth Cady Stanton, Susan B. Anthony, Matilda J. Gage, and Ida H. Harper from 1881 to 1922.

Chapter I: Mabel Newcomer, *A Century of Higher Education for Women* (New York 1959) is the most recent book on this subject. Gerda Lerner, *The Grimké Sisters from South Carolina* (Boston 1967) is a detailed biographical study of these important early feminists. The best introduction to Mrs Stanton are the two volumes of Harriot Stanton Blatch and Theodore Stanton, eds, *Elizabeth Cady Stanton as Revealed in Her Letters, Diaries, and Reminiscences* (New York 1922). On Miss Anthony see the formidable three volumes by Ida H. Harper, *The Life and Work of Susan B. Anthony* (Indianapolis 1898–1908). The remarkable and sometimes bizarre feats of women in the Civil War are recounted in Mary Elizabeth Massey, *Bonnet Brigades* (New York 1966). Victoria Woodhull has been the subject of many biographies. One of the few attempts to view her in context is in Robert Riegel, *American Feminists* (Lawrence 1963).

Chapter II: On benevolence see Robert H. Bremner, *American Philanthropy* (Chicago 1960), and A. F. Young and E. T. Ashton, *British Social Work in the Nineteenth Century,* (London 1956). The Sanitary Commission is shrewdly analysed in George M. Fredrickson, *The Inner Civil War: Northern Intellectuals and the Crisis of the Union* (New York 1965). Information on the ACA appears in Marion Talbot and Lois Kimball Mathews Rosenberry, *The History of the American Association of University Women 1881–1931* (Boston 1931). The most recent account of the General Federation of Women's Clubs is Mildred White Wells, *Unity in Diversity* (Washington 1953). Also useful is the early history by Mary I. Wood cited in the footnotes to this chapter. A contemporary book that shows how clubwomen viewed themselves is Rheta Childe Dorr, *What Eight Million Women Want* (Boston 1910).

Chapter III: The most complete study of the American settlements is Allen F. Davis, *Spearheads for Reform: The Social Settlements and the Progressive Movement 1890–1914* (New York 1967). Robert A. Woods, *English Social Movements* (New York 1891) explains at length what England had to teach America about social reform, a relationship elaborated in Arthur Mann, 'British Social Thought and American Reformers', *Mississippi Valley Historical Review*, xlii (1956), 672–92. On the mature movement Robert A. Woods and Albert J. Kennedy, *The Settlement Horizon* (New York 1922) is invaluable. Jane Addams' memoirs, especially *Twenty Years at Hull House* (New York 1910) are very revealing, as Christopher Lasch has demonstrated in his stimulating book *The New Radicalism in America 1889–1961* (New York 1965). William Rhinelander Stewart, *The Philanthropic Work of Josephine Shaw Lowell* (New York 1911) is pedestrian but includes illuminating material from her correspondence and published reports. Josephine Goldmark, *Impatient Crusader: Florence Kelley's Life Story* (Urbana 1953) and Dorothy Rose Blumberg, *Florence Kelley: The Making of a Social Pioneer* (New York 1966) are helpful, but the last word on this astonishing woman has still to be written. The best scholarly account is the as yet unpublished Louis Lee Athey, 'The Consumers' League and Social Reform, 1890–1924' (Doctoral Dissertation, University of Delaware, 1965). Gladys Boone, *The Women's Trade Union Leagues in Great Britain and the United States of America* (New York 1942) is a very useful, if uncritical, work, and one of the few to explain adequately the connections between English and American social reformers. Also informative is *Mary Dreier, Margaret Dreier Robins: Her Life, Letters, and Work* (New York 1950).

Chapter IV: The effect of woman suffrage on Colorado was fully and fairly brought out in Helen L. Sumner, *Equal Suffrage* (New York 1909), Aileen Kraditor, *The Ideas of the Woman Suffrage Movement 1890–1920* (previously cited) is a must. Charlotte Perkins Gilman was an immensely productive woman whose best known work was *Women and Economics* (Boston 1898). The liveliest account of the American militants is Doris Stevens, *Jailed for Freedom* (New York 1920). There is an abundant literature on English militancy, most recently David Mitchell, *The Fighting Pankhursts* (London 1967). Some of the most enlightening material is provided by the Pankhursts themselves, notably E. Sylvia Pankhurst, *The Suffragette Movement* (London 1931) which, though utterly lacking in self-pity, touchingly recounts the difficulties imposed on this sensible, generous women by her ex-traordinary mother and sister. There is no general study of American women in the First World War, but the longer, tougher English experience generated a great many. David Mitchell, *Monstrous Regiment* (London 1965) is comprehensive but not always fair. Sylvia Pankhurst's *The Home Front* (previously cited) views the war effort from the perspective of East London. An especially moving recital of one woman's tragic war years is Vera Brittain, *Testament of Youth* (London 1938).

Chapter V: Clarke A. Chambers, *Seedtime of Reform* (Minneapolis 1963) tells how social workers and reformers gallantly met the postwar era's challenges. In most respects, however, the liter-ature on women after 1920 is thin. Alfred C. Kinsey *et al.*, *Sexual Behavior In the Human Female* (Philadelphia 1953) has much valuable material on the sex lives of different age groups, as does Katherine Bement Davis, *Factors in the Sex Life of Twenty-Two Hundred Women* (New York 1929). Another fascinating pioneer study is Gilbert V. Hamilton, *A Research in Marriage* (New York 1929). Among contemporary efforts to understand the failure of feminism, Suzanne La Follette, *Concerning Women* (New York 1926) and Alice Beal Parsons, *Woman's Dilemma* (New York 1926) are outstanding. Ray Strachey, *The Cause* (previously cited) brings the story of English feminism up to 1928, and Vera Brittain, *Lady into Woman* (London 1954) carries it somewhat further. Viola Klein, *The Feminine Character: History of and Idealogy* (New York 1949) is a very good analysis of the feminine identity problem. Astute observations on the future of feminism appear in Victor Gollancz, ed., *The Making of Women: Oxford Essays in Feminism* (London 1917), and Wilma Meikle, *Towards a Sane Feminism* (London 1916). Virginia Woolf, *A Room of One's Own* (London 1929) is, of course, a classic.

DOCUMENTS

Duties of Women

Sarah M. Grimké, *Letters on the Equality of the Sexes and the Condition of Women*, Boston 1838. (pp. 121–8).

One of the duties which devolve upon women in the present interesting crisis, is to prepare themselves for more extensive usefulness, by making use of those religious and literary privileges and advantages that are within their reach, if they will only stretch out their hands and possess them. By doing this, they will become better acquainted with their rights as moral beings, and with their responsibilities growing out of those rights: they will regard themselves, as they really are, FREE AGENTS, immortal beings, amenable to no tribunal but that of Jehovah, and bound not to submit to any restriction imposed for selfish purposes, or to gratify that love of power which has reigned in the heart of man from Adam down to the present time. In contemplating the great moral reformations of the day, and the part which they are bound to take in them, instead of puzzling themselves with the harassing, because unnecessary inquiry, how far they may go without overstepping the bounds of propriety, which separate male and female duties, they will only inquire, 'Lord, what wilt thou have us to do?' They will be enabled to see the simple truth, that God had made no distinction between men and women as moral beings; that the distinction now so much insisted upon between male and female virtues is as absurd as it is unscriptural, and has been the fruitful source of much mischief—granting to man a license for the exhibition of brute force and conflict on the battle field; for sternness, selfishness, and the exercise of irresponsible power in the circle of home—and to woman a permit to rest on an arm of flesh, and to regard modesty and delicacy, and all the kindred virtues, as peculiarly appropriate to her. Now to me it is perfectly clear, that WHATSOEVER IT IS MORALLY RIGHT FOR A MAN TO DO, IT IS MORALLY RIGHT FOR A WOMAN TO DO; and that confusion must exist in the moral world, until women takes her stand on the same platform with man, and feels that she is clothed by her Maker with the *same rights,* and, of course, that upon her devolve the *same duties.*

It is not my intention, nor indeed do I think it is in my power, to point out the precise duties of women. To him who still teacheth by his Holy Spirit as never man taught, I refer my beloved sisters. There is a vast field of usefulness before them. The signs of the times give portentous evidence, that a day of deep trial is approaching; and I urge them, by every consideration of a Savior's dying love, by the millions of heathen in our midst, by the sufferings of woman in almost every portion of the world, by the fearful ravages which slavery, intemperance, licentiousness and other iniquities are making of the happiness of our fellow creatures, to come to the rescue of a ruined world, and to be found co-workers with Jesus Christ.

> 'Ho! to the rescue, ho!
> Up every one that feels—
> 'Tis a sad and fearful cry of woe
> From a guilty world that steals.
> Hark! hark! how the horror rolls,
> Whence can this anguish be?
> 'Tis the groan of a trammel'd people's souls,
> *Now bursting* to be free.'

And here, with all due deference for the office of the ministry, which I believe was established by Jehovah himself, and designed by Him to be the means of spreading light and salvation through a crucified Savior to the ends of the earth, I would entreat my sisters not to *compel* the ministers of the present day to give their names to great moral reformations. The practice of making ministers life members, or officers of societies, when their hearts have not been touched with a live coal from the altar, and animated with love for the work we are engaged in, is highly injurious to them, as well as to the cause. They often satisfy their consciences in this way, without doing anything to promote the anti-slavery, or temperance, or other reformations; and we please ourselves with the idea, that we have done something to forward the cause of Christ, when, in effect, we have been sewing pillows like the false prophetesses of old under the arm-holes of our clerical brethren. Let us treat the ministers with all tenderness and respect, but let us be careful how we cherish in their hearts the idea that they are of more importance to a cause than other men. I rejoice when they take hold heartily. I love and honor some ministers with whom I have been associated in the anti-slavery ranks, but I do deeply deplore, for the sake of the cause, the prevalent notion, that the clergy must be had, either by persuasion or by bribery. They will not need persuasion or bribery, if their hearts are with us; if they are not, we are better without them. It is idle to suppose that the kingdom of heaven cannot come on earth, without their co-operation. It is the Lord's work, and it must go forward with or without their aid. As well might the converted Jews have despaired of the spread of Christianity, without the co-operation of Scribes and Pharisees.

Let us keep in mind, that no abolitionism is of any value, which is not accompanied with deep, heartfelt repentance; and that, whenever a minister sincerely repents of having, either by his apathy or his efforts, countenanced the fearful sin of slavery, he will need no inducement to come into our ranks; so far from it, he will abhor himself in dust and ashes, for his past blindness and indifference to the cause of God's poor and oppressed: and he will regard it as a privilege to be enabled to do something in the cause of human rights. I know the ministry exercise vast power; but I rejoice in the belief, that the spell is broken which encircled them, and rendered it all but blasphemy to expose their errors and their sins. We are beginning to understand that they are but men, and that their station should not shield them from merited reproof.

I have blushed for my sex when I have heard of their entreating ministers to attend their associations, and open them with prayer. The idea is inconceivable to me, that Christian women can be engaged in doing God's work, and yet cannot ask his blessing on their efforts, except through the lips of a man. I have known a whole town scoured to obtain a minister to open a female meeting, and their refusal to do so spoken of as quite a misfortune. Now, I am not glad that the ministers do wrong; but I am glad that my sisters have been sometimes compelled to act for themselves: it is exactly what they need to strengthen them, and prepare them to act independently. And to say the truth, there is something really ludicrous in seeing a minister enter the meeting, open it with prayer, and then take his departure. However, I only throw out these hints for the consideration of women. I believe there are solemn responsibilities resting upon us, and that in this day of light and knowledge, we cannot plead ignorance of duty. The great moral reformations now on the wheel are only practical Christianity; and if the ministry is not prepared to labor with us in these righteous causes, let us press forward, and they will follow on to know the Lord.

CONCLUSION

I have now, my dear sister, completed my series of letters. I am aware, they contain some new views; but I believe they are based on the immutable truths of the Bible. All I ask for them is, the candid and prayerful consideration of Christians. If they strike at some of our bosom sins, our deep-rooted prejudices, our long cherished opinions, let us not condemn them on that account, but investigate them fearlessly and prayerfully, and not shrink from the examination; because, if they are true, they place heavy responsibilities upon women. In throwing them before the public, I have been actuated solely by the belief, that if they are acted upon, they will exalt the character and enlarge the usefulness of my own sex, and contribute greatly to the happiness and virtue of the other. That there is a root of bitterness continually springing up in families and troubling the repose of both men and women, must be manifest to even a superficial observer; and I believe it is the mistaken notion of the inequality of the sexes. As there is an assumption of superiority on the one part, which is not sanctioned by Jehovah, there is an incessant struggle on the other to rise to that degree of dignity, which God designed women to possess in common with men, and to maintain those rights and exercise those privileges which every woman's common sense, apart from the prejudices of education, tells her are inalienable; they are a part of her moral nature, and can only cease when her immortal mind is extinguished.

One word more. I feel that I am calling upon my sex to sacrifice what has been, what is still dear to their hearts, the adulation, the flattery, the attentions of trifling men. I am asking them to repel these insidious enemies whenever they approach them; to manifest by their conduct, that, although they value highly the society of pious and intelligent men, they have no taste for idle conversation, and for that silly preference which is manifested for their personal accommodation, often at the expense of great inconvenience to their male companions. As an illustration of what I mean, I will state a fact.

I was traveling lately in a stage coach. A gentleman, who was also a passenger, was made sick by riding with his back to the horses. I offered to exchange seats, assuring him it did not affect me at all unpleasantly; but he was too polite to permit a lady to run the risk of being discommoded. I am sure he meant to be very civil, but I really thought it was a foolish piece of civility. This kind of attention encourages selfishness in woman, and is only accorded as a sort of quietus, in exchange for those *rights* of which we are deprived. Men and women are equally bound to cultivate a spirit of accommodation; but I exceedingly deprecate her being treated like a spoiled child, and sacrifices made   to her selfishness and vanity. In lieu of these flattering but injurious attentions, yielded to her as an inferior, as a mark of benevolence and courtesy, I want my sex to claim nothing from their brethren but what their brethren may justly claim from them, in their intercourse as Christians. I am persuaded woman can do much in this way to elevate her own character. And that we may become duly sensible of the dignity of our nature, only a little lower than the angels, and bring forth fruit to the glory and honor of Emanuel's name, is the fervent prayer of Thine in the bonds of womanhood.

SARAH M. GRIMKÉ

2

'Declaration of Sentiments' and 'Resolutions' adopted by the Seneca Falls Convention of 1848

FROM the *History of Woman Suffrage,* vol. 1.

When, in the course of human events, it becomes necessary for one portion of the family of man to assume among the people of the earth a position different from that which they have hitherto occupied, but one to which the laws of nature and of nature's God entitle them, a decent respect to the opinions of mankind requires that they should declare the causes that impel them to such a course.

We hold these truths to be self-evident: that all men and women are created equal; that they are endowed by their Creator with certain inalienable rights; that among these are life, liberty, and the pursuit of happiness; that to secure these rights governments are instituted, deriving their just powers from the consent of the governed. Whenever any form of government becomes destructive of these ends, it is the right of those who suffer from it to refuse allegiance to it, and to insist upon the institution of a new government, laying its foundation on such principles, and organizing its powers in such form, as to them shall seem most likely to effect their safety and happiness. Prudence indeed, will dictate that governments long established should not be changed for light and transient causes; and accordingly all experience hath shown that mankind are more disposed to suffer, while evils are sufferable, than to right themselves by abolishing the forms to which they were accustomed. But when a long train of abuses and usurpations, pursuing invariably the same object evinces a design to reduce them under absolute despotism, it is their duty to throw off such government, and to provide new guards for their future security. Such has been the patient sufferance of the women under this government, and such is now the necessity which constrains them to demand the equal station to which they are entitled.

The history of mankind is a history of repeated injuries and usurpations on the part of man toward woman, having in direct object the establishment of an absolute tyranny over her. To prove this, let facts be submitted to a candid world.

He has never permitted her to exercise her inalienable right to the elective franchise.

He has compelled her to submit to laws, in the formation of which she had no voice.

He has withheld from her rights which are given to the most ignorant and degraded men—both natives and foreigners.

Having deprived her of this first right of a citizen, the elective franchise, thereby leaving her without representation in the halls of legislation, he has oppressed her on all sides.

He has made her, if married, in the eye of the law, civilly dead.

He has taken from her all right in property, even to the wages she earns.

He has made her, morally, an irresponsible being, as she can commit many crimes with impunity, provided they be done in the presence of her husband. In the covenant of marriage, she is compelled to promise obedience to her husband, he becoming, to all intents and purposes, her master—the law giving him power to deprive her of her liberty, and to administer chastisement.

He has so framed the laws of divorce, as to what shall be the proper causes, and in case of separation, to whom the guardianship of the children shall be given, as to be wholly regardless of the happiness of women—the law, in all cases, going upon a false supposition of the supremacy of man, and giving all power into his hands.

After depriving her of all rights as a married woman, if single, and the owner of property, he has taxed her to support a government which recognizes her only when her property can be made profitable to it.

He has monopolized nearly all the profitable employments, and from those she is permitted to follow, she receives but a scanty remuneration. He closes against her all the avenues to wealth and distinction which he considers most honorable to himself. As a teacher of theology, medicine, or law, she is not known.

He has denied her the facilities for obtaining a thorough education, all colleges being closed against her.

He allows her in Church, as well as State, but a subordinate position, claiming Apostolic authority for her exclusion from the ministry, and, with some exceptions, from any public participation in the affairs of the Church.

He has created a false public sentiment by giving to the world a different code of morals for men and women, by which moral delinquencies which exclude women from society, are not only tolerated, but deemed of little account in man.

He has usurped the prerogative of Jehovah himself, claiming it as his right to assign for her a sphere of action, when that belongs to her conscience and to her God.

He has endeavored, in every way that he could, to destroy her confidence in her own powers, to lessen her self-respect, and to make her willing to lead a dependent and abject life.

Now, in view of this entire disfranchisement of one-half the people of this country, their social and religious degradation—in view of the unjust laws above mentioned, and because women do feel themselves aggrieved, oppressed, and fraudulently deprived of their most sacred rights, we insist that they have immediate admission to all the rights and privileges which belong to them as citizens of the United States.

In entering upon the great work before us, we anticipate no small amount of misconception, misrepresentation, and ridicule; but we shall use every instrumentality within our power to effect our object. We shall employ agents, circulate tracts, petition the State and National legislatures, and endeavor to enlist the pulpit and the press in our behalf. We hope this Convention will be followed by a series of Conventions embracing every part of the country.

The following resolutions were discussed by Lucretia Mott, Thomas and Mary Ann McClintock, Amy Post, Catharine A. F. Stebbins, and others, and were adopted:

WHEREAS, The great precept of nature is conceded to be, that "man shall pursue his own true and substantial happiness." Blackstone in his Commentaries remarks, that this law of Nature being coeval with mankind, and dictated by God himself, is of course superior in obligation to any other. It is binding over all the globe, in all countries and at all times; no human laws are of any validity if contrary to this, and such of them as are valid, derive all their force, and all their validity, and all their authority, mediately and immediately, from this original; therefore;

Resolved, That such laws as conflict, in any way, with the true and substantial happiness of woman, are contrary to the great precept of nature and of no validity, for this is "superior in obligation to any other."

Resolved, That all laws which prevent woman from occupying such a station in society as her conscience shall dictate, or which place her in a position inferior to that of man, are contrary to the great precept of nature, and therefore of no force or authority.

Resolved, That woman is man's equal—was intended to be so by the Creator, and the highest good of the race demands that she should be recognized as such.

Resolved, That the women of this country ought to be enlightened in regard to the laws under which they live, that they may no longer publish their degradation by declaring themselves satisfied with their present position, nor their ignorance, by asserting that they have all the rights they want.

Resolved, That inasmuch as man, while claiming for himself intellectual superiority, does accord to woman moral superiority, it is pre-eminently his duty to encourage her to speak and teach, as she has an opportunity, in all religious assemblies.

Resolved, That the same amount of virtue, delicacy, and refinement of behavior that is required of woman in the social state, should also be required of man, and the same transgressions should be visited with equal severity on both man and woman.

Resolved, That the objection of indelicacy and impropriety, which is so often brought against woman when she addresses a public audience, comes with a very ill-grace from those who encourage, by their attendance, her appearance on the stage, in the concert, or in feats of the circus.

Resolved, That woman has too long rested satisfied in the circumscribed limits which corrupt customs and a perverted application of the Scriptures have marked out for her, and that it is time she should move in the enlarged sphere which her great Creator has assigned her.

Resolved, That it is the duty of the women of this country to secure to themselves their sacred right to the elective franchise.

Resolved, That the equality of human rights results necessarily from the fact of the identity of the race in capabilities and responsibilities.

Resolved, therefore, That, being invested by the Creator with the same capabilities, and the same consciousness of responsibility for their exercise, it is demonstrably the right and duty of woman, equally with man, to promote every righteous cause by every righteous means; and especially in regard to the great subjects of morals and religion, it is self-evidently her right to participate with her brother in teaching them, both in private and in public, by writing and by speaking, by any instrumentalities proper to be used, and in any assemblies proper to be held; and this being a self-evident truth growing out of the divinely implanted principles of human nature, any custom or authority adverse to it, whether modern or wearing the hoary sanction of antiquity, is to be regarded as a self-evident falsehood, and at war with mankind.

At the last session Lucretia Mott offered and spoke to the following resolution:

Resolved, That the speedy success of our cause depends upon the zealous and untiring efforts of both men and women, for the overthrow of the monopoly of the pulpit, and for the securing to woman an equal participation with men in the various trades, professions, and commerce.

3

'Marriage of Lucy Stone Under Protest'

FROM the *History of Woman Suffrage*, vol. I.

It was my privilege to celebrate May day by officiating at a wedding in a farm-house among the hills of West Brookfield. The bridegroom was a man of tried worth, a leader in the Western Anti-Slavery Movement; and the bride was one whose fair name is known throughout the nation; one whose rare intellectual qualities are excelled by the private beauty of her heart and life.

I never perform the marriage ceremony without a renewed sense of the iniquity of our present system of laws in respect to marriage; a system by which "man and wife are one, and that one is the husband." It was with my hearty concurrence, therefore, that the following protest was read and signed, as a part of the nuptial ceremony; and I send it to you, that others may be induced to do likewise.

Rev. THOMAS WENTWORTH HIGGINSON.

PROTEST

While acknowledging our mutual affection by publicly assuming the relationship of husband and wife, yet in justice to ourselves and a great principle, we deem it a duty to declare that this act on our part implies no sanction of, nor promise of voluntary obedience to such of the present laws of marriage, as refuse to recognize the wife as an independent, rational being, while they confer upon the husband an injurious and unnatural superiority, investing him with legal powers which no honorable man would exercise, and which no man should possess. We protest especially against the laws which give to the husband:

1. The custody of the wife's person.

2. The exclusive control and guardianship of their children.

3. The sole ownership of her personal, and use of her real estate, unless previously settled upon her, or placed in the hands of trustees, as in the case of minors, lunatics, and idiots.

4. The absolute right to the product of her industry.

5. Also against laws which give to the widower so much larger and more permanent an interest in the property of his deceased wife, than they give to the widow in that of the deceased husband.

6. Finally, against the whole system by which "the legal existence of the wife is suspended during marriage," so that in most States, she neither has a legal part in the choice of her residence, nor can she make a will, nor sue or be sued in her own name, nor inherit property.

We believe that personal independence and equal human rights can never be forfeited, except for crime; that marriage should be an equal and permanent partnership, and so recognized by law; that until it is so recognized, married partners should provide against the radical injustice of present laws, by every means in their power.

We believe that where domestic difficulties arise, no appeal should be made to legal tribunals under existing laws, but that all difficulties should be submitted to the equitable adjustment of arbitrators mutually chosen.

Thus reverencing law, we enter our protest against rules and customs which are unworthy of the name, since they violate justice, the essence of law.

(Signed),   HENRY B. BLACKWELL,
Worcester Spy, 1855.   LUCY STONE.

4

Elizabeth Cady Stanton, 'The Bloomer Costume'

FROM the *History of Woman Suffrage*, vol. I.

Fathers, husbands, and brothers, all joined in the protest against the small waist, and stiff distended petticoats, which were always themes for unbounded ridicule. But no sooner did a few brave conscientious women adopt the bifurcated costume, an imitation in part of the Turkish style, than the press at once turned its guns on "The Bloomer," and the same fathers, husbands, and brothers, with streaming eyes and pathetic tones, conjured the women of their households to cling to the prevailing fashions. The object of those who donned the new attire, was primarily health and freedom; but as the daughter of Gerrit Smith introduced it just at the time of the early conventions, it was supposed to be an inherent element in the demand for political equality. As some of those who advocated the right of suffrage, wore the dress, and had been identified with all the unpopular reforms, in the reports of our conventions, the press rung the changes on "strong-minded," "Bloomer," "free love," "easy divorce," "amalgamation." I wore the dress two years and found it a great blessing. What a sense of liberty I felt, in running up and down stairs with my hands free to carry whatsoever I would, to trip through the rain or snow with no skirts to hold or brush, ready at any moment to climb a hill-top to see the sun go down, or the moon rise, with no ruffles or trails to be limped by the dew, or soiled by the grass. What an emancipation from little petty vexatious trammels and annoyances every hour of the day. Yet such is the tyranny of custom, that to escape constant observation, criticism, ridicule, persecution, mobs, one after another gladly went back to the old slavery and sacrificed freedom to repose. I have never wondered since that the Chinese women allow their daughters' feet to be encased in iron shoes, nor that the Hindoo widows walk calmly to the funeral pyre. I suppose no act of my life ever gave my cousin, Gerrit Smith, such deep sorrow, as my abandonment of the "Bloomer costume." He published an open letter to me on the subject, and when his daughter, Mrs. Miller, three years after, followed my example, he felt that women had so little courage and persistence, that for a time he almost despaired of the success of the suffrage movement; of such vital consequence in woman's mental and physical development did he feel the dress to be.

Gerrit Smith, Samuel J. May, James C. Jackson, and Charles Dudley Miller, sustained the women, who led in this reform unflinchingly, during the trying experiment. Let the names of those who made this protest be remembered. We knew the Bloomer costume never could be generally becoming, as it required a perfection of form, limbs, and feet, such as few possessed, and we who wore it also knew that it was not artistic. Though the martyrdom proved too much for us who had so many other measures to press on the public conscience, yet no experiment is lost, however evanescent, that rouses thought to the injurious consequences of the present style of dress, sacrificing to its absurdities so many of the most promising girls of this generation.

5

Elizabeth Cady Stanton, 'Who Are Our Friends?'

FROM *The Revolution*, 15 January 1868.

SINCE turning our faces eastward from Kansas we have been asked many times why we affiliated with Democrats there, and why Mr. Train was on our platform. Mr. Train is there for the same reason, that when invited by the "Women's Suffrage Association" of St. Louis, he went to Kansas, because he believes in the enfranchisement of woman, not as a sentimental theory, a mere Utopia for smooth speech and a golden age, but a practical idea, to be pushed and realized to-day. Mr. Train is a business man, builds houses, hotels, railroads, cities, and accomplishes whatever he undertakes. When he proposes to build up a national party on educated suffrage, paid labor, American industry and greenbacks, those who know his moral probity of character and great executive ability, believe he will do all that is possible towards its accomplishment. Though many of the leading minds of this country have advocated woman's enfranchisement for the last twenty years, it has been more as an intellectual theory than a fact of life, hence none of our many friends were ready to help in the practical work of the last few months, neither in Kansas or the Constitutional Convention of New York. So far from giving us a helping hand, Republicans and Abolitionists, by their false philosophy—that the safety of the nation demand ignorance rather than education at the polls—have paralized the women themselves.

To what a depth of degradation must the women of this nation have fallen to be willing to stand aside, silent and indifferent spectators in the reconstruction of the nation, while all the lower stratas of manhood are to legislate in their interests, political, religious, educational, social and sanitary, moulding to their untutored will the institutions of a mighty continent. Why wonder that the workers in our cause turned from their theoretical friends to the Democrats in Kansas, who gave us their votes. The party out of power is always in a position to carry principles to their logical conclusions, while the party in power, thinks only of what it can afford to do; hence, you can reason with minorities, while majorities are moved only by votes. We are indebted to the Democratic party for all the agitation we have had on this question for the last four years. To a Democratic Senator from Pennsylvania, Mr. Cowan, we owe the three days' discussion on this question in the Senate of the United States; and to James Brooks in the House for the skillful manner in which he drew public attention to our petitions against the introduction of the word "male" into the Federal constitution. To the same party our thanks are due for the agitation in many of the State Legislatures, and for liberal donations, and for franking our documents to every part of the country.

While leading Democrats have been thus favorably disposed, what have our best friends said when, for the first time since the agitation of the question, they have had an opportunity to frame their ideas into statutes to amend the constitutions of two States in the Union.

Charles Sumner, Horace Greeley, Gerrit Smith and Wendell Phillips, with one consent, bid the women of the nation stand aside and behold the salvation of the negro. Wendell Phillips says, "one idea for a generation," to come up in the order of their importance. First negro suffrage, then temperance, then the eight hour movement, then woman's suffrage. In 1958, three generations hence, thirty years to a generation, Phillips and Providence permitting, woman's suffrage will be in order. What an insult to the women who have labored thirty years for the emancipation of the slave, now when he is their political equal, to propose to lift him above their heads. Gerrit Smith, forgetting that our great American idea is "individual rights," in which abolitionists have ever based their strongest arguments for emancipation, says, this is the time to settle the rights of races; unless we do justice to the negro we shall bring down on ourselves another bloody revolution, another four years' war, but we have nothing to fear from woman, she will not revenge herself! Woman not revenge herself! Look at your asylums for the deaf, the dumb, the blind, the insane, and there behold the results of this wholesale desecration of the mothers of the race! Woman not revenge herself! Go into the streets of your cities at the midnight hour, and there behold those whom God meant to be Queens in the moral universe, giving your sons and mine their first lessons in infamy and vice. No, you cannot wrong the humblest of God's creatures without making discord and confusion in the whole social system.

Horace Greeley has advocated this cause for the last twenty years, but to-day it is too new, revolutionary for practical consideration. The enfranchisement of woman, revolutionizing, as it will, our political, religious and social condition, is not a measure too radical and all-pervading to meet the moral necessities of this day and generation.

Why fear new things; all old things were once new. If the nineteenth century is to be governed by the eighteenth, and the twentieth by the nineteenth, and so on, do you not see that the world must ever be governed by dead men? Are the creeds, and codes, and customs of those who are buried beneath the sod of any importance, compared with your opinions and mine, on the vital issues of the hour in which we live? Progress is the law of life. We live to do new things! When Abraham Lincoln issued the proclamation of emancipation, it was a new thing. When the Republican party gave the ballot to the negro, it was a new thing, startling too, to the people of the South, very revolutionary to their institutions, but Mr. Greeley did not object to all this because it was new.

The reasoning of these gentlemen may be, as Weed said of Morgan, good enough to answer their purpose till after the Presidential election, but we see the cheat. We have a right to ask more substantial reasons from wise men for their opposition.

When it was proposed in Congress to amend the Federal Constitution by introducing the word "male," a protest was sent to Charles Sumner, from the strong-minded women of the nation, headed by Lydia Maria Child. He rose in his place and said, "I present this petition because it is my duty, but I consider it most inopportune." Would it have been more opportune after the deed was done, than while the amendment was under consideration?

And now, while men like these have used all their influence for the last four years, to paralyze every effort we have put forth to rouse the women of the nation, to demand their true position in the reconstruction, they triumphantly turn to us, and say the greatest barrier in the way of your demand is that "the women themselves do not wish to vote." What a libel on the intelligence of the women of the nineteenth century. What means the 12,000 petitions presented by John Stuart Mill in the British Parliament from the first women in England, demanding house hold suffrage? What means the late action in Kansas, 10,000 women petitioned there for the right of suffrage, and 9,000 votes at the last election was the answer. What means the agitation in every State in the Union? In the very hour when Horace Greeley brought in his adverse report in the Constitutional Convention of New York, at least twenty members rose in their places and presented petitions from every part of the State, demanding woman's suffrage. What means that eloquent speech of George W. Curtis in the Convention, but to show that the ablest minds in the State are ready for this onward step? We return from the West with renewed determination to give the men of this State no rest until they blot the word "male" from our Constitution. New York has taken the lead in her legislation for woman during the last twenty years, and it is fitting that she should be the first State in the Union to give her daughters the crowning right of citizenship.

6

Laura Curtis Bullard,
'The Slave-Women of America'

FROM *The Revolution*, 6 October 1870.

Slavery is not yet abolished in the United States. It is the boast of our republic that it is a nation of free men; it points triumphantly to its last great act, the emancipation of four millions of negroes, and forgets, in its pride and self-gratulation, that within its boundaries are still left at least ten millions of bond-women, who have no voice in the government, and no rights, except such as their masters have chosen to give them.

That the women in the United States are many of them comfortable and happy, as they are, is no argument in favor of the system of government under which they live.

The slaveholders of the South were, as a rule, more just and considerate in their treatment of their chattels than the laws would have compelled them to be. A certain public sentiment, as well as an instinct of human nature, demands more generosity from a superior to an inferior than would content the strict letter of legislative enactments.

This which was true of negro slavery is also true of woman slavery.

There are plenty of individual cases of barbarity, and oppression, and outrage; but, as a general rule, it is true that as many negroes were not abused by their masters, neither are many women by theirs, except in the worst of all abuses, the wresting from them of the right to individual freedom.

In one sense, the kindest of Southern slave-owners were also the most cruel; for by robbing slavery of some of its worst features, they made their chattels content with their bondage; and no social institution can be more demoralizing, or a greater curse to mankind, than one which robs its victims of the instinctive desire of a soul for liberty.

One of the saddest spectacles in our present social condition of man as master, and woman as slave, is the unconsciousness of the majority of women of their humiliating position; their indifference, so long as they themselves are comfortable, to the sufferings of others; their horror of those among them who, stung by a sense of their degradation, dare to demand freedom for themselves and for their class.

The modern world has outgrown many of the ancient ideas once held sacred by the race. The patriarchal system of government, the divine right of kings, polygamy, slavery, each of which in turn has been considered as established by God for the best interests of mankind, have had their day, and are no longer regarded as a part of the divine order. But one ancient idea still retains its hold on mankind. It is still a universally accepted theory that the position of woman should be a subordinate one. To this day, the most civilized nations of the world believe as firmly as did the early Semitic races, in the barbaric ages, that woman was made for man. The advance of civilization has changed her position somewhat. She is less the drudge, and more the plaything, or the companion of man. But it has never yet been acknowledged by any but a few of the noblest of men that she was created by God an independent being, with individual duties and individual rights, and no more made merely as a companion for man than was man made merely for a companion to woman.

Men and women were created for each other, but not alone for each other. Upon both, their Maker has imposed the duty of individual development, and it is only because their mutual companionship and association is necessary for this great end, that it can be truly said that they were made for each other. This great truth has been only half understood; and men have taught, and women have accepted, the theory that man is the central figure in creation, and woman simply an accessory. In consequence of this error men and women have suffered alike. The degradation of one-half the human race has not left the other half unharmed.

In countries where slavery exists, the ruling class are invariably demoralized by association with the subject race; and men who have put, and still keep, women in a position which dwarfs their noblest, and develops their meanest faculties, need not hope to escape the retribution which must follow, as a natural consequence—their own degradation.

The pettiness of women, and the distortion of their characters, which is produced by the confinement to one limited circle which the pressure of public opinion forces upon them, must have its effects, not only upon themselves, but on their children, their husbands, their brothers—in short, upon all the men with whom they are associated.

In the interests of the race it is most important that women should be roused to a sense of their subject condition, and to the humiliation which it involves. They should no longer accept the ideal of womanly character which society offers them, but rise to the conception of the free and independent being that God intended a true woman to be. They should no longer tamely submit to the bondage in which custom and education have for ages held them, but break off the shackles which bind them. They should demand a freedom of thought and a freedom of action equal to that which man demands for himself, and which God designed as the true means for the development of both sexes.

The enfranchisement of woman is the germ from which shall spring the reorganization of society.

One of the greatest of all the truths which have influenced the world is that of the individual rights of men, of which our republic is so grand an exponent—a truth whose leaven is already felt in every nation on the earth, and which will never cease its work until the governmental systems of the world shall be changed by its mighty power.

The recognition of the rights of man is the grandest feature of this nineteenth century; the recognition of the rights of woman is next in the natural order of evolution—a truth equally grand, equally vital, and which will, in its turn, revolutionize the social and political status of the world.

Of these rights that of the franchise is but one. Mrs. Stanton has well said on this subject, "The negro was *first* emancipated, and then suffrage was given him; and I am not sure that this is not the natural order for woman. She must demand first her deliverance from slavery, claim her right to herself, soul and body, and then ask for the suffrage."

It was a glorious day for this republic when she shook herself free from the disgrace of negro slavery, and declaring that she would have no subject race within her boundaries, broke the chains of four million bondmen! It will be a still more glorious day in her annals when the republic shall declare the injustice of a slavery of sex, and shall set free her millions of bond women!

God speed the hour!

7

Olympia Brown's attack on immigrants, given at the National Woman Suffrage Association's convention in 1889

FROM the *History of Woman Suffrage*, 4.

In Wisconsin we have by the census of 1880 a population of 910,072 native-born, 405,425 foreign-born. Our last vote cast was 149,463 American, 189,469 foreign; thus you see nearly 1,000,000 native-born people are out-voted and out-governed by less than half their number of foreigners. Is that fair to Americans? Is it just to American men? Will they not, under this influence, in a little while be driven to the wall and obliged to step down and out? When the members of our Legislatures are the greater part foreigners, when they sit in the office of mayor and in all the offices of our city, and rule us with a rod of iron, it is time that American men should inquire if we have any rights that foreigners are bound to respect.....

The last census shows, I think, that there are in the United States three times as many American-born women as the whole foreign population, men and women together, so that the votes of women will eventually be the only means of overcoming this foreign influence and maintaining our free institutions. There is no possible safety for our free school, our free church or our republican government, unless women are given the suffrage and that right speedily..... The question in every political caucus, in every political convention, is not what great principles shall we announce, but what kind of a document can we draw up that will please the foreigners? ....

When we remember that the first foot to touch Plymouth Rock was a woman's—that in the first settlement of this country women endured trials and privations and stood bravely at the post of duty, even fighting in the ranks that we might have a republic—and that in our great Western world women came at an early day to make the wilderness blossom as the rose, and rocked their babies' cradles in the log cabins when the Indians' war-whoop was heard on the prairies and the wolves howled around their doors—when we remember that in the last war thousands of women in the Northwest bravely took upon themselves the work of the households and the fields that their husbands and sons might fight the battles of liberty—when we recollect all this, and then are told that loyal women, pioneer women, the descendants of the Pilgrim Fathers, are not even to ask for the right of suffrage lest the Scandinavians should be offended, it is time to rise in indignation and ask, Whose country is this? Who made it? Who have periled their lives for it?

Our American women are property holders and pay large taxes: but the foreigner who has lived only one year in the State, and ten days in the precinct, who does not own a foot of land, may vote away their property in the form of taxes in the most reckless manner, regardless of their interests and their rights. Women are well-educated; they are graduating from our colleges; they are reading and thinking and writing; and yet they are the political inferiors of all the riff-raff of Europe that is poured upon our shores. It is unbearable. There is no language that can express the enormous injustice done to women. . . . .

We can not separate subjects and say we will vote on temperance or on school matters, for all these questions are part of government. . . . When women as well as men are voters, the church will get some recognition. I marvel that all ministers are not in favor of woman suffrage, when I consider that their audiences are almost entirely composed of women and that the church to-day is brought into disrepute because it is made up of disfranchised members. The minister would stand a hundred-fold higher than he does now if women had the suffrage. Everybody would want to know what the minister was saying to those women voters.

We are in danger in this country of Catholic domination, not because the Catholics are more numerous than we are, but because the Catholic church is represented at the polls and the Protestant church is not. The foreigners are Catholic—the greater portion of them; the foreigners are men—the greater part of them, and members of the Catholic church, and they work for it and vote for it. The Protestant church is composed of women. Men for the most part do not belong to it; they do not care much for it except as something to interest the women of their household. The consequence is the Protestant church is comparatively unrepresented at the ballot-box. . . .

I urge upon you, women, that you put suffrage first and foremost, before every other consideration upon earth. Make it a religious duty and work for the enfranchisement of your sex, which means the growth and development of noble characters in your children; for you can not educate your children well surrounded by men and women who hold false doctrines of society, of politics, of morals.

8

Elizabeth Cady Stanton, 'Patriotism and Chastity'

FROM *The Westminster Review*, vol. 135, January 1891.

The old Latin proverb, *falsus in uno, falsus in omnia,* has been made to do duty once more, used as a weapon to drive Charles Stewart Parnell from public life. It is said that he has violated the seventh commandment, and has thus rendered himself unfit for a political leader. Thousands of reformers have been holding him up in their analytical tweezers, during the last month, for a microscopic examination of his inmost thoughts and private relations. The pulpit, the press, and the people have taken the position that patriotism and chastity are convertible virtues, uniformly found in the same man, and that the lack of one precludes the exercise of the other.

But the business of the world has never been conducted on this line. In availing ourselves of the skill of our fellow-men, in any special department, we do not ask whether they possess all the cardinal virtues. If we have a difficult case in court, we inquire for the most successful lawyer; if we have a child at death's door, we seek the most skilful physician; we ask no questions as to social life in either case, but avail ourselves of knowledge and wisdom when we need it. The *Pall Mall Gazette* originated a phrase which the press generally echoed, that, "men are not built in water-tight compartments, so that they can be sound in one part and not in another." Now, the facts of life show that that is precisely the way men are built. History tells us of many men of broad culture and sympathy in all human conditions —statesmen, soldiers, scientists, and philosophers—devoted to the public good, yet faithless at their domestic altar. Lord Nelson, Lord Melbourne, the Duke of Wellington, Daniel Webster, Henry Clay, Benjamin Franklin, all rendered invaluable services to their country though they violated the popular standard of morality. Sir Charles Dilke was an able member of the House of Commons, and the women of England owe him a debt of gratitude for the persistent manner in which he helped to carry the Married Women's Property Bill. He never failed to vote in favour of Bills dealing with the protection of the civil and political rights of women. A leader in the suffrage movement once said:—"It would be more to the interest of women to have a Parliament composed of such men as Sir Charles Dilke, than one wholly of chaste angels in opposition." The press generally admits that Mr. Parnell has been a wise and skilful leader of the Irish party for the last ten years; while at the same time, it says he has had an entangling alliance in private life. Grover Cleveland was faithful to a marked degree in all the public offices he filled as Mayor, Governor, President of the United States; and yet his social life was not above reproach. With a full knowledge of the facts of his life, many distinguished moralists voted for him, and he was elected by an overwhelming majority. At one time it was thought the social scandal would jeopardise his election; but sound Yankee common sense triumphed, and the verdict was, "here is a man with a clean public record, he shall serve us!" And so well did he serve his country, that, without doubt, he will again be the Democratic nominee for the Presidency. Lord Connemara, Governor of Madras, is another example of the same principle. Though lacking in the virtues which make a good husband, he was honourable and efficient in his public duties, and so endeared himself to the people of Madras that they have sent, it is said, a petition to the Government asking that his resignation be declined.

If the women of England take up the position that there can be no true patriotism without chastity, they will rob some of the most illustrious rulers of their own sex of any reputation for ability in public affairs. The private lives of Cleopatra of Egypt, Elizabeth of England, Catherine of Russia were all below the popular standard of their own times; and yet the pages of history glow with their brilliant achievements as rulers of nations. Weighed in this new balance, the queens of literature would be robbed of their laurels. Emerson, one of the purest of men, dwells on the rare and beautiful sentiment that runs through George Sand's *Consuelo,* and who can deny the evidence of keen political insight, lofty ideas, and pure morality in the writings of such women as Mary Wollstonecraft, Francis Wright, and George Eliot:—and yet all these rejected the English code of morals.

Certainly such examples go to prove that great souls may lack some virtues, and yet in an abounding measure possess many others. We must recognise the fact that patriotism and chastity belong to different spheres of action. The former is pre-eminently a masculine virtue, to which a man is trained from his earliest years. He may, in time, be the ruler of a nation; hence he must study the laws and practise the virtues

needed to protect the public interests. He must be brave and courageous, ever ready to live or die for his country. Chastity, on the other
hand, has in all ages been considered a feminine virtue. Women have
been sedulously trained to regard this as their crowning glory, which
best fits them for family life. Hence the vast majority of women are
deficient in patriotism; they care but little for public interests; they
are generally absorbed in a narrow, personal, and family selfishness.
They are not to blame for their contracted outlook; it is the result of
their education. In this view, it is equally absurd to deny patriotism
to men because they lack chastity, as it would be to deny chastity to
women because they lack patriotism. We are all what law, custom, and
public sentiment have made us, alike fragmentary, some truth and
some error bound up in every human soul. Through our whole system
of jurisprudence we find a separate code of laws and morals for men
and women recognised and enforced by the best authorities. We find
woman, though the more important factor in the social life, always
placed in a subordinate position, and though she is declared to be the
more helpless, on her shoulders are laid the heaviest responsibilities.

"Many jurists," says Kent, vol. ii. p. 88, "are of opinion that the
adultery of the husband ought not to be noticed or made subject to
the same animadversions as that of the wife, because it is not evidence
of such entire depravity, nor equally injurious in its effects upon the
morals, good order, and happiness of domestic life. Montesquieu,
Pothier, and Dr. Taylor all insist that the cases of husband and wife
ought to be distinguished, and that the violation of the marriage vow,
on the part of the wife, is the most mischievous, and the prosecution
ought to be confined to the offence on her part.—*Esprit des Loix*,
tome 3, 186; *Traité du Contrat de Mariage*, No. 516; *Elements of
Civil Law*, p. 254."

So long as the civil and canon law—Blackstone and the Bible—
proclaim such distinctions, let us be honest and consistent, and
repudiate these authorities, rather than ostracise the individual who is
but a result of such teaching.

Like cyclones and earthquakes these sudden and violent attacks on
the reputation of great men seem to be governed by no law, but the
caprice of the elements. There never has been any true standard of
social morality and none exists to-day. The true relation of the sexes
is still an unsolved problem, that has differed in all latitudes and in
all periods from the savage to civilised man. We have thus far had
five forms of family life:—

1st. The Consanguine Family:—the intermarriage of brothers and
sisters in a group.

2nd. The Punaluan Family:—the intermarriage of several brothers to each other's wives in a group, and of several sisters to each other's husbands in a group.

3rd. The Syndyasmian Family:—the pairing of one man and woman for a season, with separation at the option of either husband or wife.

4th. The Patriarchal Family:—the marriage of one man to several wives.

5th. The Monogamian Family with legalised prostitution, our present form.

Such are the five defined systems with variations under each. As there seems to be endless complaining and contention still, even under the present system, it is fair to suppose that we may pass through four or five more experiments before finding a satisfactory solution.

In the meantime, what constitutes chastity is the vital question. Like fashion in dress, it changes with time and latitude; its definition would be as varied as is public opinion on other subjects. Some would say that all legal relations of the sexes are chaste, and all illegal relations unchaste. Some would say that only those relations sanctioned by enduring friendship and love are chaste, that all others are unchaste. It is much more easy to say, what according to our clearest thinkers is not chaste, than what is so according to the present standard. The first definition Worcester gives is continence. How many reformers even will accept this? Entire continence and no marriage is chastity for the Catholic priesthood. Unlimited license in marriage is chastity for the Protestant priesthood. A family of twelve children and an invalid wife casts no shadow on those who fill the most holy offices in the church. But a healthy, happy mother and child outside the bonds of legal wedlock, though, loving and beloved, are ostracised by the community as unchaste.

It is not my purpose or desire to say aught to lower the standard of high morality, only to ascertain in what it consists, and the most likely means by which it can be secured. To my mind, it is not by hounding men, but by the education, elevation, and emancipation of women, by training them to self-respect and a virtuous independence. It is no compliment to the strength and sagacity of women, to be always regarded as innocent victims and helpless dupes in these social catastrophes,—especially when they have reached years of discretion, and are quite able to protect their own reputation and the sacredness of their home life.

The one supreme lesson to be learned from the great upheaval that has just rent our political life is the futility of coercive measures in reformation. The spectacle of a whole nation hounding one man, and determined to administer summary punishment, is pitiful at a time, when those who love their fellow-men are asking for all the best moral appliances and conditions for the reformation of the criminal classes, instead of the old methods of punishment. Our leading thinkers in education, in prison discipline, and in the treatment of the insane have long since in no measured terms repudiated coercion and arbitrary punishment. Kindness and attraction are the corner-stones of the new system in all our educational and reformatory institutions. The child is not to be tyrannically regarded as a lump of clay to be moulded into any shape; but it is to be treated as a being of capacities and proclivities peculiar to itself, to be unfolded and developed. Force, either in the form of bodily infliction or mental lashing, has been abandoned by the experienced as wholly evil in its effects, both on the child and on the criminal. Acting on this principle, what right has a nation to turn all its enginery of denunciation on one human being for the violation of an unsettled question of morals, which even Cardinals and Bishops, Kings and Emperors ignore? The educator and the prison disciplinarian, following the old method, failed; and so long as the reform of humanity, according to that method, is attempted by public opinion, it will also fail. Indeed, these unethical systems turn the child into a dullard, the prisoner into a confirmed criminal, and force the statesman who has committed one fault into many others, force him, perchance, into such an attitude of supreme defiance that he is false to all the best feelings of his nature. While merciless hounding crushes those of tender sensibilities, it calls out savage and reckless retaliation in the more courageous, self-reliant men.

The great lesson taught by the founder of our faith is charity; without that we are but sounding brass and a tinkling cymbal. Could the Divine man, now worshipped in all our holy temples, appear again on earth, at this crisis of unhappy Ireland's history, and voice the same rebuke to the Pharisees of our day as in the past, how quickly would the pens now dipped in gall fall powerless from every hand, and the countless envenomed tongues be hushed to silence, as the nation's ear caught the stern message of charity, "He that is without sin among you, let him cast the first stone."

Charlotte Perkins Gilman, *The Home*

FROM *The Home,* New York 1903. (Excerpts).

What percentage of our human young live to grow up? About fifty per cent. What percentage are healthy? We do not even expect them to be healthy. So used are we to "infantile diseases" that our idea of a mother's duty is to nurse sick children, not to raise well ones! What percentage of our children grow up properly proportioned, athletic and vigorous? Ask the army surgeon who turns down the majority of applicants for military service. What percentage of our children grow up with strong, harmonious characters, wise and good? Ask the great army of teachers and preachers who are trying for ever and ever to somewhat improve the adult humanity which is turned out upon the world from the care of its innumerable mothers and their instincts.

Our eyes grow moist with emotion as we speak of our mothers—our own mothers—and what they have done for us. Our voices thrill and tremble with pathos and veneration as we speak of "the mothers of great men—" mother of Abraham Lincoln! Mother of George Washington! and so on. Had Wilkes Booth no mother? Was Benedict Arnold an orphan?

Who, in the name of all common sense, raises our huge and growing crop of idiots, imbeciles, cripples, defectives, and degenerates, the vicious and the criminal; as well as all the vast mass of slow-minded, prejudiced, ordinary people who clog the wheels of progress? Are the mothers to be credited with all that is good and the fathers with all that is bad?

That we are what we are is due to these two factors, mothers and fathers.

Our physical environment we share with all animals. Our social environment is what modifies heredity and develops human character. The kind of country we live in, the system of government, of religion, of education, of business, of ordinary social customs and convention, this is what develops mankind, this is given by our fathers.

What does maternal instinct contribute to this sum of influences? Has maternal instinct even evolved any method of feeding, dressing, teaching, disciplining, educating children which commands attention, not to say respect? It has not.

*   *   *   *

We have made great progress in the sense of justice and fair play; yet we are still greatly lacking in it. What is the contribution of domestic ethics to this mighty virtue? In the home is neither freedom nor equality. There is ownership throughout; the dominant father, the more or less subservient mother, the utterly dependent child; and sometimes that still lower grade—the servant. Love is possible, love deep and reciprocal; loyalty is possible; gratitude is possible; kindness, to ruinous favouritism, is possible; unkindness, to all conspiracy, hate, and rebellion is possible; justice is not possible.

Justice was born outside the home and a long way from it; and it has never even been adopted there.

*   *   *   *

Each new generation must improve upon its parents; else the world stands still or retrogrades. In this most vivid period of life how does the home meet the needs of the growing soul? The boy largely escapes it. He is freer, even in childhood; the more resistant and combative nature, the greater impatience of pain, makes the young male far harder to coerce. He sees his father always going out, and early learns to view the home from a sex-basis, as the proper place for women and children, and to push incessantly to get away from it.

From boy to boy in the alluring summer evenings we hear the cry "Come on out and have some fun!" Vainly we strive and strive anew to "keep the boys at home." It cannot be done. Fortunately for us it cannot be done. We dread to have them leave it, and with good reason for well we know there is no proper place for children in the so long unmothered world; but even in danger and temptation they learn something, and those who struggle through their youth unscathed make better men than if they had been always softly shielded in the home.

The world is the real field of action for humanity. So far humanity has been well-nigh wholly masculine; and the boy, feeling his humanity, pushes out into his natural field, the world. He learns and learns from contact with his kind. He learns about all sorts of machinery, all manner of trades and businesses. He has companions above him and below him and beside him, the wide human contact in which we grow so rapidly. If he is in the city he knows the city, if he is in the country he knows the country, far more fully than his sister. A thousand influences reach him that never come to her, formative influences, good and bad, that modify character. He has far less of tutelage, espionage, restraint; he has more freedom by daylight, and he alone has any freedom after dark. All the sweet, mysterious voices of the night, the rich, soft whisperings of fragrant summer, when the moon talks and the young soul answers; the glittering, keen silence of winter nights, when between blue-black star-pointed space and the level shine of the snow stands but one living thing—yourself—all this is cut off from the girl. The real intimacy with nature comes to the soul alone, and the poor, overhandled girl soul never has it.

In some few cases, isolated and enviable, she may have this common human privilege, but not enough to count. She must be guarded in the only place of safety, the home. Guarded from what? From men. From the womanless men who may be prowling about while all women stay at home. The home is safe because women are there. Out of doors is unsafe because women are not there. If women were there, everywhere, in the world which belongs to them as much as to men, then everywhere would be safe. We try to make the women safe in the home, and keep them there; to make the world safe for women and children has not occurred to us. So the boy grows, in the world as far as he can reach it, and the girl does not grow equally, being confined to the home.

*   *   *   *

The home, in its arbitrary position of arrested development, does not properly fulfil its own essential functions—much less promote the social ones. Among the splendid activities of our age it lingers on, inert and blind, like a clam in a horse-race.

It hinders, by keeping woman a social idiot, by keeping the modern child under the tutelage of the primeval mother, by keeping the social conscience of the man crippled and stultified in the clinging grip of the domestic conscience of the woman. It hinders by its enormous expense; making the physical details of daily life a heavy burden to mankind; whereas, in our stage of civilisation, they should have been long since reduced to a minor incident.

*   *   *   *

The position is this: the home, as now existing, costs three times what is necessary to meet the same needs. It involves the further waste of nearly half the world's labour. It does not fulfil its functions to the best advantage, thus robbing us again. It maintains a low grade of womanhood, overworked or lazy; it checks the social development of men as well as women, and, most of all, of children. The man, in order to meet this unnecessary expense, must cater to the existing market; and the existing market is mainly this same home, with its crude tastes and limitless appetites. Thus the man, to maintain his own woman in idleness, or low-grade labour, must work three times as hard as is needful, to meet the demands of similar women; the home-bound woman clogging the whole world.

Change this order. Set the woman on her own feet, as a free, intelligent, able human being, quite capable of putting into the world more than she takes out, of being a producer as well as a consumer. Put these poor antiquated "domestic industries" into the archives of past history; and let efficient modern industries take their place, doing far more work, far better work, far cheaper work in their stead.

10

National American Woman Suffrage Association, 'Declaration of Principles', 1904

FROM the *History of Woman Suffrage*, vol. 5.

The following Declaration of Principles, prepared by Mrs. Catt, Dr. Shaw, Miss Blackwell and Mrs. Harper, was adopted by the convention of the National American Woman Suffrage Association in 1904.

When our forefathers gained the victory in a seven years' war to establish the principle that representation should go hand in hand with taxation, they marked a new epoch in the history of man; but though our foremothers bore an equal part in that long conflict its triumph brought to them no added rights and through all the following century and a quarter, taxation without representation has been continuously imposed on women by as great tyranny as King George exercised over the American colonists.

So long as no married woman was permitted to own property and all women were barred from the money-making occupations this discrimination did not seem so invidious; but to-day the situation is without a parallel. The women of the United States now pay taxes on real and personal estate valued at billions of dollars. In a number of individual States their holdings amount to many millions. Everywhere they are accumulating property. In hundreds of places they form one-third of the taxpayers, with the number constantly increasing, and yet they are absolutely without representation in the affairs of the nation, of the State, even of the community in which they live and pay taxes. We enter our protest against this injustice and we demand that the immortal principles established by the War of the Revolution shall be applied equally to women and men citizens.

As our new republic passed into a higher stage of development the gross inequality became apparent of giving representation to capital and denying it to labor; therefore the right of suffrage was extended to the workingman. Now we demand for the 4,000,000 wage-earning women of our country the same protection of the ballot as is possessed by the wage-earning men.

The founders took an even broader view of human rights when they declared that government could justly derive its powers only from the consent of the governed, and for 125 years this grand assertion was regarded as a corner-stone of the republic, with scarcely a recognition of the fact that one-half of the citizens were as completely governed without their consent as were the people of any absolute monarchy in existence. It was only when our government was extended over alien races in foreign countries that our people awoke to the meaning of the principles of the Declaration of Independence. In response to its provisions, the Congress of the United States hastened to invest with the power of consent the men of this new territory, but committed the flagrant injustice of withholding it from the women. We demand that the ballot shall be extended to the women of our foreign possessions on the same terms as to the men. Furthermore, we demand that the women of the United States shall no longer suffer the degradation of being held not so competent to exercise the suffrage as a Filipino, a Hawaiian or a Porto Rican man.

The remaining Territories within the United States are insisting upon admission into the Union on the ground that their citizens desire "the right to select their own governing officials, choose their own judges, name those who are to make their laws and levy, collect, and disburse their taxes." These are just and commendable desires but we demand that their women shall have full recognition as citizens when these Territories are admitted and that their constitutions shall secure to women precisely the same rights as to men.

When our government was founded the rudiments of education were thought sufficient for women, since their entire time was absorbed in the multitude of household duties. Now the number of girls graduated by the high schools greatly exceeds the number of boys in every State and the percentage of women students in the colleges is vastly larger than that of men. Meantime most of the domestic industries have been taken from the home to the factory and hundreds of thousands of women have followed them there, while the more highly trained have entered the professions and other avenues of skilled labor. We demand that under this new régime, and in view of these changed conditions in which she is so important a factor woman shall have a voice and a vote in the solution of their innumerable problems.

The laws of practically every State provide that the husband shall select the place of residence for the family, and if the wife refuse to abide by his choice she forfeits her right to support and her refusal shall be regarded as desertion. We protest against the recent decision of the courts which has added to this injustice by requiring the wife also to accept for herself the citizenship preferred by her husband, thus compelling a woman born in the United States to lose her nationality if her husband choose to declare his allegiance to a foreign country.

As women form two-thirds of the church membership of the entire nation; as they constitute but one-eleventh of the convicted criminals; as they are rapidly becoming the educated class and as the salvation of our government depends upon a moral, law-abiding, educated electorate, we demand for the sake of its integrity and permanence that women be made a part of its voting body.

In brief, we demand that all constitutional and legal barriers shall be removed which deny to women any individual right or personal freedom which is granted to man. This we ask in the name of a democratic and a republican government, which, its constitution declares, was formed "to establish justice and secure the blessings of liberty."

11

Helen M. Winslow, 'Strikes and Their Causes'

FROM *New Cycle*, April 1895. The *New Cycle* was devoted to the interests of club women, and Mrs Winslow's paper was first read at a meeting of the Massachusetts State Federation of Women's Clubs.

"Give a man power over my subsistence," said Alexander Hamilton, "and he has power over the whole of my moral being." It was the same sentiment that led the Pilgrim fathers to leave home and friends and old associations behind and establish a New England; it was the same sentiment that led the colonists to establish a new government, founded on the principles of freedom and liberty; it is the same sentiment that, in most cases, leads the laborer of to-day to protest against the conditions that bend his neck beneath the heel of the capitalist—and results in a strike. The strike is often, perhaps always, a mistaken effort to bring about better conditions; it is too often the direct outcome of the influence of demagogues and cranks—or worse; it always entails suffering upon the innocent and deprives honest men of the chance to earn an honest living; but, since boards of arbitration as yet seldom arbitrate, and since capital is too often but the incarnation of the spirit of modern greed, is the laborer to be blamed if he looks upon the strike as his only weapon of defence against existing conditions that rob him of all power over his own subsistence and that of those dearer than self?

"No man, no body of men," says Capital, "has a right to dictate terms to me, nor any right to say whom I shall employ. The market is open and free; it is my right to do as I please." This is all true, and capital can do as it pleases because it *is* capital. But what about the rights of labor? What about the men condemned to a lifetime of hard,

unremitting toil, to long hours, stretching into endless years of hopeless drudgery, with no prospect of anything better—unless in combination with others they can force better conditions?—what of the men
who work at the lowest possible wages to support a large and rapidly-
growing family, with perhaps an aged parent or an invalid wife, and
all knowing the utter impossibility of ever saving enough to keep them
in their old age or to provide against the emergencies of accident or
illness? There are several hundred thousand women working in the
mills of New England alone today. What of them? Go farther, and
look at the coal mines of Pennsylvania, or the car shops of the Pullman
Company, if you please. Such corporations gradually obtain complete
power over the subsistence of every man in their employ. They not
only dictate wages, but they compel the men to live in their houses and
to buy all family supplies of them, and by ruinous prices and an
abominable credit system get the unfortunate or improvident as hopelessly in their power as ever was any slave in the hands of a cruel
task-master previous to 1864. And when the miserable worms turn
and go "on a strike" they sit back and "starve them into their senses,"
as one great leader gallantly puts it.

Not that there is any excuse for the methods of violence or intimida-
tion which the laborers themselves too often use. When one remem-
bers the lawlessness of the Homestead strikers and the extreme
measures of the Chicago mob of last summer, it is difficult to sympathize at all with the cause of labor and to keep from wondering where
the leaders of such movements would finally bring us were they to
have their way. And when one has carefully thought out what seems
a very good answer to the labor problem, as it presents itself in
Massachusetts, and turns to the mining population of Pennsylvania
to apply one's humane solution, why, one is all at sea again. For, with
widely differing conditions, a heterogeneous foreign element as
material and a spirit of lawlessness and ignorance, one finds the problem set to do over again and with much more complicated factors.

And yet, from a woman's point of view, it is impossible to consider
it without remembering the human suffering involved; the toiling,
hopeless old men, the weary, hard-working mothers, the young men
and women sinking lower into the average ignorance of operatives, the
little children coming up to manhood and womanhood only to settle
into lives of "rayless toil" lightened too often only by pleasures that
drag them downward. And consequently, it is impossible not to sympathize strongly with those who so undeniably constitute the "under
dog," for any contest against capital backed by an unyielding, unflinch-
ing determination to win at any cost is almost always hopeless at the
outset, although each new band of strikers tries to prove the contrary.

It has been well said that the interests of capital and labor are neither
conflicting or identical; they are reciprocal. And only by recognizing

this great truth can a right solution of the causes and cure of strikes be arrived at. Let each consider the rights of the other a little more and a long step will have been taken in the right direction. Mills are run to make money, not to educate and elevate the men and women who work in them. At the same time, those mills and factories whose operatives are most intelligent, and who are on the best possible footing as to their material surroundings, are among the most prosperous. The experience of the Briggs Brothers in England, of the Cheney Brothers in Connecticut, of the Fairbanks Company in Vermont, and of others who recognize the existence of the decalogue in the management of a great business proves this. And a strike at one of these places is an unheard of thing.

If the personal note may be pardoned, I am neither a radical nor a socialist. I was once a believer in the system of *laissez faire,* and the theory that all strikers are malefactors and unreasonable agitators. But I was once detailed by a certain paper to go to certain of our manufacturing cities, and make a study of the factory-system as it affected the common people. And when my special work was done, I said "I don't wonder these people strike from time to time; I wonder only that they submit to so much, and that so uncomplainingly. The mills themselves, in most cases, were light and well-equipped; corporations realize the necessity for this, in the great world of competition. But the tenements and lodgings of the operatives are often considered of secondary importance. I was shown through these and through the factory boarding-houses; especially those which constituted the only home of several hundred young women. The dismal exterior was attractive compared to the inside of some of these "corporation" boarding-houses. And they were for the most part alike. The hall, nothing more than an entry, was bare and dingy. Opening from it was a room that served as parlor, living and dining room. An oil-cloth was usually the floor-covering in this room, and was the only attempt at a carpet of any kind in the whole establishment. Up-stairs there were two or three floors devoted to sleeping rooms. These were very small, unpapered, dingy, and with seldom more than one window. Sometimes two and sometimes four girls occupied a room, and the furniture consisted only of the necessary bed accommodations of the poorest and often filthiest kind—of a cheap looking-glass and sometimes a bureau, sometimes a table, seldom both. On a rude stand, or oftener it was a chair, stood a tin wash-basin. On the floor beside it was a pail of water. These constituted the entire bath-room accommodations. The bare floor was clean or not as suited the taste of the landlady. "Umph," said one of these to me after she had showed me over her house, and I found myself unable to express anything she might construe as praise of her housekeeping. "You think this is a pretty poor place, don't you? Well, let me tell you it is good enough for those creatures to sleep off a drunk in." And when I asked her if drunkenness was common with her girls she replied, roughly, that never a Saturday night went by that she did not help some girl into the house, and put her to bed where she staid till Monday morning and the call to work came, and I came away wondering if there is not some duty left undone by us who are so much more fortunate. If it is not an imperative duty of intelligent, earnest men and women everywhere to consider seriously the necessity for raising the condition of these, our brethren and sisters.

It seemed to me then, and the more I have thought of the subject since—the more firmly have I been convinced that this was a wise conclusion, that by elevating the living condition and surroundings of the working classes, by giving them cleaner, healthier homes, by providing them with reading-rooms, and by the spread of that sort of Christian charity, which shall make the workingman feel that he is something more than a machine in the eyes of his employer. In short, by granting them the natural rights that according to our constitution belong to all citizens of America, we shall have taken a most important step in the progress of civilization, and the consequent settlement of the labor question. I confess that sometimes, looking at the almost hopeless ignorance, and yet worse indifference of the class of operatives in some of our large cities, my theory has sometimes seemed hardly adequate, but after all, I believe it is the right one. Such condition may delay the actual putting into practice of the movement for a new political economy that shall be combined with moral philosophy, but all the same, it is sure to come. Every decade shows more and more manufacturers putting it to a test, and always with good results.

I dare say many of my hearers have read the article in a recent number of the *Forum* by Rev. Mr. Hale, describing the condition of the tenements of the Richard Borden Company, in which the writer stated that a more filthy, indecent and disgraceful collection of tenement houses could not be found. And this was the leading company in the recent strike at Fall River. In contrast to these were cited those of Mr. Howland, of New Bedford, which that manufacturer has turned into model tenements, not from philanthropic motives, but because he believes his tenants are entitled to just as fair a consideration in return for the money they pay for rent as though they were not his operatives. It is worthy of note that during the labor troubles all around him, Mr. Howland did not reduce wages and his mills continued their work without any cessation, and with a feeling of perfect harmony among all concerned. It was those manufacturers who look upon their operatives as so many machines for piling up a fortune, that had trouble from the strikers; while he who recognized the human rights of his operatives as men and women, ran his mills straight through the fall.

Now then, what is all this to us?

Beyond the fact that a few of the fathers, husbands and brothers of us are numbered among the "captains of industry" and so indirectly the matter may influence the incomes of a few, why should we as club women give a thought to this great labor question or any of its phases? Why should we get together at a state federation meeting to listen to papers from women more or less capable of handling their subject, to listen to an address from a distinguished thinker and worker in the field, or to discuss this prosaic question of strikes? And what can women actually do about it?

Very little, at present, is the obvious answer to the last question.

But if it is true that woman is but just coming into her kingdom in any public capacity this is a question of the utmost importance to us. According to the old theory that woman's place is in the home and that her work lies in her influence upon the various masculine members of her family, there is much that she can do in the way of bringing them into broader and more humanitarian views of the rights of other men and women; and if the new idea is to prevail, and is it not already prevailing? then the club-woman has a tremendous opportunity before her.

In the first place she needs an intelligent, comprehensive knowledge of the situation from every point of view, and she needs to become capable of weighing both sides and making up her own mind, a need that applies to other matters than the labor question.

An increasing number of clubs are taking up the study of political economy and social science; and no movement connected with that much-talked-of, and, as yet, very unevenly developed being, the Modern Woman, is more promising. Classes for the study of bygone people and ancient history, of genealogy or of ancient heraldry, are quite harmless and possibly beneficial to the individual; but they are not developing women into factors of the world's progress, nor are they actively fitting women for coping with the live questions of to-day and to-morrow. It is the broad, earnest, active woman of to-day who is to be of use in the world to-morrow. And none of us can hope to be that who will not seek to understand the industrial conditions of our country.

It is the women interested in the questions of to-day who will make the best wives and mothers of to-morrow; and the power of the ballot, when it comes to woman, will only be a power to such as have the best all-round education. Those clubs which foresee this—such as the civic clubs, the Social Science clubs, the Boston Political Class, and the numerous classes all the time forming in various other women's clubs for the study of economic questions of all sorts—such clubs are doing the kind of work needed by bringing the individual woman into touch with topics too great for her, and making her feel that she is part of a modern order of things which demand that every one who can, in either a public or private capacity, do aught to relieve misery, to combat evil, to assert the right, to redress the wrong, is bound to do it with her whole heart and soul.

The day will doubtless come when arbitrators will arbitrate, when strikes will be looked upon by the laboring man as a weapon of the ignorant past, and when he will have a speedier and more humane way of remedying his wrongs. It rests with the coming woman, if not with the present one, to hasten this condition of things by the spread of intelligent sympathy for the workingman, and the leaven of Christian love for all humanity, as it rests with her to prove whether her advent into public life is really to make the world better for the masses of human beings yet to come.

12

Josephine Woodward, 'Woman's Clubs from a Reporter's Point of View'

FROM *The Club Woman,* vol. 3, December 1898.

I am fond of applause, and I feel that I should make the most of my pleasant greeting, for it may be all that I shall get to-day; however, I feel that I ought to be willing to forego the thrills of pleasure that would come through the gratification of my vanity for the greater luxury of honest speaking.

Newspapers lie so much (you all say we do—we all know that we do) that the prospect of being permitted to speak the truth for twenty minutes looms up before me with all the seductiveness of a wild dissipation, a mad orgie, a debauch. I shall revel for a few moments, and then hereafter I shall know whether you mean what you say when you wish from the bottom of your hearts that newspaper reports could be depended upon.

I would like to call your attention to the fact that the title of my paper is "Woman's Clubs from a Reporter's Point of View"—not "the" reporter's.

I don't wish to interfere with the influence of my sisters of the press by making them in any measure responsible for my own opinions.

I will only use one prop for support: the expressed belief that the Cincinnati club women—to whom I am indebted for so many courtesies, but more than everything else, whose friendship I enjoy— will at least guarantee that malice had no place in my heart.

I am only a poor, stupid fool who believes in the doctrine of laziness and the religion of happiness, and who believes that the greatest success in life is to love everybody worth loving, and to have everybody worth being loved by love you; who believes that it is better to eat a piece of your cake every single day of your life than to save it up until the end of the year and find it stale; only a poor, weak-minded person, who would "rather be pleasant than President"—even of a woman's club.

Once, a long time ago, before club women had taught me how to lie cheerfully and glibly, and before I had taught myself the value of silence, I undertook to give in print my honest opinion of some club proceeding or other.

I have never tried it since. The truth crushed to earth that day now rises for the first time.

Since that tragic day, when I was led from the path of truth and duty by a club woman, I have made it a practice, in reporting club proceedings, to find out what the president of the club, or the chairman of the department, would like to have said, and then say it, no matter what my own judgment may be. It simplifies matters immensely.

And if the lady who reads the paper of the day has an account of it already prepared for publication, I accept the contribution to club literature with a glad hand.

It usually reads something after this fashion: "Mrs. Blank's review of Tolstoi and his works was the most brilliantly comprehensive essay it has been our good fortune to hear in many a day. This gifted woman is probably better qualified to speak of the great Russian author and what he has written than any other critic in this vicinity, since she has the most beautiful silver samovar in town, and invariably takes lemon in her tea, even when she is alone."

I may possibly blue pencil the samovar and the tea, but the "brilliantly comprehensive" and the "gifted woman" go to the printer's in her own handwriting.

Sometimes my conscience even troubles me because I haven't added something—some little tribute of my own—I do like to be pleasant.

Then there are always the poor and the sick and the lame and the timid women to be considered and encouraged.

That is what women's clubs are for—to encourage those who need encouragement. All the club members ask is that the press shall do the encouraging.

It is so much easier and less compromising, and, of course, altogether quite the same thing, ethically considered, for a club member to ask the reporter to "Please say something pleasant about poor, little Mrs. Brown—she's so unfortunate, you know; just look at her clothes"; than it would be for this same club member to go to poor, little Mrs. Brown and pat her on the back and say, "Good for you; I'm glad you belong to our club and I'm glad I know you. I'm coming to call on you."

It is no hardship for the average reporter to lie under these circumstances. (The average reporter has worn shabby clothes herself.) To tell the truth, I love to lie for the poor little Mrs. Browns of the clubs. Of all the club members who need encouragement, the poor, the sick, the lame, the timid, I would rather praise the woman who is too poor to buy good clothes to wear. She needs sympathy the most for she gets the least. It has become a passion with me to lie for her—you can't ask too much of me on her account—only I wish that some of you would occasionally do a little lying on your own accounts.

In fact, I am here to-day, ladies, to ask you to pause in your mad careers before it is too late. There is yet time while there remains one club reporter uncorrupted by your system. Some of you may know of one. I do not.

But the sweet opportunity to lie in behalf of a poor little Mrs. Brown is unfortunately of rare occurrence, for there aren't very many poor little Mrs. Browns in city clubs.

They can't get in.

For the woman's club, so far as my observation of it goes in this part of the country, is still an aristocracy.

There are queens of clubs, and the number of high cards is out of all proportion to the sequences. I have yet to know of a woman proving herself brilliant enough and amiable enough and respectable enough to be invited to dinner by a club woman who didn't already know her socially.

The club woman of social position has a speaking acquaintance on the street. She calls when Mrs. Brown dies and looks at her through her lorgnette and says "Yes, a member of our club—so bright," and then notices that she is wearing the same dress, and how threadbare the carpet is under the coffin. Very likely the poor thing died because she was so lonesome. Killed by a club frost!

The yearning for companionship is strong in every human heart. Women's clubs are probably the outgrowth of just such a need, but they have not recognized it and have mistaken the beginning, the means, and the end. The law of natural selection and compatibility is as strong as the yearning for companionship, and on this basis may be excused the exclusiveness of women's clubs; but there are reasons for inclusiveness. "The greatest good to the greatest number," is the motto of so many clubs, and yet sometimes, in her pessimistic moments, the club reporter imagines that the average woman goes into the club for the sole purpose of keeping somebody else out. That is, if a woman needs to know a lot of nice women, she must be black-balled by them.

Women's clubs have claimed to be democratic and have built up aristocracies. They imagine themselves reformers and satisfy themselves with the imagination. They pose before the world as seeking the accomplishment of great good, and when they see themselves in print, with all their theories aired and expounded, they are willing to believe that the good has been accomplished. They have acquired a reputation for activity at the expense of truth, and it is not fair or honest.

The lying done by club reporters at the instigation—nay, not only the solicitation, but the entreaties and commands of club women—is not altogether a laughing matter by any means. It involves more than you think. It involves a lack of honest purpose and it involves the growth of the club, not to mention the demoralization of the club reporter, to which I first referred.

It is a curious fact that the same women who say that newspapers ought to be honest, and who decry untruths and shams, who are fiercest in their denunciation of misleading statements in print, do not hesitate to dictate misleading statements in regard to their clubs. They are not willing to grant the newspaper the privilege of judgment, and yet this is the same judgment which they insist should be brought into public service on other subjects. It may not be unfailingly correct, but it is generally unbiased and tolerably ripened by experience, and as fit to be trusted in one case as another. At least fair treatment might be expected from it.

To look upon the reporter as a natural enemy is a mistake. She may seem to you a bit inclined to iconoclasm and not quite sufficiently enthusiastic in espousing your views, but an enemy—no. Why not be honest with her? She probably never thinks anything worse about you than that she would rather be an idler's club and be idle than be a literary club and not be literary.

I sometimes think that the mind's eye of the average reporter may be nearsighted, and that many things that appear of ample proportions to other eyes seem small to it at the same distance; or it may be that the eye itself is too small, like the eye of the canary bird or the butterfly—the picture thrown upon it is too minute to seem important. It may be that people with such eyes take naturally to reporting, and it may be that the use of the mind's eye for reportorial purposes produces, in time, a condition which borders on astigmatism and may be accountable for the pangs we sometimes suffer—the sort of pangs I suffer, for instance, when I am called up by telephone, after midnight, by a club woman who begs me to mention in glowing terms an address that has seemed maudlin to me, or to speak of a singer whose voice has really caused me pain, as having "contributed in no small measure to the pleasure of the afternoon; or when she implores me, if I love her and wish ever to be admitted to the club again, to say nothing—not a word—about the differences of opinion that have taken place that afternoon at the club, when it has been the only really interesting meeting of the year—the only time when there has been any opportunity for writing an interesting report. It is only a difference in the point of view.

By the way, if any of you have ever attempted to interview a club woman on any other subject than that of her own paper, you can more readily understand my inclination to doubt the general good of clubs. The club reporter is apt to incline to the belief that the women's clubs take themselves too seriously.

The differences between women's clubs and men's clubs is that men's clubs were never intended to be serious, but have always been taken seriously by women, while women's clubs are serious, but never have been taken seriously by men.

Most women's club meetings are like most American dinners and afternoon teas, and the other set pieces of our social system—absolutely lacking in a certain quality of gay, good-humored daring, and full of a conventionalism that is both material and dull.

You find chairmen of departments of sociology and municipal government presiding as if they were serving little cakes and weak tea.

The club reporter has to do something every single day of her life, and so she must be excused if it sometimes seems to her that the clubs are satisfied with infinite nothings—that they miss opportunities, that the members fritter conversation and stare superciliously at all expressions of original thought. The club circle doesn't always seem to her so broad and luminous as it does to you; but, as I said before, there may be something wrong with her eyes.

To confess the whole truth, the objects of women's clubs bewilder me, and their solemnity appalls me, and I don't know why they want me to tell so many fibs about them.

I have been reporting club meetings for four years, and I am tired of hearing reviews of the books I was brought up on. I am tired of amateur performers at occasions announced to be for purposes either of enjoyment of improvement. I am tired of suffering under the pretence of acquiring culture. I am tired of hearing the word "culture" used so wantonly. Culture seems to me like the nut which sheds its burr with no special or very "prickly" manifestation when the kernel is ripe. I am tired of the essays that let no guilty author escape quotation.

I have been unhappy over the spectacle of celebrities—men of genius—converted into club women while being entertained as guests of honor.

You must pardon a club reporter if she hasn't much sympathy with theories. She has to practice so much, and she is often so tired that she cannot understand how anybody can even contemplate the doing of anything that involves labor not absolutely necessary to the support of life. She may be pardoned if she sometimes wonders why you haven't learned the restfulness of silence, and, paradoxical though it may seem, why you don't more quickly learn the value of open discussion—if she wonders why you are afraid of each other, and why you are so seldom gay—if she sometimes thinks that you glory in achievement without regard to the value of the achievement.

But whether I have been able to discover that women are happier, honester or more content, better cooks, or more agreeable companions, I will concede that I have watched the evolution of the timid, shrinking woman, who has been snubbed first by her father and brothers and later by her husband, and have rejoiced to see her spread her wings and soar in the sky of appreciation. And I have watched the involution of the woman accustomed to the flattery of an over-fond mother and foolish sisters and have rejoiced to see her get the dust rubbed off her wings—for it was artificial dust, not the real black and gold and pink. But I have not been permitted to tell about her. You took your chances on me. I have sometimes referred to women's clubs as "a body of women banded together for the purpose of meeting together." A reporter, you know, comes in contact with all classes of people and in touch with all sorts of measures for public improvement. Is it her fault alone, I wonder, if she sometimes fails to grasp "the significance of the club movement"?

13

Martha E. D. White, 'Work of the Woman's Club'

FROM *Atlantic Monthly*, vol. 93, May 1904. Excerpts.

It would be interesting to know if the impulse to organize that first resulted in a Woman's Club in 1868 had its basis in any fundamental and common need of the women of that period. That two clubs, the New England Women's Club of Boston, and Sorosis of New York, were formed almost simultaneously, would point toward such a conclusion. That some of the leaders in the movement were suffragists, that the individual members were women who had been intellectually quickened and trained in practical experience by the events of the civil war, and that the time to enjoy the results of such organization had been gained by the improved domestic economy, will suggest some basis for speculation as to the underlying causes. The superficial and stated reason for being, in the constitutions of those early clubs, was unanimously "for mutual, or general, improvement, and to promote social enjoyment."

With this simple and egoistic platform, the club idea gained adherents very rapidly in New England and the Middle States. Study clubs were formed in large cities and remote villages, each with its encumbering constitution, and rules of order that seemed specially designed to retard the business of the day.

Outwardly, for twenty years, the woman's club remained an institution for the culture and pleasure of its members; but within, the desire for a larger opportunity was gradually strengthening. Parliamentary practice gave women confidence in their ability to lead larger issues to a successful conclusion. The inherent longing for power, coupled with confidence in the wisdom and beneficence of whatever woman should do, brought the leaders of the club movement to a conception of social service. To effect this, further organization was necessary. It was then, in 1890, that a union of individual clubs was formed into a chartered body, known as the General Federation of Women's Clubs. Closely following this culmination, the women of Maine formed the first union of the clubs of that state into a state federation. Other states joined in the movement, each state federation as it organized becoming a unit of the General Federation. There are now represented in this body thirty-nine states and territories and five foreign countries, with 3288 clubs having a membership of about 275,000 women.

The organization of the General Federation is complete, making it possible, given the responsible person in office, to get immediately into touch with every individual member. Its character is unique; racially heterogeneous, sectionally widespread, theoretically of no politics, it is pledged to work for the improvement of its members in every line of human culture and for all wise measures relating to human progress.

To be a member of such an organization must stimulate the imagination, deepen the sympathies, and go a long way toward overcoming that provincialism of mind with which our country has constantly to reckon. This subjective work was the early endeavor of the federations; but for eight years, since the Biennial held in Milwaukee, and also since the state federations found their social consciences, the effort has been toward the concrete issue. "Something must be done to justify our existence," has been the constant cry of officers, federation bulletins, and committee reports. To see the general preparedness to do passing on to an active doing may well cause a certain dismay in the mind of the onlooker.

The amused toleration that has for long characterized the thought of those unfortunates who were outside the club movement is changing to a somewhat anxious curiosity, and not without cause. It makes little difference to the community that the club has set aside the colored lithograph in favor of a Preraphaelite photograph in carbon, or that it studiously regards the possibilities of Hamlet's madness. Even vacation schools and college scholarships as an issue fail to arouse serious comment. But when the clubs begin to appear in legislative committee rooms, bearing yards of signatures, and when they question why the employees of bakeshops are permitted to work seventy or eighty hours a week, their potential power becomes a factor to be seriously considered.

The spectacle of 275,000 women splendidly organized, armed with leisure and opportunity, and animated by a passion for reform, assumes the distinction of a "social force." Forces must be reckoned with, and the work and the worth of the woman's club movement are becoming important public interests.

The work of the woman's club is threefold: to educate its members, mentally and morally; to create public opinion; to secure better conditions of life. Its worth, personal and social, is in proportion to its effectiveness in securing these ends.

The first clubs were study clubs; all clubs are in some degree study clubs, the culture idea having been the most tenacious. The early club, and the parlor club of to-day, would frequently devote a season to the study of one book, or one author, or some theory of economics or epoch in history. Their study may not have been either profound or judiciously chosen, but the woman herself really believed in it, and was being as studious as she could easily be.

The members took great interest in naming their clubs. The heroines of antiquity, the modern literary celebrities, Geek words that look so simple but mean so much, flowers of the field, all were pressed into the significant service of this organization.

The club members of long ago did not bring ponderous dignity with them to their meetings. They were gay, girlish, and, it may be, frivolous. Their programmes and calendars reveal a schoolgirl's indifference to the decorous habits of an older society. Happily there are still sections of our country where the president appears in the Year Book as "Mrs. Bob," or "Mrs. Mayme," and where the Recording Secretary naïvely writes herself "Mrs. Katie;" where the "Clio Club" devotes the season to the study of "Robert Louis Stevenson and of Nature;" where "Browning Clubs" read "Shakespeare and the Magazines," and where a "Current Events Class" studies "The Bible."

The simple club, with its accessories of tea and poetry, has given way to, or been absorbed in, the Department Club, a club that needs no distinguishing title, but is, par excellence, the Woman's Club.

The department club has taken unto itself the sphere of human knowledge, or, to be specific, and according to the records of 1902, it devotes itself in general to nine named lines of work: Literature, Music, Art, Education, Current Topics, Finance, Philanthropy, Household Economics, and Social Economics. The average scope of endeavor of all the clubs of the country is six departments to each club, the majority undertaking five subjects, and a goodly number being undaunted by the nine.

The theory that underlies the department club is, that the members will naturally gather around the standing committee with whose work they are in especial sympathy, study groups being thus formed; while from time to time each committee will introduce some eminent person to speak to the whole club of his speciality. Practical work will be assigned to the group to which it belongs, and so all possible interests of society will have their hospitable centre from which community betterment will radiate. That the theory is workable has been proven by the efficient practice of such clubs as the Cantabrigia in Massachusetts, the Chicago Woman's Club, and the Woman's Club of Denver. The common practice is far from the ideal. The individual members do not cumulate, nor does the standing committee radiate. The season's work consists, instead, of an expensive programme in which the amusement idea is overlaid by the serious character of the subjects presented. Few groups of study are formed, and these are likely to be on culture subjects. The concrete work of the club is spasmodic, and dependent for its performance almost entirely on the personnel of the standing committee, which is annually changing. The one permanent feature is the lecture; that cannot be escaped, nor can it be related.

*   *   *   *

The dubiety of thought that results from the mixed club programme is further complicated by the occasional mistiness of the club vocabulary. For instance, there is the term Social Economics. In 1902 thirty state federations and 369 clubs announced this science to be one branch of their work. Investigation does not reveal that the term means to any club a particular science. On the contrary, it seems to be a nebulous term covering a diversity of interests more or less misunderstood. A certain blunting of mental sensitiveness will result from such inaccuracy, even if clubs escape the criticism of intellectual dishonesty.

*   *   *   *

To stimulate and direct public opinion is a natural function of the woman's club. Its members are curious about local conditions, and directly interested in the administration of civic affairs. They have experienced in some measure the power of organized and directed effort, and believe in the inherent rightness of their own theories. Lacking the means of direct authority, they seek to gain, by influence and persuasiveness, a determining voice in the conduct of public affairs. On the other hand, the fact that there is a woman's club at all gives evidence to the community that women have time to give that special attention to civic problems which is denied to most men. Our domestic life has approximated the ideal of the ambitious husband in Miss Jewett's story,—the one who had realized his keenest desire, that his wife "could set in her rocking-chair all the afternoon and read a novel." Because American women have this leisure, the community looks to them, more and more, to hold the sensitive plate of public welfare, and to be responsible for the initiation of better methods and manners in civic life. Women's clubs necessarily, then, find their chief scope of altruistic work in creating public opinion.

It is of singular importance that this should be a wise public opinion. The leaders of the club movement are recognizing this necessity,—

a fact evinced by the precautionary advice with which they surround their plans for work. The elimination of the tramp is the special object of the Social Service committee of a prominent state federation. Once he might have been eliminated *viva voce,* or by withholding his morning coffee. But the new intelligence of organized women demands that the case shall be studied. Individual clubs are asked to collect local data. They are urged to undertake no public action without consultation with the committee. The help of able sociologists is invited, and the cooperation of organizations that made a special study of the "Tramp Evil" is secured. By these means the committee undertakes to prevent any hasty or unwise action, and to supply to each community some fundamental knowledge on which wise public opinion may be based. As a sign of the times in the club world, this is a significant incident. Nor is the action of this committee isolated; instead, the same method is coming to be adopted for each remedial measure authorized by the federations. It is yet too early to see definite, quotable results of this plan of work in individual clubs. Past constructive work has been too often due to the quiescent acceptance of whatever measures might be proposed, rather than to their intelligent consideration. Should the new leaven work, the worth of the woman's club to a community would be tremendously increased. Its habits of study would be revolutionized. Its claim to be a "promoter of the public welfare" would be established.

But even without the personal enlightenment that counts for so much, women's clubs have been a potent factor in determining public opinion. As organizations, they have realized that "in public opinion we are all legislators by our birthright." And in practice, they have found that they could actually legislate by means of this power. Legislative work is undertaken by all the state federations, in urging and securing the passage of laws that deal with the conditions of women and children. In Massachusetts, Connecticut, and Illinois, the state federations have promoted the passage of a bill giving joint and equal parental guardianship to minor children. The Juvenile Court Law has been secured in California, Illinois, Maryland, and Nebraska. The Louisiana Federation has worked successfully for the Probationary Law, and in Texas an industrial school has been established. Laws to raise the standard of public morality, to segregate and classify defective and delinquent classes, to secure the services of women as factory inspectors, police matrons, and on boards of control, are other measures for which women's clubs have successfully worked.

While it is difficult to determine the degree of women's participation in this large body of corrective legislation, careful investigation proves that they were, at least, an important single factor. In some instances, the officers of the state federation framed the bill and secured the necessary guidance at every step of its passage; in others, petitions and public agitation were the agencies employed. An inland newspaper in describing the passage of a bill, whose sponsors had been the women's clubs, said, "It was passed in a rush of gallantry in which gush, good sense, and sentimentalism were combined."

The reporter perceived a number of the elements that have entered into the support given by men to women's measures. And while a more elegant exposition might be made of underlying motives, it is hardly possible to give one more discriminating. Whatever the psychical basis of their legislative influence may be, their success demonstrates the fact that politics is possible to a non-political body; that a third party, without vote or direct participation, may come, in a democracy, to have a determining authority in corrective legislation.

Securing the passage of laws is the extreme instance of what organized women have accomplished through the medium of public opinion. Many other concrete illustrations drawn from local conditions might be given; but they would all serve to illustrate that the woman's club is determining the mind of the community in its relation to many educational, philanthropic, and reformatory questions. How important, then, becomes right thinking in the club,—not solemn, arrogating, feminine, self-inclusive thinking, but gay, self-forgetful, reflective, human thinking.

A club to which I belong at one time concentrated its very serious efforts to prevent the further destruction of song birds. We interested the children in the public schools. We argued with the husbands and fathers, and particularly with the bachelor sportsmen. We wrote columns in the local paper, and succeeded in arousing much public sympathy for the songsters. Soon after we bought and appeared in our new millinery. An irreverent joker counted fifty aigrettes floating from fifty new bonnets, and proposed to our president that he come to do a little missionary work in the club in behalf of birds. It was fortunate for our club that its president had a sense of humor, else we might be still wearing aigrettes and distributing pamphlets for the protection of song birds.

The federation of one of the more enlightened states has recently undertaken to enter the field of direct politics. I quote the advice it gives to its constituents:—

"Before senators and representatives are even nominated, it is very essential that club women look up the record of the various candidates in their districts, and satisfy themselves as to their position regarding women upon boards of control of state institutions. Find out how they voted last year. Information will be gladly furnished by members of this committee. Then strive to create a sufficient public sentiment in your own locality to defeat, at the party caucus, any nominee known to oppose women representatives upon Boards of Control." It is this partial, local, and partisan type of mind that the woman's club supposedly tries to correct. That it has not succeeded, as yet, in doing this, may be due to the greater attention given to objective causes than to subjective conditions, or it may be an expression of the mere femininity of the movement.

The field for constructive work in the women's clubs—work in which they have direct and controlling authority—is limited. To create better conditions of life means for them commonly to use the indirect agencies we have been considering. In philanthropy and public education, they have found their chief opportunity for responsible effort, and in both fields women's clubs have been of conspicuous service. They have been hospitable to all forms of philanthropy, creating, by their aggregation of nonsectarian people, a new centre of public beneficence. They have added frequently to the educational equipment of a community, the kindergarten, manual training, and domestic science; and this not always by persuasion, but through the establishment and support of these branches of education, until such time as the community should be convinced of their usefulness and voluntarily assume their responsibilities. More than in any other way, the women's clubs have benefited the schools by creating better hygiene and aesthetic conditions in school buildings and grounds. They have made it possible for the children to become familiar with good art, with the beauty of cleanliness, and with the charm of a growing vine or flower.

But it is in the work for the extension of libraries that women's clubs have most fully demonstrated their ability to further an educational project. Many states in the Union have made no provision for the establishment of free libraries, and in others, where there is the necessary legislation, local conditions prevent their adequate establishment. Realizing keenly what a dearth of books means to a community, women's clubs have promptly initiated in many states systems of traveling libraries to satisfy the needs of the people until free libraries could be established on a permanent basis. In Oklahoma and Indian Territory the federation collected one thousand volumes. These were classified and divided into fifty libraries, and each was sent on its enlightening pilgrimage. Kansas is sending to its district schools and remote communities 10,000 books divided into suitable libraries. The women of Ohio circulate 900 libraries; Kentucky is sending sixty-four to its mountaineers. In Maine the traveling library has become a prized educational opportunity. Its success has secured the appointment of a Library Commission and the enactment of suitable library legislation. This movement is extensive; and as an indication of what organized women can do, when the issue is concrete and appealing, it is significant. At a recent federation meeting in Massachusetts, no orator of the day made so eloquent an appeal as did the neat and convenient case of good books that invited our inspection before it should be sent to a remote community in the Tennessee Mountains.

Except in the two lines of work we have just considered, women's clubs are not zealous in undertaking to create better conditions of life by direct and authoritative measures. To many causes they give tacit assent. A veteran club officer said to me recently, "I am ashamed to bring a petition before my club; the members will sign anything."

"But do they do everything?" I asked.

"No," she answered, "they seem to think that to sign a petition is tantamount to securing the end desired. Having signed, the matter is closed so far as they personally are concerned."

An instance which will illustrate this curious personal apathy toward causes that are furthered by the federations, and to which the club members abstractedly assent, is found in the history of their relation to industrial conditions. Six years ago the General Federation undertook to help the solution of certain industrial problems, notably to further organization among working-women; to secure and enforce child labor legislation where needed; to further attendance at school; and to secure humane conditions under which labor is performed. State federations have acted in accordance with the General Federation's plans to appoint standing industrial committees, procure investigations, circulate literature, and create a public sentiment in favor of these causes. In Illinois this indirect power was of much aid in securing a Child Labor Law. In other communities something has been accomplished by way of enacting new laws or enforcing existing ones, showing that organized women readily avail themselves of the chance for indirect service in promoting the intelligent efforts of the federations.

On the other hand, there are three opportunities by means of which women's clubs and their members can directly effect in a limited and local sense that industrial amelioration for which as federations they work so zealously. The first is found in the industrial conditions of the South, where it has been proved that the establishment of schools that offer manual training combined with some study of books, and with practical work in gardens and kitchens, will offset the attraction the factory has had for the children in its vicinity. These schools are called "Model Schools," and have been successfully inaugurated in Georgia. Their need is financial, and Southern women have brought the nature and needs of this work, which is, in a broad sense, an industrial reform, to the notice of women's clubs in the North. In 1903 the clubs of Massachusetts established their first school at Cass, Georgia, and assured its maintenance for two years. But there is no other evidence that this significant opportunity for industrial amelioration has received that prompt and direct support that might warrantably have been expected.

The Child Labor Committee of the General Federation has furnished individual clubs with a second direct opportunity. This committee finds that the argument most frequently encountered while attempting to enact Child Labor legislation has been that the earnings of little children are needed to support widowed mothers. Therefore the committee requests clubs to investigate local conditions, and whenever an apparent case of this nature is found, "to persuade the children thus employed to return to school, undertaking to pay the amount of the weekly wage, which the child formerly earned, to his widowed mother." This money is to be called and regarded as a scholarship. The plan resembles one that has been carried on successfully by the state authorities in Switzerland for twenty-five years; therefore it is neither a visionary nor impracticable scheme, but one in which women could realize their traditional responsibilities toward the children of the community, and in which women's clubs could find a beneficent opportunity for direct and constructive work toward industrial amelioration. Eight such scholarships have been established in Chicago. There is no further evidence that any woman's club has undertaken to carry out this plan.

The third instance is comprised in the unique opportunity for individual, as well as united, service offered to women by the Consumers' League. This is the case of the individual purchaser, and of the product in one line of manufactured goods. For some years the Consumers League has argued upon the community the righteousness of buying only such goods as have been produced under humane conditions, believing that the final determiner of these conditions is the purchaser. But the claims of the Consumers' League are well known, and it is also known to all women that "white goods" bearing the League's significant label can be bought in open market for prices that are entirely fair. Many state federations and the General Federation are pledged to further the work of the League. Single clubs give exhibitions of white goods, and form small local groups of membership. But the next step, the step that concerns the individual and makes the 275,000 members of women's clubs consistent purchasers of these goods, is not taken. The "bargain counter" is the same scene of conflict as of yore; and the woman who belongs to an organization pledged to industrial reform is a lively participant in this warfare of questionable economy.

The weakness of the club movement is this lack of real contact of ideals between the federations and the single club. The latter is satisfied, selfish, absorbed in its own local concerns; the federation appeals are a disquieting interruption to its orderly programme; while the federations, counting on their numerical strength, and believing in the ultimate awakening of the club, flatter it into an acquiescence that is mistaken for cooperation. In undertaking to awaken interest in so many lines of work, the federations jeopardize all interests, and minimize the value of each. If the women's clubs of 1904 could come together on the platform of some common and fundamental social need, as did their progenitors, the club writ large in its federations would no longer be an elaborate organization for the dissemination of propaganda, but would at once become that which it now may seem to be,—a social force. Its incoherencies would be explained, its complex methods and motives would be simplified, and its constitutional rank might be assigned.

I asked my grocer recently what he thought of our woman's club. And he, with careful precision, answered me, "I think your lady's club is very dressy." While I was still revolving the grocer's answer, I chanced to see these words of an eminent educator: "When the history of this period comes to be written, it will be recognized that from 1870 to 1900 was a period of greater significance than any former two hundred years; and out of the whole time of thirty years, that which will be recognized as the most significant, as the most far-reaching, will be the movement that is represented by the women's clubs."

The adjudication of the two points of view—the club woman and the club movement—may still furnish scope for the altruistic endeavor of the Woman's Club.

14

Grover Cleveland, 'Woman's Mission and Woman's Clubs'

FROM *Ladies Home Journal*, vol. 22, May 1905. This article by a former President of the United States caused a great stir at the time of its publication.

It cannot be denied that we have fallen upon days when florid and exaggerated optimism is exceedingly fashionable among the American people. Conservatism seems to be at a discount, and those who seek to win popular approval or support are shrewdly apt to confidently insist that our political, economic and social conditions have advanced to a point from which the highest human achievements are easily in sight.

Great latitude may harmlessly be allowed to this sort of congratulatory optimism; and it is certainly an easy thing to float with the current of prevalent inclination by assenting to the jaunty suggestion heard on every side that old things have passed away and all things have become new. This concession to the substitution of new things for old should, however, be modified by the proviso that such substitution means not merely change, but substantial and beneficent progress. Nor should the least toleration be awarded to the assumption that moral traits or the relationships interwoven with all that ennobles and dignifies civilized humanity are within the range of useful change or reconstruction. Honesty, good faith, charity, patriotism and belief in God are among the things that can never, without defiance of Divine purposes, be submerged by human progress, or supplanted by any substitutes contrived by the wit of man. So, also, love and affection were planted by the hand of God, and endued by Him with eternal life; and they bear their sweetest and most wholesome fruit when undisturbed by blind and blighting efforts to unnaturally stimulate their growth in the soil and atmosphere of man's material advancement. They are as old as the human race, and they create the relationships that underlie the foundations of organized society.

THE SCOPE AND CHARACTER OF WOMAN'S MISSION

Among these relationships none compares in importance and vital influence with those of wife and mother. This proposition should be so clearly recognized and so apparent in the light of our instinctive perception as to need no other support; and, more than this, its mere statement should suggest to every well-regulated mind the sacred mission of womanhood.

At first blush it would appear easy to deal with the topic we have in hand. One who can remember a mother's love and a mother's care in childhood, or who has known in later days the joys a devoted wife brings to the life of man, ought to be able to calculate upon general experience so largely tallying with his own that he need not fear protest or dissent in treating of the scope and character of woman's mission. It is a melancholy fact, however, that our subject is actually one of difficult approach; and it is a more melancholy fact that this approach is made difficult by a dislocation of ideas and by false prospectives on the part of women themselves. To those of us who suffer periods of social pessimism, but who, in the midst of it all, cling to our faith in the saving grace of simple and unadulterated womanhood, any discontent on the part of woman with her ordained lot, or a restless desire on her part to be and to do something not within the sphere of her appointed ministrations, cannot appear otherwise than as perversions of a gift of God to the human race. These perversions have made their appearance; and they differ in direction and degree as greatly as the temper accompanying them changes with the extent of their threatened departure from the path of God's beneficence.

Those who, seeking to protect the old and natural order of things as they relate to women, reverently appeal to the division of Divine purpose clearly shown when Adam was put in the Garden of Eden to dress it and keep it, and Eve was given to him as a helpmeet and because it was not good that man should be alone, are apt to encounter the half-pitying scorn of certain successors of this helpmeet; and if they attempt to fortify their position by referring to the fact that, as part of the punishment visited upon our first parents for their disobedience, it was decreed that in the sweat of his face should the man eat bread, and in sorrow should the woman bring forth children, they must not be surprised if they are met by the indignant outburst: "And so you think a woman's only use is to bear children!" It must be confessed the inclination is very strong to meet this in like temper, by retorting that no woman who estimates motherhood as less than her highest, holiest function and privilege is fit to be a mother. The following dispatch from Berlin, recently published, is most refreshing and ought to teach a salutary lesson:

"The little Princess Victoria, daughter of the Emperor and Empress, is suffering from a severe attack of influenza, which the Empress also contracted while nursing the child. Her Majesty has been obliged to cancel various public engagements."

THE QUESTION OF A WOMAN'S VOTE

The restlessness and discontent to which I have referred is most strongly manifested in a movement which has for a long time been on foot for securing to women the right to vote and otherwise participate in public affairs. Let it here be distinctly understood that no sensible man has fears of injury to the country on account of such participation. It is its dangerous, undermining effect on the characters of the wives and mothers of our land that we fear. This particular movement is so aggressive, and so extreme in its insistence, that those whom it has fully enlisted may well be considered as incorrigible. At a very recent meeting of these radicals a high priestess of the faith declared: "No matter how bad the crime a woman commits, if she can't vote, and is classed with idiots and criminals and lunatics, she should not be punished by the same laws as those who vote obey." This was said when advocating united action on the part of the assembled body to prevent the execution of a woman proved guilty of the deliberate and aggravated murder of her husband. The speaker is reported to have further announced as apparently the keynote of her address: "If we could vote we'd be willing to be hanged." It is a thousand pities that all the wives found in such company cannot sufficiently open their minds to see the complete fitness of the homely definition which describes a good wife as "a woman who loves her husband and her country with no desire to run either"; and what a blessed thing it would be if every mother, and every woman, whether mother, wife, spinster or maid, who either violently demands or wildly desires for women a greater share in the direction of public affairs, could realize the everlasting truth that "the hand that rocks the cradle is the hand that rules the world."

There is comfort in the reflection that, even though these extremists may not be amenable to reformation, there is a fair prospect that their manifest radicalism and their blunt avowal of subverting purposes will effectively warn against a dangerously wide acceptance of their theories.

The real difficulty and delicacy of our topic becomes most apparent when we come to speak of the less virulent and differently directed club movements that have crossed the even tenor of the way of womanhood. I do not include those movements which amount to nothing more than woman's association or coöperation in charitable, benevolent and religious work, largely local in its activities and in all its qualities and purposes entirely fitted to a woman's highest nature and best impulses. I speak more especially of the woman's clubs of an entirely different sort which have grown up in all sections of our land, and which have already become so numerous that in the interests of their consolidated management a "National Federation of Woman's Clubs" has been created. I speak also of the vast number of associations less completely organized, but not less exacting of time and attention, whose professed purposes are in many instances the intellectual improvement or entertainment of the women composing their membership. Doubtless in numerous cases the objects of these clubs and associations are shown in such a light and are made to appear so good, or at least so harmless, that a conscientious woman, unless she makes a strong fight against self-delusion, may quite easily persuade herself that affiliation with them would be certainly innocent and perhaps even within the dictates of duty. The danger of self-delusion lies in her supposition that she is consulting the need of relaxation or the duty of increased opportunity for intellectual improvement, when in point of fact, and perhaps imperceptibly to herself, she is taking counsel of her discontent with the humdrum of her home life.

ARE WOMEN RETALIATING ON MEN?

We certainly ought not to be too swift in charging the tendency toward club affiliation on the part of our women to a deliberate willingness to forget or neglect their transcendent mission or home duties. Unquestionably this tendency is partly due to the widespread and contagious fever for change or rearrangement which seems to leave no phase of our people's life untouched. I believe it has also been largely provoked and intensified by the increase of club life among the husbands and fathers of our land, and by their surrender to such business preoccupation or the madness of inordinate accumulation, as results in the neglect of wives and those to whom, under all rules of duty and decency, they owe attention and companionship—thus creating a condition of man's guilt which tempts retaliation in kind. So far as woman's club indulgences may be retaliatory they might challenge considerable toleration if punishment were visited only upon the guilty; for it may be safely assumed that among those who are most disturbed by the growth of woman's clubbism the sentiment is universal that man's neglect of woman is a dastardly offense, and that the whipping-post for wife-beaters would be a wholesome feature of

our criminal law. They believe, however, not less universally, that
women who seek to punish man's violation of duty by their own home-
neglecting resort to club pursuits or diversions may be said to take the
law in their own hands in a most daring way. As in other cases of like
procedure, the guilty are not always punished, but those who are
innocent and helpless are made to suffer; and, saddest of all, the saving
womanly traits that distinguish us above other nations, and the
strength and beauty of our domestic life, are put in peril.

WOMAN'S DANGER OF THE CLUB HABIT

No woman who enters upon such a retaliatory course can be sure
that the man she seeks to punish will be otherwise affected than to be
made more indifferent to home, and more determined to enlarge the
area of his selfish pleasures. She can be sure, however, that cheerless-
ness will invade her home, and that if children are there they will be
irredeemably deprived of the mysterious wholesomeness and delight
of an atmosphere which can only be created by a mother's loving
presence and absorbing care. She can also be certain that, growing out
of the influence which her behavior and example are sure to have upon
the conduct of the wives and mothers within the range of her companionship, she may be directly responsible for marred happiness in other
households, and that as an aider and abettor of woman's clubs she
must bear her share of liability for the injury they may inflict upon the
domestic life of our land. It must be abundantly evident that, as
agencies for retaliation or man's punishment, woman's clubs are
horribly misplaced and miserably vicious.

To the honest-minded women who are inclined to look with favor
upon such of these clubs as indicate beneficent purposes or harmless
relaxation it is not amiss to suggest that these purposes and characteristics are naturally not only of themselves expansive, but that
membership in one such organization is apt to create a club habit
which, if it does not lead to other similar affiliations, induces toleration and defense of club ideas in general. It is in this way that many
conscientious women, devoted to their home duties and resentful of
any suspicion to the contrary, through apparently innocent club
membership subordinate their household interests, and are lost to the
ranks of the defenders of home against such club influences and consequences as the unbiased judgment of true womanhood would unhesit-
atingly condemn. The woman is fortunate and well poised who, having
yielded to whatever allurements there may be in a single club
membership, can implicitly rely upon her ability to resist persuasion
to additional indulgence, and can fix the exact limit of her surrender
to its infatuation. It is quite evident that she ought not take the first
step toward such membership before considering the matter with a

breadth of view sufficient to take in all its indirect possibilities, as well as its immediate and palpable consequences.

WOMAN'S CLUBS NOT ONLY HARMFUL, BUT A MENACE

I am persuaded that without exaggeration of statement we may assume that there are woman's clubs whose objects and intents are not only harmful, but harmful in a way that directly menaces the integrity of our homes and the benign disposition and character of our wifehood and motherhood; that there are others harmless in intent, but whose tendency is toward waste of time and perversion of effort, as well as toward the formation of the club habit, and the toleration or active patronage of less innocent organizations; that there are also associations of women whose purposes of charity, religious enterprise or intellectual improvement are altogether laudable and worthy. Leaving this latter class out of account, and treating the subject on the theory that only the other organizations mentioned are under consideration, I believe that it should be boldly declared that the best and safest club for a woman to patronize is her home. American wives and American mothers, as surely as "the hand that rocks the cradle is the hand that rules the world," have, through their nurture of children and their influence over men, the destinies of our Nation in their keeping to a greater extent than any other single agency. It is surely not soft-hearted sentimentalism which insists that, in a country where the people rule, a decisive share in securing the perpetuity of its institutions falls upon the mothers who devote themselves to teaching their children who are to become rulers, lessons of morality and patriotism and disinterested citizenship. Such thoughts suggest how supremely great is the stake of our country in woman's unperverted steadfastness, and enjoin the necessity of its protection against all risks and all temptations.

THE REAL PATH OF TRUE WOMANHOOD

I am in favor of according to women the utmost social enjoyment; and I am profoundly thankful that this, in generous and sufficient measure, is within their reach without encountering the temptations or untoward influences so often found in the surroundings of woman's clubs.

For the sake of our country, for the sake of our homes, and for the sake of our children, I would have our wives and mothers loving and devoted, though all others may be sordid and heedless; I would have them disinterested and trusting, though all others may be selfish and cunning; I would have them happy and contented in following the Divinely appointed path of true womanhood, though all others may grope in the darkness of their own devices.

15

Mary Antin, 'Russia'

FROM *Thirteenth Biennial Convention* (The General Federation of Women's Clubs, 1916). Miss Antin was a young socialist who had written what was, perhaps, the most beautiful account of an immigrant's experience, *The Promised Land* (1912). She was both Jewish and radical, and by inviting her to speak at the GFWC's biennial convention clubwomen showed their liberality and ideological openness. Miss Antin's speech was, however, not only the best but almost the last of its kind. After America entered the war, and especially after the Russian revolution, such addresses, common enough in the Federation's early years, became increasingly rare.

This once I am afraid. I am afraid to hear my voice. There are nearly three million Jews in America. I have been asked to speak for them. It is not for the whole of Russia that I can speak, because when I lived in Russia my world was limited to a little corner where they kept the Jews, so if my message out of Russia is only partial, you have the Russian system to call to account for it.

On the whole the Russian immigrant in this country is the Jewish immigrant, since we are the most numerous group out of Russia. But to speak for the Jews—the most misunderstood people in the whole of history—ten minutes, in which to clear away 2,000 years of misunderstanding! Your President has probably in this instance, as in other instances, been guided by some inspiration, the source of which none of us may know. I was called by name long before your President notified me that she would call me to this assembly, I was called by name to say what does the Jew bring to America—by a lady from Philadelphia. Miss Repplier, not long ago, in an article in her inimitable fashion, called things by their name, and sometimes miscalled them, spoke of "the Jew in America who has received from us so much and has given us so little." This comment was called down by something that I had said about certain things in American life that did not come up to the American standard. "The Jew who has given so little"—tonight I am the Jew—you are the Americans. Let us look over these things.

What do we bring you besides our poverty and our rags? Men, women, and children—the stuff that nations are built of. What sort of men and women? I shall not seek to tire you with a list of shining names of Jewish notables. If you want to know who's who among the Jews, I refer you to your biographical dictionary. You are as familiar as I am with the name of Jews who shine in the professions, who have done notable service to the state, in politics, in diplomacy, and where you will. If you read the newspapers and magazines, you are as well acquainted as I am with the sort of life the Jews on the whole live in this country.

You know as well as I what numbers of Jewish youth are always taking high ranks, high honors in the schools, colleges and universities. You know as well as I do in what numbers our people crowd your lecture halls and your civic centers, in all those places where the spiritual wine of life may be added to our daily bread. These are things that you know. I don't want you to be thinking of any list of Jewish notables.

A very characteristic thing of Jewish life is the democracy of virtue that you find in every Jewish community. We Jews have never depended for our salvation on the supreme constellations of any chosen ones. It was well with us only when and wherever the masses were disciplined to the spiritual code of our people. Little did we count on the supreme constellations of the shining ones—always we had honor, our scholars, our philosophers, but not because we hoped through their virtues to arrive at a balance, with their virtues to balance the shortcomings of the mass. Our shining ones were to us always examples by means of which the whole community was to be disciplined to what was Jewish virtue.

Take a group of Jews anywhere, and you will have the essence of their Jewishness, though there be not present one single shining luminary. The average Jew presents the average of whatsoever there is of Jewish virtue, talent or capacity.

What is this peculiar Jewish genius? If I must sum it up in a word, I will say that the Jewish genius is a love for living out the things that they believe. What do we believe? We Jews believe that the world is a world of law. Law is another name for our God, and the quest after the law, the formulation of it, has always permeated our schools, and the incorporation of the laws of life, as our scholars noted it down, has been the chief business of the Jewish masses. No wonder that when we come to America, a nation founded as was our ancient nation, a nation founded on law and principle, on an ideal—no wonder that we so quickly find ourselves at home, that presently we fall into the regulation habit of speaking of America as our own country, until Miss Repplier reproves us, and then we do it no more. I used formerly when speaking of American sins, tribulations, etc., I used to speak of them as "ours"; no more—your sins. I have been corrected.

Why then, now that we have come here, to this nation builded on the same principle as was our nation, no wonder that we so quickly seize on the fundamentals. We make no virtue of the fact—it is the Jewishness in us—that has been our peculiar characteristics, our habit. We need no one from outside of our ranks to remind us of the goodly things we have found and taken from your hands. We have been as eloquent as any that has spoken in appreciation of what we have found here, of liberty, justice, and a square deal. We give thanks. We have rendered thanks, we Jews, some of you are witnesses. We know the value of the gifts that we have found here.

Who shall know the flavor of bread if not they that have gone hungry, and we, who have been for centuries without the bread of justice, we know the full flavor of American justice, liberty and equality.

To formulate and again formulate, and criticise the law,—what do our Rabbis in the Ghetto beside the study of law? To them used to come our lawyers, to our Rabbis, not to find the way how to get around the law, but to be sure that we were walking straight in the path indicated by the law. So today in America we are busy in the same fashion.

The Jewish virtues, such as they are, are widespread throughout the Jewish masses. Here in New York City is congregated the largest Jewish community in the whole world, and what is true of the Jews of New York, is true of the Jews of America, and the Jews of the world. If I speak of the characteristics of Jewish life on the East side, one of the great characteristics is its restlessness in physical form, due to the oppression of city life, and the greater restlessness, due to the unquenchable, turbulent quest of the truth, and more truth. You know that the East side of New York is a very spawning ground for debate, and debating clubs. There are more boys and girls in debating clubs than in boys' basket ball teams, or baseball teams. I believe in boys playing baseball, but I also believe in that peculiar enthusiasm of our Jewish people for studying the American law, just as they used to study their own law, to see whether any of the American principles find incorporation in American institutions and habits. We are the critics. We are never satisfied with things as they are. Go out and hear the boys and girls. They like to go to school and learn the names of liberty, and equality and justice, and after school they gather in their debating circles and discuss what might be the meaning of these names, and what is their application to life. That is the reason there is so much stirring, rebellion, and protest that comes out of the East side.

In the great labor movement, it is the effort of the people to arrive at a program of economic justice that shall parallel the political justice. Consider for a moment the present condition of the garment-making trade. That is a Jewish trade. Ages ago when the lords of the nations, among whom we lived, were preventing us from engaging in other occupations, they thrust into the hands of our people the needle, and the needle was our tool, why through the needle we have still thought to give expression to the Jewish genius in our life.

This immense clothing industry—a Jewish industry primarily—is today in a better condition as regards unionization, is further on the road to economic justice than any other great industry that you could name. Mind you, the sweatshop we found here when we came here. We took it just as it was, but the barring of the sweatshop and the organization of the clothing industry in such fashion that it is further in advance, more nearly on a basis that affords just treatment to all concerned—that has been the contribution of our tailor men and tailor women. We have done this thing. This very afternoon you heard from Henry Moskowitz of the Protocol. The Protocol is a piece of machinery for bringing about justice in this great industry. We have invented that thing, we Jews. We are putting it in operation, we are fighting for its perpetuation. Whatsoever good comes from it, we have done it.

We are not only busy criticising and finding fault, we know not only what is wrong, but how to right the wrong. The life of the East side is full of this protest. The Socialistic movement in this country, which is the protest against conditions in this country, is almost a Jewish movement—a very radical movement, and is greatly recruited from the Jewish ranks, and many radical movements are initiated by the Jewish people.

A public speaker of wide experience said he counted it a feather in his bonnet if he could put over his doctrine in Cooper Union. And, when talking to a Jewish audience you have got to know what you are talking about. The spirit of the law—that appeals to us—the formulation—and the next thing is to see that it is incorporated.

Consider us, if you will, in the most barbarous sense, but I point to this as our great contribution, we are always protesting, and if you want to know the value of that contribution, I remind you that the formulae of the rights of men, which was a criticism of things as they used to be, and a formularizing of things as they ought to be, was at least as efficient as all the armies of the continent put together in the revolutionary war. The Spirit of '76 is the spirit of criticism. We Jews in America are busy at our ancient business of pulling down false gods.

M. Carey Thomas, 'Present Tendencies in Women's College and University Education'

FROM *Publications of the Association of Collegiate Alumnae*, vol. 3 February 1908 (Excerpts). Miss Thomas, the president of Bryn Mawr College, was the leading female educator of her day. Dr Clarke, whose book *Sex in Education* (1873) she attacks, argued that education weakened the reproductive capacity of women, and was, therefore, a danger to the race.

Anniversaries like this which compel us to pause for a moment and review our progress come with peculiar significance to women of my generation. I doubt if the most imaginative and sympathetic younger women in this audience can form any conception of what it means to women of the old advance guard, among whom you will perhaps allow me to include myself, to be able to say to each other without fear of contradiction that in the twenty-five years covered by the work of the Association of Collegiate Alumnae the battle for the higher education of women has been gloriously, and forever, won.

The passionate desire of the women of my generation for higher education was accompanied throughout its course by the awful doubt, felt by women themselves as well as by men, as to whether women as a sex were physically and mentally fit for it. I think I can best make this clear to you if I refer briefly to my own experience. I cannot remember the time when I was not sure that studying and going to college were the things above all others which I wished to do. I was always wondering whether it could be really true, as everyone thought, that boys were cleverer than girls. Indeed, I cared so much that I never dared to ask any grown-up person the direct question, not even my father or mother, because I feared to hear the reply. I remember often praying about it, and begging God that if it were true that because I was a girl I could not successfully master Greek and go to college and understand things to kill me at once, as I could not bear to live in such an unjust world. When I was a little older I read the Bible entirely through with passionate eagerness, because I had heard it said that it proved that women were inferior to men. Those were not the days of the higher criticism. I can remember weeping over the account of Adam and Eve because it seemed to me that the curse pronounced on Eve might imperil girls' going to college; and to this day I can never read many parts of the Pauline epistles without feeling again the sinking of the heart with which I used to hurry over the verses referring to women's keeping silence in the churches and asking their husbands at home. I searched not only the Bible, but all other books I could get for light on the woman question. I read Milton with rage and indignation. Even as a child I knew him for the woman hater he was. The splendor of Shakspere was obscured to me then by the lack of intellectual power in his greatest woman characters. Even now it seems to me that only Isabella in *Measure for Measure* thinks greatly, and weighs her actions greatly, like a Hamlet or a Brutus.

I can well remember one endless scorching summer's day when, sitting in a hammock under the trees with a French dictionary, blinded by tears more burning than the July sun, I translated the most indecent book I have ever read, Michelet's famous—were it not now forgotten, I should be able to say infamous—book on woman, *La Femme*. I was beside myself with terror lest it might prove true that I myself was so vile and pathological a thing. Between that summer's day in 1874, and a certain day in the autumn in 1904, thirty years had elapsed. Although during these thirty years I had read in every language every book on women that I could obtain, I had never chanced again upon a book that seemed to me so to degrade me in my womanhood as the seventh and seventeenth chapters on women and women's education of President Stanley Hall's *Adolescence*. Michelet's sickening sentimentality and horrible over-sexuality seemed to me to breathe again from every pseudo-scientific page.

But how vast the difference between then and now in my feelings, and in the feelings of every woman who has had to do with the education of girls! Then I was terror-struck lest I, and every other woman with me, were doomed to live as pathological invalids in a universe merciless to woman as a sex. Now we know that it is not we, but the man who believes such things about us, who is himself pathological, blinded by neurotic mists of sex, unable to see that women form one-half of the kindly race of normal, healthy human creatures in the world; that women, like men, are quickened and inspired by the same great traditions of their race, by the same love of learning, the same love of science, the same love of abstract truth; that women, like men, are immeasurably benefited, physically, mentally, and morally, and are made vastly better mothers, as men are made vastly better fathers, by subordinating the distracting instincts of sex to the simple human fellowship of similar education, and similar intellectual and social ideals.

It was not to be wondered at that we were uncertain in those old days as to the ultimate result of women's education. Before I myself went to college I had seen only one college woman. I had heard that such a woman was staying at the house of an acquaintance. I went to see her with fear. Even if she had appeared in hoofs and horns I was determined to go to college all the same. But it was a relief to find this Vassar graduate tall and handsome and dressed like other women. When, five years later, I went to Leipzig to study after I had graduated from Cornell, my mother used to write me that my name was never mentioned to her by the women of her acquaintance. I was thought by them to be as much of a disgrace to my family as if I had eloped with the coachman. Now, women who have been to college are as plentiful as blackberries on summer hedges.

*   *   *   *

We did not know when we began whether women's health could stand the strain of college education. We were haunted in those days by the clanging chains of that gloomy little specter, Dr. Edward H. Clarke's *Sex in Education*. With trepidation of spirit I made my mother read it, and was much cheered by her remark that, as neither she, nor any of the women she knew, had ever seen girls or women of the kind described in Dr. Clarke's book, we might as well act as if they did not exist. Still we did not *know* whether colleges might not produce a crop of just such invalids. Doctors insisted that they would. We women could not be sure until we had tried the experiment. Now we have tried it, and tried it for more than a generation, and we know that college women are not only not invalids, but that they are better physically than other women in their own class of life.

*   *   *   *

We did not really know anything about even the ordinary everyday intellectual capacity of women when we began to educate them. We were not even sure that they inherited their intellects from their fathers as well as from their mothers. We were told that their brains were too light, their foreheads too small, their reasoning powers too defective, their emotions too easily worked upon to make good students. None of these things has proved to be so.

*   *   *   *

We are now living in the midst of great and, I believe on the whole beneficent, social changes which are preparing the way for the coming economic independence of women. Like the closely allied diminishing birth rate, but unlike the higher education of women, this great change in opinion and practice seems to have come about almost without our knowledge, certainly without our conscious co-operation. The passionate desire of the women of my generation for a college education seems, as we study it now in the light of coming events, to have been a part of this greater movement.

Vida Scudder, 'Class-Consciousness'

FROM *Atlantic Monthly*, vol. 118, March 1911 (Excerpts). Miss Scudder was a pioneer settlement resident and a well known educator. She was also one of the few feminists to become a socialist. Her essay outlines the intellectual reasons which deterred most American women from joining her.

I

Jane Addams, in *Twenty Years at Hull House,* implies that the two doctrines of economic determinism and class-consciousness have deterred her from accepting socialism. Now, the form in which these doctrines were currently presented by earlier socialists was sufficiently crass to repel any one idealistically inclined. Yet, looked at closely, economic determinism at least is a very innocent bogey. When we assume our free power to control social progress, we may proceed under a great delusion. So may we in assuming that we move about lightly in space, while really an incredible weight of atmosphere presses from every point upon us. It would be foolish to worry about the weight, however, when we are catching a trolley; and fatalistic ideas, whether attacking us from the side of sociology, theology, or science, are cheerfully disregarded the moment we enter the race of life. Determinism simply assures us that the threads of moral purpose are knit into the woof of the universe, instead of trailing vacuously through space. Just as we have deeper faith in a spiritual nature than our fathers, who clung to special creations, our children will find the privilege of cooperating with the Will disclosed to reverent study of the changing order, higher than the effort to impose on that order methods invented by private preference. 'Cercando libertà,' was Dante's aim: the generations move onward; attaining it only in measure as, to use Wordsworth's fine phrase, they come to know themselves 'free because embound.'

When the early exponents of economic determinism uttered their thrilling call, 'Proletarians of all lands, unite!' it was a call to free men. But was that call a wise one? Shall we echo it? The question raises the vital issue of class-consciousness as a desirable factor in social advance. Only with the advent of the two theories together, did the Utopian socialism of the earlier nineteenth century become an effective force. As that force advances, enters practical politics, permeates life, the doctrines are phrased less crudely, but they are not abandoned; and class-consciousness at least proves itself to-day no academic theory, but a driving power.

To indorse it, is a serious matter. It means that we welcome discontent, it might call us to rejoice in revolt. It demands that we hail with satisfaction, instead of dismay, the steady dogged rise of proletariat claims to higher wages, shorter hours, larger compensations in injury. It means that while we may be mildly pleased with the announcement of a new profit-sharing scheme on the part of employers, our hearts leap with more confident gladness when an increase of wages has been won by a group of employees. We shall approve of any shrinking in the ranks of free labor, any accession to the ranks of the organized; shall encourage the spread of radical and subversive teaching among the working people, make an Act of Thanks for Milwaukee, note with joy the socialist propaganda in New York, and desire by all rightful means to persuade the helpless unthinking mass of the Workers that power and responsibility are in their hands.

*   *   *   *

The majority of educated men are obviously not yet at this point. The change is amazing, but it is still wavering; nor do men yet recognize the underdrift of sympathy in which they are caught. This drift is the recognition that the working classes must achieve their own salvation, and that such salvation demands not only fragments of improvement grudgingly bestowed, but a general pressure, if not toward social equality, then at least to the point where a 'living wage' shall secure the chance to all manhood to rise to its highest level.

As the drift slowly becomes conscious, people grow troubled. For they see that it involves two things:—

First, the sharp belief that privilege must be cut down before our general life can flourish. Now, the finer idealism does not shrink from this idea in itself. Disinterested men, including many who have a stake in the game, are coming to admit it; many are even inclined to accept the central socialist tenet, that no effective cure for our social evils will be found until a large proportion at least of wealth-producing wealth be socially owned. Many people disagree with this proposition, but it no longer shocks the common mind. The sacred and inalienable righteousness of the principle of private property was once even among radical thinkers an assumption to be built on; it is becoming a thesis to be proved.

But there is another implication from which the moral sense recoils: that is, from encouragement of class-consciousness as a militant weapon. For are we not coming to object to any weapons at all? Just when the old political militarism is coming to be at a discount in the idealist ranks, this new form of war—conflict in industrial relations— makes its appearance among pitiable mortals; and our enthusiasm is enlisted to foster in the working people the very traits which civilization is struggling to leave behind! True, ballot rather than bomb is the weapon commended, physical violence is honestly deplored by both sides, and even extremists ardently hope that we may spell our Revolution without the R. None the less are the passions educed by the whole situation essentially those of the battlefield; men exult in wresting advantages from their antagonists, they are trained to regard one another as adversaries, not brothers. And this is the very age theoretically agog for peace! The good people who would fain see all social progress proceed from the growing generosities of realized brotherhood, find a mere travesty of their desires in gains won through self-assertion. Shall the lovers of peace sympathize with a movement for quickening discontent and making hatred effective? Shall we lend our approval to destroying whatever meekness the poor may have, and summon them to curse that Poverty which a certain word calls blessed? It is time to call a halt!

There is doubtless some unconscious prejudice on the side of privilege in all this. But there is something better too, and every honest socialist knows it. The theory of class-consciousness does offend the conscience of the moralist as often as the sister doctrine of economic determinism offends the intellect of the philosopher.

II

Frank confession behooves us at the outset. Class-consciousness is a weapon, and to applaud it does involve a militant attitude. If people say that it is *ipse facto* discredited thereby, we can only enter a plea for consistency. Virtuous disapproval of the working-class struggle sits ill on the lips of those who point out with zest the stimulating qualities of the competitive system and vote enthusiastically for the increase of armaments. It is a curious fact that the man who talks Jingo politics most loudly, and defends with most vigor the admirable necessity to commerce of the triumph of the strong, is habitually the very person most outraged at the pressure of a united proletariat group toward fredom. Yet he may be hard put to it to persuade the man from Mars that to fight for one's country is glorious while to fight for one's class is an inspiration of the devil. Good Paterfamilias, sweating to discomfit your competitors for the sake of your darlings at home, how convince our visitor that in defending the interests of your family you fulfill a sacred duty, while your employee, fighting for the interests of his industrial group, flings a menace at society?

*   *   *   *

As for warfare, we all agree that its moral values are provisional, and look eagerly to that promised time 'when war shall be no more.' But while the vision tarries, no one who accepts that provisional value in one field should disallow it in another. Most of us moreover hold it to be a real value, and still thrill unabashed to martial strains. Why did Thackeray present soldiers as the only men among the weak egotists of Vanity Fair to preserve a standard of selfless honor? Why did Tennyson hail the clash of arms as the only means of transforming the smug clerks of England into her patriots? Not because these authors approved a militant ideal, but because they knew such an ideal to be nobler than prosperous sloth and self-absorption. Battle is deep embedded in our finiteness. As Hellen Gray Cone nobly puts it,—

> In this rubric, lo! the past is lettered:
> Strike the red words out, we strike the glory:
> Leave the sacred color on the pages,
> Pages of the Past that teach the Future.
>   On that scripture
> Yet shall young souls take the oath of service.
>
> God end War! But when brute war is ended,
> Yet shall there be many a noble soldier,
> Many a noble battle worth the winning,
> Many a hopeless battle worth the losing.
>   Life is battle:
> Life is battle, even to the sunset.

The Apocalypse which ends with Jerusalem, Vision of Peace, is chiefly occupied with chronicling in succession of awesome symbols the eternal Wars of the Lord. In the Teachings of Christ there are three bitter sayings against smooth conventionality for one against violence, for the context shows that the saying about non-resistance is personal, not social, in application. We may not dismiss class-consciousness as evil on the mere score that it arouses the passions of war. To determine its value, its end must be questioned, and the qualities evoked by the conflict must be scanned.

III

Let us take the last task first, for in fulfilling it we may almost hope to reassure those gentle folk,—notably on the increase even while nominal Quakerism declines,—the lovers of peace at any price. We may not approve war for the sake of its by-products alone, but when these are valuable we may find in them some consolation for such war as is bound to exist. The class-conscious movement has two precious results: its inner disciplines, and its power to widen sympathies.

Even the most recalcitrant grant the value of an army from the first point of view. Military life affords a unique training in the very virtues most needed by a democratic state: humility and self-effacement; courage, and swift power of decision,—the qualities of subordination and of leadership. We all hope to foster these qualities through the opportunities of peace, but so far our success is so imperfect that we can hardly disregard the help presented by the crises of war. Nowhere is this help more striking than in the class-conscious movement. Consider those class-conscious groups called trade-unions. Seen from without, especially in time of stress, a union may appear actuated by the worst impulses: ruthless in pressing unreasonable demands, callously indifferent to inconveniencing the public, stubbornly self-seeking. Seen from within, the aspect alters. Here is no longer a compact unit fighting for selfish ends, but a throng of individuals, each struggling no more for himself than for his neighbor. In such an organic group—composed, be it remembered, of very simple and ignorant people—you shall see each member submitted to severe discipline in the most valuable and difficult thing in the world,—team-work.

Wordsworth found in Nature the over-ruling power 'to kindle and restrain,' and it is not far-fetched to say that this same double function, so essential to the shaping of character, is performed for working people by the trade-union. It kindles sacrifice, endurance, and vision; it restrains violent and individualistic impulse, and fits the man or woman to play due part in corporate and guided action. Those who have stood shoulder to shoulder with the women during one of the garment-workers' strikes that have marked the last two years, have watched with reverence the moral awakening among the girls, born of loyalty to a collective cause. It was the typical employer, defending the American fetish of the Open Shop, who remarked,—when his clever Italian forewoman asked him, 'Ain't you sorry to make those people work an hour and a half for twelve cents?'—'Don't you care. You don't understand America. Why do you worry about those peoples? Here the foolish people pay the smart.' And it was the spirited girl who replied to him, 'Well, now the smart people will teach the foolish,'—and led her shop out on strike.

Which better understood America and its needs? There is no question which had learned the truth that freedom consists, not in separateness but in fellowship, not in self-assertion but in self-effacement. The employer of so-called 'free labor' denies this sacred truth: for the liberty he defends is that of the disintegrating dust, not that of the corpuscle of living blood. By his vicious doctrine, 'each man free to make his own bargain,' he is doing his best to retard the evolution of the workers towards the citizenship of the future. . . .

*   *   *   *

Socialism, the other great class-conscious force, is as yet little found among us except when imported. Menacing enough, the anarchical type that drifts to us from southern Europe; as ignorant as indifferent concerning American conditions; expecting, like many another creed, to save the world outright by the application of a formula. Yet here too, we may already discern assets to be cherished. Memory rises of illumined eyes belonging to a young Italian. Brought up, or rather kicked up, in a stable at Naples, a young animal when twenty, unable to read, careless of all except the gratification of desire, he found himself errand-boy in a restaurant frequented by a small socialist group. Then came the awakening: 'How behave longer like a beast, Signora? I could not disgrace the comrades! How should Luigi get drunk? There was the Cause to serve. I served it there, I serve it here. I now live clean. Life is holy.' Luigi had experienced that purifying, that rare, that liberating good allegiance to an idea! Thinking goes on in all class-conscious groups: and while we feebly try to moralize and educate the poor, forces are rising from their very heart, generated by the grim realities of the industrial situation, competent to check self-absorption and widen horizons.

Nor in our straits can we afford to despise the international passion of socialism, for it is a strong force at work among the people, capable of kindling in them the sense, so needed here, of universal brotherhood. Adjustment of loyalties between old countries and new is a delicate problem sure to be increasingly pressing among us. No good American wants the old forgotten; no right-thinking immigrant should wish the new ignored.

> True love in this differs from gold and clay,
> That to divide is not to take away.

He who loves two countries is richer than he who loves one only; but as matter of fact our newcomers usually end in loving none. These spiritual exiles present the pathetic spectacle, not of one man without a country, but of great throngs.

At the North End in Boston, Denison House conducts a Sunday lecture course for Italians. The control disclaims responsibility for opinions presented on this practically free forum. Yet American members consented with some reluctance to invite a speaker representing a society organized to strengthen the bond to Italy, and suspected of discouraging naturalization. With anxiety of another type, we asked a socialist club to send its orator for our next meeting. But what the speaker did was to talk with fire and eloquence, grateful to his grave Latin audience, on the theme of the necessity to the Italian in the United States of a new patriotism broad enough to disregard old lines, and to express itself in loyal American citizenship, and in cooperation with all that was progressive in the life of the United States. The inspiration of class-conscious internationalism was plain in the speech, and it did more to quicken a civic conscience than any words of ours could have achieved.

IV

Noting these things, comparing them with the dreary barrenness of the psychical life which obtains among the unaroused masses, how can we fail to see in the class-struggle one of those inspiriting forces which are the glory of history? ... It is the very newness of the force that shocks and terrifies. Race and nation have long broken humanity into groups on perpendicular lines. Class introduces a broad horizontal division. The mighty emotions it generates move laterally, so to speak, interpenetrating the others. They may be competent to overcome in large degree, as we have claimed, the deep-seated antagonisms, racial, political, religious, that separate men and hinder brotherhood. But is not a danger involved? These older loyalties were, after all, in their essence sacred. Does not loyalty to class threaten bonds rightly and jealously cherished? Will it not dull the allegiance of men to family, nation, and church? ...

Socialists themselves well illustrate the danger. The negative attitude toward family ties, marked enough among certain socialist groups, springs to be sure from other sources and is not relevant here to consider. But it is sober fact that socialism is, among many of its adherents, replacing all other religions, and filling the only need they experience for a faith and an ideal. We may in fairness ascribe this situation to temporary causes, and dismiss the difficulty, noting that all the best leaders stress the purely nonpartisan and secular nature of the movement. But we have still to reckon with the indifference of the movement to patriotism, an indifference rising into antagonism in the earlier stages. Marx, in the *Communist Manifesto*, said that the working people have no fatherland. Bakunin could write: 'The social question can only be satisfactorily solved by the abolition of frontiers.' This strong language, however, marked the infancy of the movement and is increasingly discarded. Patriotism has deep roots, and socialists are men. The issue has been hotly discussed in those socialist conventions where a rare and refreshing interest in great intellectual issues obtains. And 'The view is gaining ground among socialists,' says Sombart, 'that all civilization has its roots in nationality, and that civilization can reach its highest development only on the basis of nationality.' It is this growing conviction which makes the socialists sympathetic champions of oppressed peoples like the Poles and Armenians. 'The socialist purpose,' says a prominent leader, 'is to give to the proletariat an opportunity of sharing in the national life at its best. Socialism and the national idea are thus not opposed: they supplement each other.' . . .

*   *   *   *

V

Class-consciousness then can be dismissed on the score neither of its militant implications, nor of the menace it offers to older devotions. Both in its political aspect and in its more intimate reaches of private experience, we find it to be at once a disciplinary and an awakening force; it kindles and restrains.

But now we must go further. We have been dwelling mainly on the qualities it evokes, and the opportunities it offers. We have not yet asked ourselves squarely the final, the crucial question: What end does it propose?

To answer, we must turn from its inner reactions to its outer relations, and take into account the other combatants in the class-war.

By common consent, the term class-conscious is usually applied to the working people. But in accurate speech, it should not be so limited, for it describes quite as truly the stubborn struggle of the employing class to maintain supremacy. The persistence of this class in defending its prerogative is as natural a product of the industrial situation as the pressure of the proletariat. Why is not the emotion as right and admirable when experienced by employer as by employed?

It is more admirable, many will hasten to reply. We need not at this point answer the obviously partisan cry. But if we are to convince the dispassionate man, our supposed interlocutor, that our own cry is less partisan, if we are to justify that strong undertow of sympathy toward the popular cause of which we spoke at the outset, we must lean on an instructive assumption. This is the conviction that the time when the defense of prerogative was valuable to society as a whole is nearing its end, and that the ideal of the proletariat, not that of the capitalist, is implicit in the truly democratic state.

Do we or do we not want to put an end to class in the modern sense?

This is the real, if paradoxical issue. The situation is curious and interesting. As we have already hinted, those who deplore most angrily the rise of class-consciousness in the proletariat foster it most eagerly in their own camp, and would with the greatest reluctance see class-distinctions disappear. On the other hand, the leaders who labor most earnestly to strengthen working-class solidarity do so because they hate class with a deadly hatred, and see in such solidarity the only means of putting an end to it altogether. If we agree with them to the point of holding that class, like war, is provisional, it would seem that these are the people to whom our sympathy is due.

Professor Royce has well shown us that the aim of all minor loyalties is to bring us under the wing of that mother of all virtues, loyalty to the Whole. One draws a long breath at this grandiose, appealing image of the unachieved end of all human striving. Which serves it best,—socialism with its class-conscious connotations, or capitalism with its repudiation of the new bond? The question implies the answer. The capitalist movement has avowedly no aim beyond self-protection and the maintenance of a new type of benevolent feudalism. The working-class movement, on the other hand, is probably the only form of group-consciousness yet evolved in history, to look beyond its own corporate aim. It is inspired by a passion of good-will for all men, and never loses sight of a universal goal. Nay, it is concerned with the welfare of the very enemies whom it is fighting, for it is aware that rich as well as poor are today so fast in prison that they cannot get out. Have we not good reason then to honor it and to exalt it above even patriotism in our thoughts?

The man fighting for his country does not look beyond that country's welfare. But the wider outlook is an integral part of the class-conscious inspiration. The popular movement marches to the tune of Burns:—

> It's coming yet for a' that
> That man to man the warld o'er
> Shall brithers be for a' that.

> L'Internationale
> Sera le genre humain, —

is the rallying cry of the people. What they seek is not the transfer of privilege, but the abolition of privilege; and while they work first for the emancipation of their own class, they believe not only that this class comprises the majority of mankind, but that its freedom will enable all men alike to breathe a more liberal air. With the disappearance of privilege, all possibility of the class-war would of course vanish, for the very sense of class as based on distinction in industrial assets and opportunities would be replaced by new groupings founded, one would suppose, on more subtle and intimate affinities of pursuit, capacity, and taste. In all history-creating movements, the urge of life has been the impelling force; nor can we deny that it has on the whole worked for good to the whole as well as to the part. But it is the great distinction of socialism that, while frankly accepting and fostering such primal passion, it is at the same time more or less clearly aware of a more disinterested aim. Class will never become to our minds a permanent factor in social life, on a level with nation or country. In this fact we may find a legitimate reason for the distrust of class-consciousness that prevails. But, thinking more deeply, in the same fact is the indorsement and justification for the only movement which is to-day setting its face toward the destruction of class distinctions, and which has thus for its very object the annihilation of that sense of separateness which as a weapon it must temporarily use.

VI

We need then have no fear lest class-consciousness, any more than economic determination, catch us in the net of materialism.

*   *   *   *

We have done full justice to the teaching that expounds the importance of the economic base, and vindicates the forces rooted in economic necessity and self-interest. But another question is waiting, nor can we close without asking once more whether all productive forces are directly related to this base, or whether we may reserve a place for the effective power of pure altruism.

Whether we look out or in, the question for most of us is answered in the asking. Heroic devotion springing from ranges quite out of the economic sphere fills the human annals; and this not least in the case of social progress. From the days of John Ball to those of John Howard, philanthropists who have waged brave successful battle against abuses, reformers who have lifted the general life to a higher level, have appeared from any and every social stratum, drawing their inspiration from depths greater than class can reach. All through history, the pressure of the unprivileged toward freedom has been supplemented at critical moments by the undercurrent of sympathy in the hearts of the privileged, and the one group has supplied leaders to the other. It would almost seem that the socialist movement is particularly rich in such leaders. Marx, if you come to that, was not a working man; nor Lassalle, nor Morris, nor Kropotkin, nor many another who in prison or exile has proved himself true to the workers' cause. Among contemporary leaders it is safe to say that the large majority are from the middle class. Looking at the high proportion of 'intellectuals' among effective socialists, one is even a little bewildered. Yet the situation is simple. It is evident, whatever radicals may say to the contrary, that if the proletariat could produce its own leaders there would be no need of social revolution.

The cry of the dispossessed is compelling. The working classes must show the way to social advance. They alone, free from sentimentality, the curse of the privileged, and from abstract theorizing, the curse of the scholastic, have that grim experience of the reaction of economic conditions on the majority from which right judgment can be born. But if their function be to furnish momentum, and corporate wisdom, the power of individual initiative and directorship will often in the nature of things be generated among those governing classes in whom these gifts have been fostered. If education and administrative experience are valuable enough to share, it is obvious that the dumb proletariat must to a certain extent look to the classes that possess them for the revelation of its own sealed wisdom and the guidance of its confused powers. The enlightened energy of those who come from other groups to serve it should not be slighted. Their high impulses, their rich devotions, are also, to ultimate vision, within, not without, the evolutionary process,—a process broader, deeper than current Marxianism admits. In them that wider loyalty, toward which class-consciousness itself is groping, has been born already, and to assert that they have no part in social advance and that the working class must produce unaided the new society, would be to deny democracy at the root.

The best, the final work of democracy will be to give us all the freedom of the City of the Common Life. This all Americans know in theory. Let us beware lest we deny it in deed by withholding our faith from the great class-conscious movement of the working people, which alone holds in practical form the ideal of a world where divisions based on economic accident and arbitrary causes shall be obliterated, and life be lifted to new levels of freedom. The instinctive sympathy with proletarian movements should cast aside timidity and incertitude, and realize that its roots strike deep into a true philosophic and religious conception of social advance. It should imply, not only indorsement, but cooperation. So only the effective reality of our national assumptions can be vindicated, and the day hastened when the Greater Loyalty shall be ruler of the world. So we can prove that the ideal central to this Republic at its outset was no histrionic Tree of Liberty cut from its native soil, to wither even as the echoes of the encircling dance and song should die away, but a growth firm-planted in the fruitful earth, and slowly, surely developing till it becomes a Tree of Life whose leaves shall be for the healing of the nations.

18

Anna Howard Shaw: remarks on emotionalism in politics given at the National American Woman Suffrage Association convention in 1913

FROM the *History of Woman Suffrage*, vol. 5.

By some objectors women are supposed to be unfit to vote because they are hysterical and emotional and of course men would not like to have emotion enter into a political campaign. They want to cut out all emotion and so they would like to cut us out. I had heard so much about our emotionalism that I went to the last Democratic national convention, held at Baltimore, to observe the calm repose of the male politicians. I saw some men take a picture of one gentleman whom they wanted elected and it was so big they had to walk sidewise as they carried it forward; they were followed by hundreds of other men screaming and yelling, shouting and singing the "Houn' Dawg"; then, when there was a lull, another set of men would start forward under another man's picture, not to be outdone by the "Houn' Dawg" melody, whooping and howling still louder. I saw men jump up on the seats and throw their hats in the air and shout: "What's the matter with Champ Clark?" Then, when those hats came down, other men would kick them back into the air, shouting at the top of their voices: "He's all right!!" Then I heard others howling for "Underwood, Underwood, first, last and all the time!!" No hysteria about it—just patriotic loyalty, splendid manly devotion to principle. And so they went on and on until 5 o'clock in the morning—the whole night long. I saw men jump up on their seats and jump down again and run around in a ring. I saw two men run towards another man to hug him both at once and they split his coat up the middle of his back and sent him spinning around like a wheel. All this with the perfect poise of the legal male mind in politics!

I have been to many women's conventions in my day but I never saw a woman leap up on a chair and take off her bonnet and toss it up in the air and shout: "What's the matter with" somebody. I never saw a woman knock another woman's bonnet off her head as she screamed: "She's all right!" I never heard a body of women whooping and yelling for five minutes when somebody's name was mentioned in the convention. But we are willing to admit that we are emotional. I have actually seen women stand up and wave their handkerchiefs. I have even seen them take hold of hands and sing, "Blest be the tie that binds." Nobody denies that women are excitable. Still, when I hear how emotional and how excitable we are, I cannot help seeing in my mind's eye the fine repose and dignity of this Baltimore and other political conventions I have attended!

Florence Kelly, 'Modern Industry and Morality'

FROM *Modern Industry in Relation to the Family, Health, Education, Morality*, New York 1914 (pp. 124–8).

One sinister consequence of the anonymous, impersonal ownership of business, and the accompanying degradation of the workers to the position of "hands," is their own acceptance of this position. Filthy or diseased meat, adulterated eatables, short-weight packages, though the product of their labor appear them to be no concern of theirs. They feel no share in the guilt of the employing concern under whose orders, and in whose pay, they put alum in bread, formaldehyde in milk, tin, lead or iron in silk (in the process of dyeing), or shoddy in place of wool in garments to be worn by other working people. Steel workers know when there are blow holes in armor plates, but they regard it as no affair of theirs. The negotiation is between the steel manufacturer and the Navy Department, and the wage earner's experience has awakened in him no patriot's rage against such treason. If he thinks at all of the matter, it is perhaps to reflect that wars are fought to the profit of financiers, and at cost of working people, whichever side wins. Or the steel worker may sullenly remember that he has long been begging the Government to abolish contract work and make its own steel plate.

In any case, the irresponsible state of mind of employing corporations and indifferent "hands" is more threatening to civilization than the actual harm inflicted by alum, formaldehyde, shoddy, blow holes and all the other poisons and dishonest products. And this indifference, like the moral confusion of the general public concerning gifts derived from these and similar sinister sources for the higher education, philanthropy and religion, is a normal product of modern industry.

Our confusion is well illustrated in relation to our concept of murder.

The Old Commandment in the New Order

The Commandment, Thou Shalt Not Kill, is still valid in our laws to the extent that the individual murderer of an individual person pays with his life for his crime, the hangman or electrocutioner being held—somewhat whimsically—exempt from the effect of the Commandment. But wholesale killing in industry as in war remains unpunished.

Our morality has been sapped by precept and practice, by living in a society in which the moral foundations of industry are false and corrupting. The human mind accepts without revolt that to which it is accustomed from childhood. Cannibals were not horrified at eating their grandparents. Soldiers do not recoil from murder, they plan it systematically years in advance; and on the field of battle they bayonet men as butchers stick pigs. And gentle grandmothers give little children paper or tin soldiers as playthings, and read of bayonet charges with enthusiasm.

Owners of tenement houses do not count themselves infanticides, though the death rate of babies in tenements is twice as large as elsewhere. On the contrary, the real estate interests fight as one man every requirement of tenement house sanitation which seems to threaten to cut into their incomes. The landlords' resistance to improved housing is uninterrupted and nation wide.

Although dirty milk is a permanently active cause of disease and death, the milk producers and dealers succeeded in 1913 in defeating legislation calculated to assure greater cleanliness in the rural treatment of the milk supply of New York City.

Builders, managers, stock and bond holders of factories are not punished as murderers, though a hundred and more men and women perish by fire and smoke in a single work room. In connection with the most terrible of factory fires, the owners of the building have been absolved by the courts of New York State from all criminal responsibility for the monstrous slaughter, and the firm is still doing business.

When hundreds of women and children on a Sunday School outing in the East River perished by drowning, many of the victims were lost because the cork safety belts carried on the boat were weighted with lead or iron, substances cheaper than cork in belts bought and sold by weight. Only the captain of the Slocum was punished. Manufacturers and dealers in cork safety belts appear to be free to continue to furnish their death-dealing wares.

We are by way of forgetting the Iroquois Theatre in Chicago in which children were suffocated at a matinée. The manager—far from having been punished for failing to supply the needed precautions for safety—appeared before a legislative committee at Springfield, ⌐ 1911, insolently to oppose, and demand the repeal of, the beneficent Illinois statute which keeps young children off the stage.

Some years ago a speculator cornered the ice supply in summer in New York City. The price rose, poor mothers could not buy ice, and the list of deaths of babies lengthened, for milk without ice is poison in the tenements in summer. Later for an offence unrelated to this, the speculator was sent to a federal penitentiary for a long term. Upon the representations of reputable physicians that the convict was about to die, the President pardoned him. Our moral sense is dulled by modern industry, and the President in pardoning a single influential one among hundreds of sick convicts, and one whose record was, perhaps, the most anti-social of all, did but act in accordance with prevailing standards.

It is silly and confusing to tilt at Big Business, as though bigness in itself were the sole or the chief active element in our political and industrial immorality. The pushcart peddlers and news vendors who have stands on city street corners are animated by precisely the same business motives as the gas trust, the surface car companies and all the other large exploiters of the cities. And their very numbers make the little offenders perhaps the more insidiously poisonous to the community, in these days of transition to new forms of industry calling for new and loftier morality. The source of corruption in large and small alike is irresponsibility, the relation to the community of freebooting exploiters in a society which sends those who fail to the almshouse and the potter's field.

Unsigned Editorial, *The General Federation of Women's Clubs Magazine,* Vol. 16, June 1917

This editorial, which appeared just after America entered the Great War, fairly reflected the temper of moderate women in the crisis, and the general attitudes which sustained them during it.

[handwritten: ascribes to old ideas of wom. but says for this occasion will change]

[handwritten: private vs. public]

Women are natural pacifists. Love and harmony are the factors that make the home within our gates, and so it has been our pleasure and privilege to run inside and close the gate, leaving the confusion and discord and misunderstanding on the outside to settle themselves. But no more of this. The bugle call to service has penetrated the walls of home, and out through the gates have come the women, realizing long before we we are told that the war is our own special affair, that it is here, and that we are no slackers. We shall meet it, experience it, and come through it, greatly changed. The heedless, happy-go-lucky thinking of the past is no longer for us. We shall work out the war with blood and tears just as Europe is working it. We shall exchange our material thinking for something quite different, and we shall all be kin. We shall all be enfranchised, prohibition will prevail, many wrongs will be righted, vampires and grafters and slackers will be relegated to a class by themselves, stiff necks will limber up, hearts of stone will be changed to hearts of flesh, and little by little we shall begin to understand each other. Those of us who have money will learn what money is for. We shall all take a course of training in self-denial, and we shall find that giving is getting. We shall recognize blessings when we meet them, and no introduction needed. We shall send our beloved men to the front. We shall learn to pray understandingly, to be grateful, to give all we have on the altar of our country.

[handwritten: diff.s groups among wom.]

Already we tiptoe in at night, we mothers, and look at our boys as they sleep. They never will know just how we feel, nor of the dull pain tugging at us somewhere in consciousness.

Women realize that we are living in an ungoverned world. At heart we are all pacifists. We should love to talk it over with the war-makers, but they would not understand.

Words are so inadequate, and we realize that the hatred must kill itself; so we give our men gladly, unselfishly, proudly, patriotically, since the world chooses to settle its disputes in the old barbarous way. We are even rather proud of the minority who stand for principles of preservation, and are not ashamed to say so, even though they are called cowards. It is this minority that shall provide the leaven for a new civilization after this war is worked out. We understand when they say they shall not commit murder, for war is murder. We are rather glad they look at it in that way, for something must come of it if they stand fast. The war-makers do not understand them, since the language of peace is unknown, "peace without honor." We do not talk a great deal, we women. We are standing by our President, standing by our Uncle Sam and by Columbia. We are no slackers. But we know that somebody has done things all wrong, and that it is high time we awoke. We know now how much we are needed in the world's affairs.

Is she speaking for herself?
What about the movements?

21

Carrie Chapman Catt, 'John Hay, Mrs. Catt, and Patriotism'

FROM *The Woman Citizen,* 10 November 1917. This response to charges that suffragists were failing to support the war effort shows Mrs. Catt at her disingenuous best. Her strategy required her to pay a maximum of lipservice to the war effort, while at the same time diverting to it as few suffragist resources as possible. The reader may judge for himself how successful she was in reconciling these two policies.

"John Hay, the father of the national president of the anti-suffragists, *drafted a peace treaty while this country was at war with Spain. He* said he might get lynched for it, but just the same he did it. He believed that the war with Spain was a necessary and righteous war; but he detested war; he believed in peace.

"So do I, though I believe this war with Germany is still more necessary and still more righteous than the war with Spain.

"If I am a traitor, so was he."

This is one volley of the broadside which Mrs. Carrie Chapman Catt pours into the anti camp in final answer to the misstatements and falsehoods that have emanated from anti sources calling to question Mrs. Catt's loyalty for the reason that before this country went to war with Germany she believed in and worked for peace.

Mrs. Catt's letter, sent to Mrs. James W. Wadsworth, Mrs. Margaret C. Robinson, and Miss Alice Hill Chittenden, joint disseminators of the canards against her, follows in full:

"I thank you for the correction, even though begrudgingly made, that it is not I, but my cause which you connect with the I. W. W.'s through 'other prominent leaders.' The three prominent leaders you name in support of your claim demonstrate anew my contention that, being hard pushed for legitimate argument, you are skilfully juggling facts with fancies for the apparent purpose of 'camouflage.' No one of these three persons is a member of the National American Woman Suffrage Association, which includes at least 98% of all organized suffragists.

"If you can clear the skirts of all anti-suffragists from connection with anti-draft agitation by declaring that Annie Riley Hale resigned from your body before she was arrested, the same rule must clear suffragists from many questionable connections with which you charge them. These three persons you mention may or may not have spoken with or for the I. W. W.; it does not matter; they are not our representatives. It is a poor rule that doesn't work both ways. Millions of men and women are suffragists and one should no more hold this great army responsible for the acts and opinions of any one of these millions than call all anti-suffragists thieves because their sponsor, Gov. Ferguson of Texas, has just been impeached for misappropriation of public funds.

"You say that you have the right to accept reports as reliable if when they appear in 'the reputable press' suffragists do not take the trouble to correct or deny them. In that case, to leave no outstanding falsehood in the present controversy without its proper denial, I submit the following:

"To every single or collective insinuation, implication, or direct charge, published or spoken in any place at any time by professional anti-suffrage campaigners, or 'the reputable press,' which has conveyed the impression that I, or any other officially responsible leader of the National Suffrage Association, has, by word or deed, been disloyal to our country, I make complete and absolute denial here and now, and spare the reader the tedium of detail.

"There are only two points raised in your reply to my letter which seem worthy of further attention.

"You charge that the I. W. W.'s are stronger in suffrage states than elsewhere 'because the doubling of their strength through the votes of their women makes their class vote a powerful political weapon.' As all the world knows, the I.W.W.'s came into existence in Massachusetts, and Eastern leaders have stirred their activities in the Western states. Why? Because in the West grow the trees out of which ships are built, and the wheat and other grain and fruit crops which feed the world. The I.W.W.'s are not after votes but destruction, in order to block the progress of the war. To attempt to make women voters in the West responsible for this national problem is too pitifully silly to merit further comment.

"The other point is in regard to Rosika Schwimmer. Rosika Schwimmer is a Hungarian Jewess, a journalist by profession, belonging to a respected family in Budapest. She was in England when the war broke out, as correspondent for several continental papers. Shocked by the sudden appearance of war and its threat of world-wide devastation, she believed that it could be averted and that, like Joan of Arc, she was called of God to see that this was done.

"By cable to the women leaders of organizations all over the world, and especially of suffrage associations, she asked consent to sign their names to an appeal to President Wilson to urge the United States Government to intervene. People in many countries at that moment were turning to this country in the hope that, if it would call for an armistice, long enough to find out what the trouble was, arbitration might be secured.

"I repeat once more that Frau Schwimmer did not come to this country by my invitation or suggestion or that of any other American. More, to the best of my knowledge, she was not sent by any person or persons, organization or government on the other side. She came solely on her own initiative. The petition to the President was her idea and the signatures were gathered by her. She arrived about September 3, 1914, presenting her petition within a few days.

"I repeat that she was not an official of the International Woman Suffrage Alliance. She had been employed as an international press secretary by that organization, but had resigned within a month after her appointment.

"When she came to America she undertook some suffrage campaign work as part of the arrangement that had closed her connection with the I.W.S.A. Please understand that I am setting forth these facts as in no sense an apology for the I.W.S.A.'s employment of Frau Schwimmer, but merely that the whole history of the case may be understood. So far as I know, Frau Schwimmer was exactly what she represented herself to be, a woman working for peace on her own initiative, with no diplomatic entanglements whatever. Also, that there may be no ground for further misrepresentation about the appeal to the president, I reproduce it here intact:

" 'September 14, 1914.

" 'To His Excellency, The President of the United States.

" 'Sir: We come to you representing the women of many lands who have sent to our London Headquarters urgent appeals that our officers should urge the United States Government to lead a movement to end the present European war.

" 'We entreat you, therefore, in the name of our common civilization to combine the neutral nations under your own wise leadership in an insistent demand to all belligerent powers to call an immediate armistice until mediation has been given a fair opportunity to find a just settlement of international differences.

" 'Let the demand be repeated again and again until it is heeded. If at first such action calls forth criticism, an international sentiment will surely be created which will transform criticism into gratitude, and it will at least bring courage and hope to the millions whose hearts are breaking with despair.

" 'Men of families of our leaders in fifteen countries are at the front. We learn that the homes of some are now hospitals for the wounded, and all European suffrage headquarters are transformed into relief stations. The stories these women tell us of suffering, want, destruction of property, disease, atrocities and brutal attacks upon women, are well-nigh unbelievable in this twentieth century. We accept these scattered testimonials of women we know well, as certain indications that civilized Europe has relapsed into barbarism. Under these circumstances no diplomatic conventions should be allowed to stand in the way of the most expeditious means of securing mediation.

" 'The women of the world are looking to you, the leader of the only great neutral nation to find a way of mediary interference.

" 'The petitions which we present have been voluntary and unorganized. Not less significant than the entreaties which we have received is the absence of appeals from Austria, Servia, Germany, Finland, Galicia and Bohemia. These countries are silent only because they cannot speak, but we know their sentiment so well that we dare to assure you that mediation hastened by outside intervention will be as welcome to the women of these lands as to those whose names are hereto appended.

" 'That the petitions of these women might reach you quickly and surely, Madam Rosika Schwimmer of Hungary, has come to this country for the express purpose of presenting them to you.'

"This appeal was signed by the presidents and secretaries of the following women's organizations: Women's National Political Union of Australia; National Suffrage Association of Canada; the three leading suffrage associations of Denmark; the French Union of Suffrage Societies; the three leading Hungarian suffrage associations; the Norwegian Council of Women; Norwegian Women's Peace Society; Italian Women's Suffrage Association; the Russian Women's League for Woman's Rights; Froken Signe Bergman for 300,000 Swedish women; the Civil Union of Great Britain; the National American Woman Suffrage Association; the West German Women's Suffrage Association; the Dutch Woman Suffrage Society, and the National Council of Swiss Women.

"At that time Germany had committed no offense against the United States and our relations were friendly with her, as with all the belligerent countries. Meetings of protest against war had been held but a short time before in Berlin, Vienna, Petrograd, Paris and London, and in every land there were still those who hoped that the sickening sorrows of a long war might yet be prevented.

"In this connection I wish to call your attention to the fact that the late John Hay, the father of the president of the national association of anti-suffragists, had his own experiences with people who challenged his loyalty and cursed him, he says, 'for being the tool of England against our good friend Russia.' See his letter to J. W. Foster, under date of June 23, 1900. 'These idiots,' he added, 'say I am not an American because I don't say, "To hell with the Queen," at every breath.'

"In May, 1898, when the country was at war with Spain, John Hay actually had the temerity to draft a peace project although he knew, he said, he would be lucky if he escaped lynching for it.

"Are you willing to apply to Mrs. Wadsworth's father the chain of alleged reasoning that you apply to me and, because of his great faith in and hope for peace, call him a traitor to his country?

"John Hay was one of the first advocates of peace; he believed in peace and said so.

"So do I.

"If I am a traitor to my country, so was he.

"To continue: Shortly after Frau Schwimmer came to America events followed each other so rapidly that the situation changed almost hourly.

"Frau Schwimmer and Mrs. Pethick Lawrence of England, were both welcomed by suffrage and other associations, but their peace meetings, it must be remembered, were held in a nation then at peace with the world.

"The Woman's Peace Party was organized in January, 1915. Out of it grew an international meeting at the Hague, held the next April. Delegates were there assigned to visit all the belligerent countries and secure audiences with the proper authorities in an effort to find some common ground on which all would agree to pause long enough to 'parley' over possibilities of adjustment of differences between the nations. Jane Addams with others went to Berlin, Vienna and London. Frau Schwimmer, with Miss Chrystal MacMillan, a well-known British woman, went to Russia. She did not see any Russian authorities or agents except in company with her Scotch companion, who is now mourning the death of her soldier brother, and who could scarcely be charged with intent to betray Russia into the hands of Germany.

"Rosika Schwimmer again returned to this country under engagement to a lecture bureau under whose auspices she spent the autumn, leaving on the Ford peace ship December 4, 1915. While here she may have seen German, Russian and other officials and agents, for her hope that some one could be found who could make an armistice a reality was not yet extinguished, but I do not know of such meetings.

"If Rosika Schwimmer was a spy or an agent, suffragists and all others who befriended her were deceived. Personally, I believe her to have been entirely honorable in every motive. She was nearly distraught over the failure to find means to end the war; and that is the worst that can be said of her.

"With the effort to urge the United States to intervene in the early weeks of the war I, with millions of other Americans, was in sympathy. I ceased to be in sympathy with any effort of that or similar nature after our relations with Germany became strained. A question of national honor entered into the situation then which had not been there before.

"An overwhelming amount of damaging evidence has been laid before the American people since December, 1915. To juggle words so as to give the impression that the events, facts, and opinions which were perfectly appropriate before that date apply to 1917, when they are wholly out of accord, is too flagrant a case of 'red herring' to pass muster with intelligent people.

"I wish to make my own stand quite clear to you and to any others interested. I believe war for our country was unavoidable, and that the safety of democratic institutions all the world around now depends upon its outcome; that there should be national unity in order to get through it as soon as possible; that a premature peace will only perpetuate war; that the only good which can possibly eventuate from the war is the spread of democracy and the resulting certain elimination of war from the crimes of the world; that democracy means 'the right of those who submit to authority to have a voice in their own government'; and that woman suffrage is a part of this great world struggle; for their can be no real democracy which leaves women out.

"In time of war when sedition and treason are possible and must be hunted out in defense of national unity, it is an unpardonable and wellnigh seditious offense, to attempt to arouse and spread suspicion, with its consequent unrest, anxiety and distress, by the charge that a very large class of supposedly honorable citizens are disloyal. You will remember that in New York alone more than one million women have declared themselves suffragists. When such numbers of persons are accused of disloyalty, the charge either falls to the ground by the weight of its enormous falsity, or it lessens and weakens the stability of public faith necessary to the proper support of the government.

"If it be true that suffragists are striving for 'peace at any price,' secretly hindering the draft, the Red Cross, the Liberty Loan, aiding and abetting the I.W.W., etc., the government might as well throw up its hands now, for no country could wage a successful war with such vast groups of the population ranged in opposition. As a matter of fact you know that your charges are untrue and your offenses are in consequence the more serious. It is the anti-suffragists, fighting against democracy at home who are the 'menace to the situation,' not the suffragists who are striving for democracy at home and straining every nerve and sinew in support of the fight for democracy abroad."

Ethel Puffer Howes, 'The Meaning of Progress in the Woman Movement'

From *Annals of the American Academy of Political and Social Science,* vol. 143, May 1929.

It is altogether fitting that there should be at this time a stock-taking of what is known as the woman movement. The last ten years have seen an extraordinary flux in the position, the activities, and most of all in the inner attitudes of women. A natural impulse is to conjure with the word progress; to tell over the new legal freedoms and powers, and the new occupations of women, and to expound the achievements of outstanding individuals. But if this survey is to be a serious reckoning, it must first ask in what sense the quality of progress may be ascribed to these multitudinous changes, or, pressing further, in what progress in the woman movement may rightly be held to consist.

What *is* progress? No concept in the field of social thought has been more eagerly disputed. A recent listing of variant definitions of social progress topped the hundred in number. Nevertheless, for application to a special movement within the social field, the dictionary definition (Webster's) gives a fair clue: "A moving or going forward; an advance toward better or ideal knowledge or condition or that conceived of as better." In the words of a sociologist, "We shall be unable to define concepts of progress ... except in relation to standards of value."[1] Progress, then, in post-war phrase, in an advance toward an objective, which objective is some ideal condition.

Has the woman movement an objective in this sense? Is there an ideal condition of womankind, clearly envisaged, which is to be sought as a goal, an end? The first answer of most women to this question is likely to be an indignant affirmative. But it is one that must, I believe, be qualified.

[1] Odum, H., *The Quest for Social Guidance* (1928).

FREEDOM FROM LEGAL AND POLITICAL DISABILITIES

The great spokesmen of the woman movement have demanded freedom from disabilities. Women have rebelled against their chains, and all that they have currently asked is to be allowed to cast them off. When their condition was something less than human—without legal right in their own persons or their children, without the privilege of mental or any systematic training—they demanded the redress of these manifest injustices. It was a negative aspiration, cast in a negative form. As expressed by Mary Wollstonecraft in the opening of her *Vindication of the Rights of Women* (1798):

> Contending for the rights of woman, my main argument is built on this simple principle, that if she be not prepared by education to become the companion of man, she will stop the progress of knowledge and virtue.

The *Vindication* is in fact a brilliant presentation of the fundamentals of education, illustrated by women's disabilities. Freedom from the ban on rational thinking was what was sought for women.

The negative aspect is still more marked in the next great women's manifesto, put forth by the first Woman's Rights Convention of 1848. It is primarily a declaration of woman's wrongs at the hands of men, wrongs which called for redress. The fact that the demand for the vote was only included as an after thought at this convention is a well-known bit of suffrage history; but the way in which that first convention was precipitated is also significant. The moment came through Elizabeth Cady Stanton's sudden denunciation of the wretched conditions of daily life for all women, wives and mothers, as she had seen them among poor women in her remote country dwelling. It was while on a visit to her friends Lucretia Mott and Jane Hunt that this denunciation took definite form, and she so fired her friends to action, as told in Mrs. Blatch's *Life,* that the call to convention was issued from that meeting.

That great landmark of the woman movement, Mill's *On the Subjection of Women* (1869), tells its story in the title, and the burden of the argument is summarized as follows:

> The disabilities of women are the only case, save one, in which laws and institutions take persons at their birth and ordain that they shall never in all their lives be allowed to compete for certain things. ... Among all the lessons which men require for carrying on the struggle against the inevitable imperfections of their lot on earth, there is no lesson which they more need than not to add to the evils

which nature inflicts, by their jealous and prejudiced restrictions on one another.

All negatives!

FREEDOM FROM ECONOMIC DISABILITIES

The next guidepost in the woman movement was *Women and Economics* (1896), Charlotte Perkins Gilman's epoch-making book. Women are oversexed (she says in substance), taught to rely on feline arts, restrained in their human impulse to do and to make, because their real disability is economic, not political. "The economic dependence of the human female on her mate," that "sexuo-economic relation," poisons love and marriage, family and social life, at their source. Hence, her program of economic independence is one of removing disabilities like the preceding. Much more, of course, is implied than is expressed, and Mrs. Gilman, in this and other writings, has anticipated most of the practical efforts for the management of women's lives which the new century has seen. Thus it would appear that the great interpreters of the woman's movement in the past have seen their goal as escape from a condition, rather than as the establishment of a positive concept or ideal of women's nature and work.

That this idea has continued into the present and still largely dominates the woman movement is seen in the following words of Mrs. Carrie Chapman Catt in an article in *Current History*, for October, 1927:

> What is the woman movement and what is its aim? It is a demand for equality of opportunity between the sexes. It means that when and if a woman is as well qualified as a man to fill a position, she shall have an equal and unprejudiced chance to secure it. . . . What will bring the revolt to a close? . . . absolute equality of opportunity only will satisfy and therefore close the woman movement.

PROGRESS IN REMOVING DISABILITIES

Now it is certainly true that the successive practical steps by which women attained freedom from their disabilities in comparison with men, or, positively, the right to own property, to make contracts, to study and practice professions, to vote, have in every case been clearly set forth as objectives. From one point to another, then, there has been progress in this limited sense, that the immediate objective was clearly defined, and was attained. Mrs. Catt's own statement, however, is indubitable testimony to the fact that the positive "ideal condition" for women, which shall be a goal, a beacon, a guide to what she may, can, or shall do, or endeavor to do, has never as yet been a definite part of the woman's program. Progress in the full sense can, then, not be attributed to the woman movement, because no real objective has been set or attained. The "woman question" has never had an answer. And the proof of this is that never in the history of the woman movement were the conflicts in ethical motives more acute, the trends in education more contradictory, or the lack of clear thinking on fundamental meanings more notorious, than now.

This confusion was voiced by Dr. Harry Emerson Fosdick in sharper terms in a recent sermon, from a newspaper report of which I quote:

There has been among us and there is now an insistence for freedom so widespread as to create the moral climate in which we all live. Many people, however, forget that there are two stages in the fight for freedom: first, the achievement of it; and, second, the using of it when you have achieved it.

Think of the new freedom of woman. She has been emancipated in every realm of her life, legal, economic, and political. And yet has all this freedom solved a single ultimate problem for women? Only in the sense that it has presented American womanhood with an opportunity which may make womanhood or break it.

WHEREIN PAST OBJECTIVES HAVE BEEN INADEQUATE

Dr. Fosdick is right. It is not too much to say that there is no more general grasp of these "ultimate problems" than in 1798, 1848, 1869, or 1920, when the vote was gained. Moreover, whereas a few years ago there was at least unanimity among thinking women as to the next step, that constituency is today facing two ways without realizing it.

There is, on the one hand, the original drive for ever wider opportunities for women: education to be carried to any point which a specific activity may require; with every *apparent* intention of serious pursuit of it—but with no least provision, either in professional machinery, in social framework, or even in current acknowledgment of need, for relating the individual occupation to the physical functions and emotional needs of women. The current rejoinder—"but we are now teaching women the basic arts of the family"—is precisely meaningless in this connection. The selective vocation is approached as if it were to be "the occupation of a celibate"—to paraphrase Herbert Spencer—until the moment comes, always by chance, when the use of training is abandoned, and the individual reverts to domestic pursuits. Education in home-making is of course good in itself; but it gives only the turn of the screw to what an English feminist calls "the intolerable choice" between married love and concrete achievement.

The serious higher education or professional training of women today is literally founded on self-deception; a solemn farce in which all the actors consent to ignore the fact that the most natural, necessary, and valuable of human relations will in all probability soon ring down the final curtain. Of the inhibiting effect of this subconscious expectation of the break, both on education and achievement, I have written elsewhere. Suffice it to say that the most extraordinary and unexplained situation in the whole history of women is this ostrich-like attitude of women themselves, and women's educators above all, to the pressing need of conscious constructive control of the ever-imminent conflict between work and the love life.

This confusion in the objectives of women on the level of higher education is repeated in the field of women in industry. Not even the leaders of working-women know what to advise for them, as is clearly set forth in a publication of the Women's Bureau.[2] They are said to be:

> . . . . victims of an ever-changing public opinion. The least that the married woman who works should expect from industry is a consistent attitude toward her employment so that she may know what she is to expect. . . .

But, "the decrease in poverty incident to the employment of mothers," set over against the bad social consequences of the over-fatigue of the mother and the loss in childcare, has never been evaluated. The ultimate value for the industrial woman is still undetermined. Very recently a vivid picturing, by a social expert, of the dislocation in the personnel direction and organization of young women workers caused by their lack of real interest in anything but ultimate marriage, left the impression that this wholly natural interest was something which permanently vitiated the woman's labor situation. Rather would I say that the present *impasse* showed up the opportunity for constructive thinking on the part of the official leaders of women.

Alongside this age-old disregard of the fundamental impingement of nature on work, we have a recent tremendous efflorescence of the domestic and parental interests; a tendency to deprecate all systematic training except that for family living and to identify this with "training for life." This tendency derives, in the line of theory, from Rousseau's romantic view of woman's rôle, through Ellen Key and Havelock Ellis. Rousseau, who professed that education should be guided by the needs and rights of the personality of each individual, nevertheless applied this principle only to his *Émile*—his *Sophie* was never considered in any light save as Émile's life-companion.[3] Havelock Ellis is led by his

---

[2] *Married Women in Industry*, Mary A. Winslow (1924).
[3] Cp. Monroe, *History of Education*.

studies in the differentia of sex to assume a complete fundamental difference in mentality and character and to expand this toward the conclusion that the whole end of woman is her biological and emotional activity. To quote from Havelock Ellis' account of Ellen Key, in which he voices his own agreement with her,

> Women, indeed, need free scope for their activities—and the earlier aspirations of feminism are thus justified—but they need it, not to wrest away any tasks that men may be better fitted to perform, but to play their own part in the field of creative life which is peculiarly their own. . . . The really fundamental difference between man and the woman is that he can usually give his best as a creator, and she as a lover, that his value is according to his work and hers according to her love. . . . Women are entitled to the same human rights as men [continues Ellis], and until such rights are attained "feminism" still has a proper task to achieve. But women must use their strength in the sphere for which their own nature fits them.[4]

Ellen Key's name is most widely associated with her special doctrines of "the cult of the child," "the right to motherhood." It may be questioned, however, if they will have as great importance for the concept of woman's function as the general trend of her teachings, which seek to lead women to abandon the field of varied creative opportunity and concentrate on family devotion. We get the reverberation of this plea in those new expressions of educators who are beginning to say, apparently to wide approval, "Let us now educate women *as women!*" This should not be thought to mean merely the desire to give women the necessary equipment for wifehood and motherhood —no, it is intended as a redirecting of women's education, and so of women's destiny. Here at least we have come to a foreshadowing of that ultimate concept for which we looked in vain before.

President Eliot [of Harvard] is forthright in his expression of this view:

> It is not the chief happiness or the chief end of woman, as a whole, to enter these new occupations, to pursue them through life. They enter many which they soon abandon; and that is good— particularly the abandonment. . . . The prime motive of the higher education of women should be recognized as the development in woman of the capacities and powers which will fit them to make family life more . . . productive in every sense, physically, mentally, and spiritually. To this modification of the higher education of women as we have seen it during the past generation may we not all look forward with abundant hope?

[4] *The Task of Social Hygiene* (1912).

This was said by President Eliot in 1907[5] and it is now reprinted as a college publication by another president, with the comment that "it deserves a place in predictive prophecy."

WHERE WE MAY LOOK FOR PROGRESS IN THE WOMAN MOVEMENT

We have here at last the confrontation of two principles: the one, still confused, unfinished, entailing obvious conflict and contradiction; the other, definite enough, an "ultimate" in the sense required—if we can accept it. Where, then, shall we seek "progress" in the woman movement?

The people who want a quick return on their thinking are increasingly throwing in with the last view. It is so easy to rest in the dictum—since we all agree—that a woman's chief happiness is the vocation of wife and mother. But it needs only what Ellen Key calls "incorruptible realism" to see that the irresistible march of events is against it. First of all, the alleged sex division, in the effective sense, is gone. Science no longer sustains the dictum of Havelock Ellis; biology, genetics, and psychology are now on the side of the relative dissociation of abilities from sex-characters. Secondly, we see the psychological impossibility of denying *development* to youth that is eager to learn, to act, and, for the most part, to work, or that needs to work. Thirdly, the psychological impossibility of restraining the *exercise* of a faculty which has once been developed, without danger of ill effects, even tragic ills. A hundred years ago, such a policy might have had some success, because women then did not as a class realize that their abilities were, broadly, equivalent to men's. But there is now no more chance of diverting those who thirst after knowledge and skill and the use of that skill, than of turning democracy permanently back to despotism. A real solution must be accepted in principle by at least the superior half of any class to be affected. Fourthly, the fact is inescapable that with early marriage and motherhood—an essential element in "the single vocation of motherhood" program—the termination of that active vocation will arrive just at the time when the woman herself is at the zenith of her powers. Result, either a frantic attempt to hold on to her vocation (with all the "fixation" and "mother-in-law" evils which modern mental hygiene has too fully shown us); or, resolute self-withdrawal, with the torture of twenty or more remaining years of futilities, social and cultural. Superfluous women! Every provocative magazine is full of stories about them.

No, the romantic program is a glorious picture of the possibilities of the wife and mother *relation*, but is not the solution of the ultimate destiny of the woman who has a mind, talents, energy and a long life to be lived in a world of creative doings. Therefore, it is to be hoped

[5] *Women's Education*—A Forecast.

that the present distraction and uncertainty in the field of education, which this doctrine has mediated, will on sober second thought be overcome by its better understanding.

It is enough to read attentively Key's great book, *Love and Marriage,* to see the impossibility of releasing women's individual powers through education, and then diverting them completely from their end, without disaster.

Yet that disaster is what we are now inviting, not on principle, but through pure obstinate stupidity, in opening all doors to women, without providing for the woman's love life as the ordinary social setting does for man's. Various writers set up a straw-woman, the "brain-woman." It is as futile to deny that the present social framework does not allow the natural and necessary development of woman's affectional life, along with the natural continuous development and exercise of her individual powers. The man demands of life that he have love, home, fatherhood and the special work which his particular brain combination fits. Shall the woman demand less?

Here we are at the heart of the problem. I would say to Dr. Fosdick, that the reason why the emancipation of women has brought no "ultimate," is because women as a class have been too humble, too timid, to claim as an ultimate principle of life for themselves, what every man has without asking. The true concept of woman is of a being with a mind, with *specific* talents which need to be developed *and used*; and with a soul and body, a psychophysical organism which, too, needs to be developed *and used*; and until this principle is accepted as ultimate, as shaping not only education, but social forms, we shall look in vain for progress.

Whatever subvarieties of occupation of "the whole woman" develop, for individuals, is immaterial. It may well be that nine-tenths of womankind will find fulfillment in the specific vocation of "collective motherliness," to use the phrase of Ellen Key. But this would be, on our view, merely one type of the general principle of integration. The ultimate principle of integration would demand full provision, in all educational plans, professional codes, and social arrangements for the ideally complete woman which would eliminate forever the necessity of an "intolerable choice."

Here is the place for John Dewey's definition of the problem of progress as one "of discovering the needs and capacities of collective human nature—and of inventing the social machinery which will set available powers operating for the satisfaction of those needs."

INVENTING THE SOCIAL MACHINERY

It is far from a small matter of special devices or personal adjustments by which women may participate in both professional and family life; it is a matter of transforming the whole social setting and the inner attitudes of men and women to accept the two-fold need of women as fundamental. The absolute first necessity is to see the problem for what it is; a fundamental one for education and ethics, not a mere question of management. The invention or achievement of successful methods by which, at various stages, adjustment may be assured, is important, indeed, but important primarily as a *vindication of possibility,* as *an illustration of meaning,* as *an aid to establishment of principle.*

A PRACTICAL EFFORT TO COORDINATE WOMEN'S INTERESTS

"The individual can prescribe a life of reason more readily than he can follow it. But an environment can be formed in which desirable conduct becomes a reflex response."[6] It is toward the forming of the environment for successful integration (now in general effectively inhibited); to making integration both possible and natural, that the Institute for the Coordination of Women's Interests at Smith College is dedicated.

That is why the satisfactory organization, in a college project, of a new type of service for homes, of a cooperative nursery group, of a cooked food supply adjusted to moderate incomes, means not so many bits of ground won in home economics, but so many props in the social framework so necessary to any ultimate solution. All our analyses of the professions for their adjustment to women's needs, all our case histories of successful integrations of professional and home interests find herein their meaning and enter as elements into the synthesis.

The Institute's problem is thus intimately related to the fundamentals of education. The form which the principle of integration in women's lives takes, for collegiate education, is the principle of continuity in intellectual work. The practical corollaries of this principle are proving immense. It entails, for instance, replanning the curriculum for educational continuity, resulting in the new plan of the Graduate Project. It rescues women from the mental dryness of the post-college years from which so many women suffer.

We have only begun to realize that the true coordination of women's interests, the demand for integration, is a sword to cut such knotty problems of social ethics as partnership in marriage, the spacing of children, the objectives of women in research and administration, commerce and art. But the one unassailable ground won, from which all can ultimately be reached, is the acknowledgment of the principle of the integration of the full circle of the powers and needs of women.

[6] Cattell, *A Statistical Study of American Men of Science.*

Index

Declaration of Independence, 16, 17, 22
Declaration of Principles, 22
Declaration of the Rights of Women, The, 15
Despard, Charlotte French, 83
Dilke, Sir Charles, 64, 67
Dilke, Lady Emilia, 64
Disraeli, Benjamin, 30, 72
Divorce, 22, 27, 40, 41
Dix, Dorothea, 35
Dorr, Rheta Childe, 85 n.
Douglass, Frederick, 22
Dreier, Mary, 65

East London Federation, 86–87
Eastman, Crystal, 79
Education. See Higher education
Ellis, Edith, 41
Ellis, Havelock, 95
Englishwoman's Journal, 22
Equal rights amendment to the Constitution, 92

Fawcett, Dame Millicent, 72, 81
Female Humane Association, 34
Feminine Mystique, The, 95
Finney, Mrs Charles G., 34
Frankfurter, Felix, 62–63
Free Church League, 86
Free love. See Marriage reform and sexual freedom
Freud, Sigmund, 96
Friedan, Betty, 95
Fry, Elizabeth, 34
Fuller, Margaret, 21

Garrison, William Lloyd, 19, 24, 38
General Association of Congregational Ministers of Massachusetts, 21
General Federation of Trade Unions, 67
General Federation of Women's Clubs, 43–54, 90
Gilman, Charlotte Perkins, 41, 49, 74, 95, 96
Gladstone, William E., 31, 72
Goldmark, Josephine, 61
Goldmark, Pauline, 61
Gompers, Samuel, 64, 66
Gouges, Olympe de, 15
Grimké, Angelina, 19, 21, 25
Grimké, Sarah M., 19, 21

Henry Street (Nurses) Settlement, 57–58
Higher education, 19, 43–47, 57, 93
Hobhouse, C. E. H., 85
Howe, Julia Ward, 24, 51, 73
Hull House, 57, 61

International Federation of Working Women, 90–91
International Labor Conference, 90
International Ladies' Garment Workers Union, 65

James, Henry, 82
Jewish League, 86
Jones, Mother, 69

Kelley, Florence, 61–63, 73, 74
Kelley, William D., 60
Kenney, Annie, 83
Kingsley, Canon Charles, 63
Kraditor, Aileen, 73

Labor, U.S. Dept. of, 62
Labour Party, 68, 69, 83, 86, 87, 89, 91, 93
Ladies' Association for the Female Prisoners In Newgate, 34
Letters on the Equality of the Sexes and the Condition of Women, 21
Liberal Party, 32, 72, 86, 87
Livermore, Mary, 23, 38
Lloyd George, David, 85, 86
London Charity Organization Society, 35
London Trades Council, 64–65
London University, 44
Lowell, Josephine Shaw, 36, 59
Lyon, Mary, 20

MacArthur, Mary, 64, 66–68
Maiden Tribute of Modern Babylon, The, 38, 40
Manchester Women's Suffrage Committee, 30
Marriage and Divorce Act, 22
Marriage reform, 25–29, 41
Married Women's Property Act, 38
Married Woman's Property Bill, 22
Martineau, Harriet, 17, 21, 63
Matriarchate or Mother-Age, The, 41
Maximum hour legislation, 62–63
May, Samuel J., 97
McDowell, Mary, 56
Militants. See Women's Social and Political Union and Woman's Party
Mill, John Stuart, 30, 37, 43
Minimum wage legislation, 61–62
Moore, Mrs Philip North, 51–52
More, Hannah, 34
Mormons, 26
Mott, Lucretia, 22
Muller v. Oregon, 62

Nathan, Maud, 59
National American Woman Suffrage Association, 29, 49, 51, 72–80

94

William L. O'Neill, editor

THE WOMAN MOVEMENT

Feminism in the United States and England

In this unusual book, Mr. O'Neill traces the development
of the movement for women's rights in America and,
to a lesser extent, in England. Beginning with Mary
Wollstonecraft's attack on British institutions in 1790,
he relates in narrative—and illustrates with twenty-two
documents—the continuing struggle through the 1920's
and on to the "permissive" society in which we live.
"The Victorians had resolved to destroy the double
standard of morals by compelling men to be as chaste
as women," Mr. O'Neill writes. "This proved to be
unfeasible . . . If men and women could not be equally
chaste, they could, at least, be equally promiscuous."

The story covers all facets of the movement: the struggle
for the vote, for property rights, for education, for women
in industry, and for temperance and social reform. The
reader will find the cross-cultural comparisons of the
feminist movement in England and America particularly
valuable.

"Masterly. . . . Here at last is a study of feminism which
asks penetrating questions and treats the subject from a
focus larger than simply one aspect of American reform
history. . . . O'Neill [has] a sensitive understanding of the
feminine point of view. . . . This small book is an important
challenge to scholarship in the field. It should not be
missed."—Gerda Lerner, *Journal of American History*

Cover Design by Chestnut House/Miles Zimmerman

Quadrangle Books/Chicago

N70947